OFFICIAL COPY.

[*Crown Copyright Reserved.*

$\dfrac{40}{\text{W.O.}}$
1823

HANDBOOK

OF

ARTILLERY INSTRUMENTS.

1914.

LONDON:
PRINTED UNDER THE AUTHORITY OF HIS MAJESTY'S STATIONERY OFFICE
BY HARRISON AND SONS, 45–47, ST. MARTIN'S LANE, W.C.,
PRINTERS IN ORDINARY TO HIS MAJESTY.

To be purchased, either directly or through any Bookseller, from
WYMAN AND SONS, LTD., 29, BREAMS BUILDINGS, FETTER LANE, E.C., and
54, ST. MARY STREET, CARDIFF; or
H.M. STATIONERY OFFICE (SCOTTISH BRANCH), 23, FORTH STREET, EDINBURGH; or
E. PONSONBY, LTD., 116, GRAFTON STREET, DUBLIN;
or from the Agencies in the British Colonies and Dependencies,
the United States of America, the Continent of Europe and Abroad of
T. FISHER UNWIN, LONDON, W.C.

1914.

Price One Shilling and Sixpence.

PREFACE.

This book has been compiled with the object of bringing together descriptions of all instruments which are used by the Royal Artillery alone.

Descriptions of instruments which are also used by other units will be found in the following books :—

Signalling Apparatus ..	Training Manual. Signalling.
Telephones	Instructions in Army Telegraphy and Telephony.
Mekometers	Handbook of the Mekometer.

"Apparatus, training gunlayers" is described in "Instructions for use of Laying Teacher," issued with Army Orders, dated 1st March, 1911.

Coast Defence Range-finders are described in a separate Handbook, viz., "Manual of Coast Defence Range Finding."

Electrical stores are described in "Notes on Electricity," 1911.

Scott's sights, which are obsolescent, are not described in this book, but details of them may be found in the Handbook for Telescopic Sights, 1904.

The theory of optics has not been entered into, except in a very few cases. When required, reference should be made to "Notes on Optics."

It is hoped that the book will be found of use for instructional purposes, for assisting artificers and others, who have to adjust or repair the instruments, and for general reference for those who use or have charge of the instruments.

It is impossible to give all the details of each instrument, but those given should be sufficient for most purposes.

The correct nomenclature has been given to all parts mentioned, and should be of assistance when new parts are being demanded. The name of the maker, date of manufacture and number of the instrument for which the parts are required, should be stated in the demands, as small details of the instruments vary from time to time.

Attention is particularly called to the subject of taking instruments to pieces (see page 170).

The book is corrected up to April, 1914. Any alterations or additions which may be suggested should be forwarded to the Chief Inspector, Royal Arsenal, Woolwich.

CONTENTS.

	PAGE
Chapter I.—Telescopes. General principles. Collimating. Detailed description of various natures	1
Chapter II.—Binoculars. General principles. Detailed description of various natures	33
Chapter III.—Directors. Observation of Fire Instrument. Slide rules. Plotters	41
Chapter IV.—Clinometers. General principles. Detailed description of various natures. Tests and Adjustments	72
Chapter V.—No. 7 dial sight. General principles. Detailed description	83
Chapter VI.—Field Telemeter. Description. Drill. Adjustments ...	99
Chapter VII.—One-man Range-finders	126
Chapter VIII.—Angle of Sight Instrument. Bubbles. Collimator. Iris diaphragm. Illumination of telescope cross wires, &c. Sighting Rules. Stop Watches	159
Chapter IX.—Care and preservation of instruments	170
Chapter X.—Repair and adjustment of instruments. General method of obtaining a horizontal line. Fixing cross wires, &c. Replacing a broken bubble	173
Appendix A.—Notes on reflecting prisms	179
Appendix B.—Tests for Range Takers	182
INDEX	184

PLATES.

	OPPOSITE PAGE
I.—Telescope, Sighting, No. 1, Mark II, in parts	14
II.—Telescope, Sighting, No. 1, Marks I* and III	15
III.—Telescope, Sighting, No. 2, Mark I	16
Telescope, Sighting, No. 4, Mark II	16
IV.—Telescope, Sighting, No. 4, Mark II, in parts	17
V.—Telescope, Sighting, No. 5, Mark II	18
VI.—Telescope, Sighting, No. 6, Marks I and III	19
VII.—Telescope, Sighting, No. 7, Mark I	22
Telescope, Variable Power, No. 1, Mark I	22
Telescope, Field Artillery, Mark IV	22
Telescope Garrison, Mark I	22
VIII.—Telescope, Sighting, No. 7, Ross Pattern. Arrangements for varying the power	24
IX.—Telescope, Variable Power, No. 1, Ottway Pattern. Arrangements for varying the power	25
X.—Stand for No. 1 V.P. Telescope	26
Stand for No. 2 V.P. Telescope	26
Case for No. 2 V.P. Telescope	26
Case for No. 2 V.P. Telescope Stand	26
XI.—Telescope, Stereoscopic, Front View	30
XII.—Telescope, Stereoscopic, Rear View	31
XIII.—Binocular, Mark IV, in parts	35
Binocular, Mark V	35
XIV.—Binocular, Night	36
Binocular, Prismatic, No. 1, Mark I	36
XV.—Binocular, Prismatic, No. 2, Mark I, in parts	37
XVI.—Binocular, Prismatic, No. 2, Mark I	39
Binocular, Prismatic, No. 3, Mark I	39
XVII.—Director, No. 1, Mark II, on Stand, Telescope, Field Artillery	41
XVIII.—Director, No. 2, Mark I	42
XIX.—Director, No. 2, Mark I	43
XX.—Director, No. 3, Mark I, on Mark I Stand	45
XXI.—Director, No. 3, Mark I, on Mark I Stand	45
XXII.—Stand, Mark II, for Director, No. 3	49
XXIII.—Apparatus, Observation of Fire, Instrument	54
XXIV.—Apparatus, Observation of Fire, Instrument	55

	OPPOSITE PAGE
XXV.—Apparatus, Observation of Fire, Stand, Sight Arm and Compass	56
XXVI.—Apparatus, Observation of Fire, Slide Rule, Mark VI ...	64
XXVII.—Rule, Slide, 10-inch, Mark I	68
XXVIII.—Field Plotter, Mark IV...	70
XXIX.—Field Plotter, Mark IV...	71
XXX.—Clinometer, Inspector's, Mark II	72
Clinometer, Large, Mark I	72
Clinometer, Field, Mark II	72
Clinometer, B.L. 10 pr., Mark I	72
XXXI.—Clinometer, Field, Mark III	79
Clinometer, Sight, Mark I	79
XXXII.—No. 7, Dial, Sight	83
XXXIII.—No. 7, Dial, Sight. Section	93
XXXIV.—No. 7, Dial, Sight, in pieces	95
XXXV.—Artillery Telemeter	100
XXXVI.—Artillery Telemeter	100
XXXVII.—Artillery Telemeter, Mark IV...	103
XXXVIII.—Artillery Telemeter, Mark IV, on stand	103
XXXIX.—Stand for Mark IV Artillery Telemeter	106
XL.—Zeiss Artillery Range-Finder...	149
XLI.—Zeiss Artillery Range-Finder	149
XLII.—Barr and Stroud Range-Finder	151
XLIII.—Barr and Stroud Range-Finder	151
XLIV.—Barr and Stroud Range-Finder, Dismantled	152
XLV.—Stand, Artillery Range-Finder, Mark I	154
XLVI.—Stand, Artillery Range-Finder, Mark I	154
XLVII.—Stand, Artillery Range-Finder, Mark I	154
XLVIII.—Stand, Artillery Range-Finder, Mark II, in case	155
XLIX.—Laths, adjusting Artillery Range-Finder	155
L.—Angle of Sight Instrument	158
LI.—Stop Watches. Sighting Rule	168

HANDBOOK
OF
ARTILLERY INSTRUMENTS.

CHAPTER I.
TELESCOPES.

The following are the principal telescopes for use with Artillery. The list does not include signalling, or range-finding telescopes, or those which form part of instruments which are described elsewhere:—

Name.	Magnification.	Field of View.	Remarks.
Sighting No. 1, Mks. I, I*, II and III	3 diameters	10°	Fitted with a pointer. For sights of garrison guns
Sighting No. 2, Mk. I	5 "	5°	Fitted with a pointer. For sights of 4·7" Q.F. guns on travelling carriages and 6" B.L. Howitzer, 30 cwt. The focus of the object glass could be adjusted, but is now fixed.
Sighting No. 3, Mks. I and II	10 "	3½°	Fitted with a pointer. For sights of garrison guns.
Sighting No. 4, Mks. I, II and III	5½ "	5½°	Fitted with a pointer. For 13 and 18-pr. Q.F. guns.
Sighting No. 5, Mks. I and II	12 "	3°	Fitted with a pointer. For 60-pr. B.L. guns.
Sighting No. 6, Mks. I, II, III and IV	5 "	5°	Fitted with a pointer and clinometer level. For 15-pr. B.L.C. guns, Q.F. 15-pr. guns with Territorial Force only. The focus of the object glass of the Mark I could be adjusted, but is now fixed.
*Sighting No. 7, Mk. I	5 to 21 "	6° to 1¼°	Fitted with a pointer. Superseding Nos. 1 and 3.
Sighting No. 8, Mks. I and II	3 or 10 " approximately	10° or 3½° approximately	Converted No. 1 or 3. Fitted with a pointer. For use with Apparatus Training Gun Layers.
Field Artillery, Mks. II*, II**, III and IV	35 diameters	55'	Fitted with a sighting wire which can be placed either horizontally or vertically.
Garrison, Mk. I	35 "	55'	For look-outs.
*Variable power, No. 1, Mk. I	7 to 21 "	4° 30' to 1° 30'	Fitted with a diaphragm having graticules 1', 10', 30', 60' and 90' respectively on either side of the axis of the telescope. For siege artillery.

Name.	Magnification.	Field of View.	Remarks.
*Variable power, No. 2, Mk. I	7 to 21 diams.	4° 30′ to 1° 30′	For heavy artillery. This telescope is generally similar to "Telescope V.P. No. 1" but has no graticules.
*Stereoscopic	10 ,,	4°	Binocular pattern. The right eyepiece is fitted with a diaphragm having two horizontal graticules one minute above and one minute below the optical centre respectively, and three vertical graticules, one being on the optical centre and the others 30 minutes to either side. The diaphragm can be revolved until the horizontal graticules are vertical. For observing fire from 9·2″ B.L. guns.

All the above telescopes except those with a Variable power and the Stereoscopic (marked with a star—*—) are made on the same optical principles, but vary in size, magnification, field of view, weight, &c. With the exception of the "Sighting No. 2," "Sighting No. 6 Mark I," "Field Artillery" and "Garrison" pointers or diaphragms are fixed in the focal planes of the object glasses.

It will be noticed that, when the magnification is great, the field of view is small, and *vice versa*. One telescope can be compared with another by multiplying its magnification and field of view together and comparing the product with that of another. This product is called the "Apparent field of view."

Thus, comparing the "Sighting, No. 6 Mark I" with the "Stereoscopic" the products are 25 and 40 respectively. This indicates that the "Stereoscopic" is in some respects the better telescope. The "Sighting, No. 6 Mark I" is of old design and had to be made to small dimensions.

It does not follow, however, because the product of the magnification and field of view is large, that the telescope is necessarily good. It is possible that owing to faulty design, a large proportion of the light which passes through the object glass does not reach the eye. If some of the rays of light do not tend to come to focus in the focal plane, they are cut off by stops inside the telescope body, as otherwise they would render the image indistinct or coloured.

The size of the object glass, or rather the size of the portion that is being made use of (which is called the effective aperture), also has a great effect on the optical properties of the telescope. The larger the effective aperture the more brilliant the object looked at will appear to be, provided the magnification is the same.

The length of the telescope affects the definition. Short telescopes usually have bad definition except in the centre of the field of view.

Some telescopes have two eyepieces, one giving a high power and the other a low power. Whichever is used the image comes to focus at the focal plane of the object glass (where there is often a pointer or diaphragm). With the high power eyepiece the image is much magnified, and its brilliancy diminished by the light from it being spread over a large area. With the low-power eyepiece the image is not magnified so much, and the light from it not so much dispersed, and it will consequently appear more brilliant.

With some of the most modern telescopes, the magnification (and corresponding field of view) can be varied within certain limits. After focussing on an object, the power can be altered until the object appears to be most distinct. The magnification of the pointer or graticules will vary with the power that is being employed, but the graticules will remain the same angular distance apart.

The magnifying power of a binocular or telescope is often described as being × 6, × 10, &c., which means that an object seen through it appears to be 6 or 10 times as large, both in height and width, as it did when seen by the unaided eye; or the magnification of the instrument is said to be 6 or 10 diameters.

Service telescopes are nearly all of the Terrestrial pattern, *i.e.*, the image is seen the correct way up, and not inverted as in Astronomical telescopes.

The principal lenses in a telescope* are :—

OBJECT GLASS LENSES.

The object glass consists of two lenses.

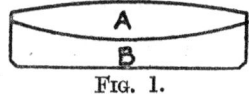

FIG. 1.

A (Fig. 1), which is made of crown glass and is usually convex on both sides, and (B), which is made of flint glass, its front surface being made to fit accurately against (A) and its rear surface being either flat, concave, or convex. The lenses are not cemented together, as is often the case with binocular object glasses.

If the object glass were made of one piece only, the rays of light in passing through it would be split up into rays of different colours.

The rays of light passing through the object glass will come to focus, and form an image, in the focal plane of the object glass, and if pointers, graticules or cross-wires are used they will usually be situated in this plane.

With telescopes, which require collimating, it is very necessary that the object glass should not be revolved or moved in any direction with reference to the remainder of the telescope or the collimation will be upset. The following precautions must therefore be taken :—

(1) The object glass must be prevented from revolving in its cell. This is effected by cutting a small groove or feather way in the edge of the glass, and fitting a small feather inside the object glass cell.

---

* This does not apply to Variable Power and Stereoscopic Telescopes.

(2) The object glass cell must always be screwed home to the same place in its adapter. In some cases the outside edge of the object glass cell and its adapter are marked with lines which should be made to correspond, but in practice it is often found to be impossible to screw the cell far enough home, or that the cell is loose in the adapter when the lines correspond. Before removing the cell for cleaning, &c., temporary marks should be made, and when the cell is replaced these marks should be made to correspond again.

(3) Never remove the object glass from its cell for cleaning, &c., unless it is absolutely necessary, as when it is being replaced, a different part of its edge may be in contact with the inside of the cell, and its optical axis be moved into a new position in the telescope, thus upsetting the collimation.

To ensure the two lenses of the object glass being correctly assembled they are marked in one of the following ways (Fig. 2).

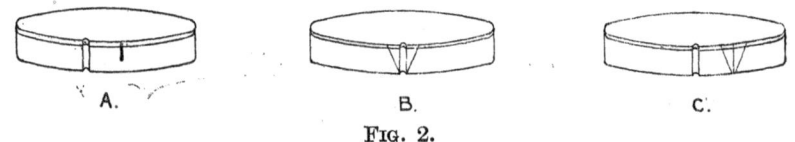

Fig. 2.

(A) Short lines on the edge of each lens, which should be continuous, the feather way being to one side.
(B) A broad arrow extending across the edges of both lenses, the shaft forming the feather way.
(C) A broad arrow as in (B), but with the feather way to one side.

The greatest care must be taken when assembling the lenses that the two correct surfaces are in contact, or when the counter cell is being screwed home they may fracture.

In nearly all cases the front surface of the object glass is convex.

EYEPIECE LENSES.

There are usually four lenses in the eyepiece (Fig. 3), which may be divided into two sets, the eyepiece proper, whose function is to magnify the image, and the erector which causes the image to appear erect. Two lenses are used in each set, as they give better definition and colour correction than single lenses.

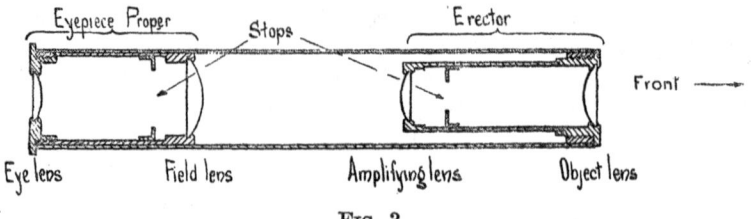

Fig. 3.

Fig. 4 shows how the rays of light from a point on an object are refracted by the various lenses. It will be noticed that images of the point are formed at G and F. It is in planes passing through these points that cross wires, pointers, &c., would be fixed, usually at G.

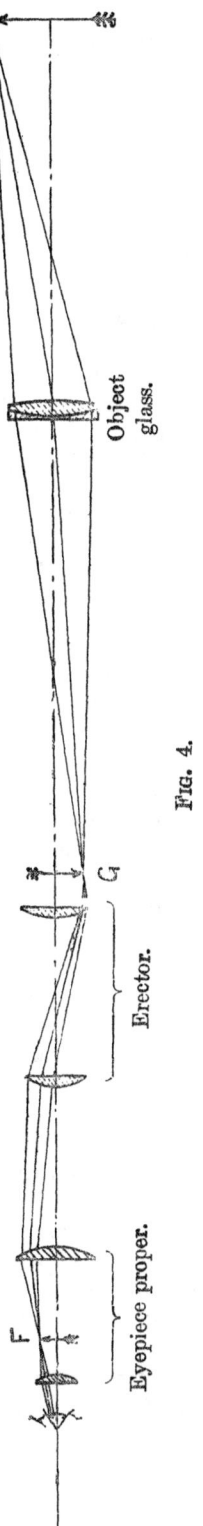

Fig. 4.

The "eyepiece proper" used is known as a Huygens or negative eyepiece. A cross wire immediately in front of it cannot be focussed.

FOCUSSING.

A telescope is correctly focussed when :—

(1) The cross wires, pointer or graticules are in the focal plane of the object glass (*i.e.*, the plane in which an image of the object is formed).

(2) The cross wires, graticules or pointer and object are distinctly seen by the observer.

Some telescopes have the pointer, graticules or cross wires permanently fixed in the focal planes of the object glass. This is the case with practically all telescopes of low power, which are not required to be used for short ranges. This is the case with all those mentioned on pages 1 and 2 with the exception of the "Sighting No. 2 Mark I" and the "Sighting No. 6 Mark I," "Field Artillery" and "Garrison."

Others allow of the object glass being moved away from, or brought nearer to the pointer, graticules or cross wires. (To prevent repetition the pointer only will be referred to below.) This is usually the case with high-power telescopes used with range-finders, &c., where very accurate focussing is necessary.

To focus a telescope.—Withdraw the eyepiece until the pointer is very distinct. (If the telescope is of "Fixed focus" pattern, a distant object should also appear to be distinct, because the pointer is permanently fixed in the focal plane of the object glass.) If any adjustment for the focus of the object glass is provided, rack the object glass in or out until a distant object is also distinct.

Lay the pointer on a well defined distant object and move the eye up and down and sideways, and note if the tip of the pointer remains on the same part of the distant object. If it does so the focus is correct. If it does not, re-adjust the focus of the object glass and eyepiece until it does. If, with a "fixed focus" telescope the pointer does not remain on the distant object, the relative positions of the object glass and pointer require adjusting by an artificer.

By this test we have been seeing whether the pointer is in the focal plane of the object glass. The same effect can be shown by considering a sheet of paper as the focal plane of an object glass, and a mark on it as the image there of some object. Using a pin as a pointer; if it touches the mark on the paper, it will always appear to be on the mark from whatever position it is viewed. If, however, the pin is moved a short distance from the paper it will not appear to be in line with the mark except when viewed from one direction.

If a telescope is not correctly focussed (and this may be the case even if the pointer and the object appear quite distinct) the pointer will appear to be in line with different parts of the object if the observer moves the position of his eye. The telescope is then said to have *Parallax.*

When a telescope is correctly focussed for one observer and is to be used by another observer, it is not necessary to re-adjust the object glass, but only the eyepiece.

COLLIMATION.

Definition.—The line of collimation is a line between the optical centre of the object glass and the tip of the pointer or intersection of the cross wires. A telescope is said to be in collimation when the line of collimation coincides with, or is parallel to, the mechanical axis of the telescope, *i.e.*, the axis of the bearing bands.

When telescopes are used for range-finding or sighting, it is very important that the collimation should be correct.

Test.—Place the telescope in its bearings on the sight bar or instrument, and after careful focussing lay the tip of the pointer or intersection of the cross wires on a well defined distant object. Revolve the telescope slowly and note whether the tip of the pointer or intersection of the cross wires remains on the same point of the distant object. If it does the collimation is correct. If it does not, the collimation must be adjusted as explained below.

Some telescopes, *e.g.*, the No. 6 Sighting Telescope, have no bearing rings and cannot be collimated, but their pointers can be adjusted, so that the line of sight through the telescope is brought parallel to the axis of the gun.

MEANS OF ADJUSTING COLLIMATION.

There are two main principles upon which the collimating arrangements are constructed, viz. :—

(1) The pointer being fixed, and the object glass being mounted in eccentric rings, by one of which an up and down movement can be given, and by the other a sideway movement.

    It is claimed that telescopes constructed on this principle do not easily get out of collimation. They are, however, rather difficult to collimate.

(2) The object glass being fixed, the diaphragm to which the pointer or cross wires are fixed can be moved in two directions at right angles to one another by means of adjusting screws, which usually pass through the body.

(1) ECCENTRIC RINGS.

The general arrangement of this principle is shown in Figs. 5 and 5A.

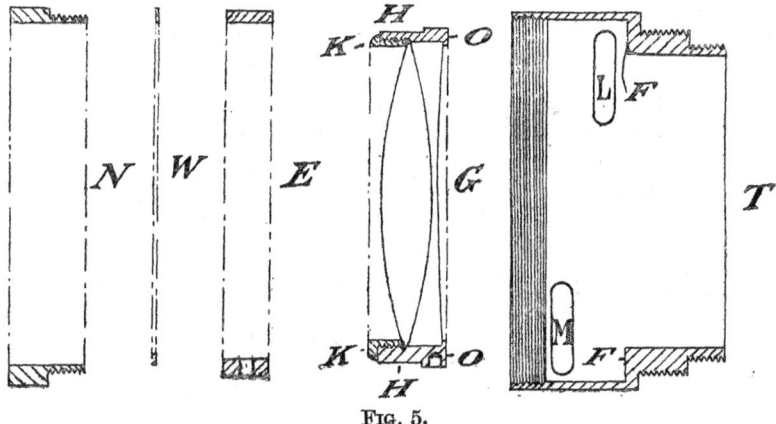

FIG. 5.

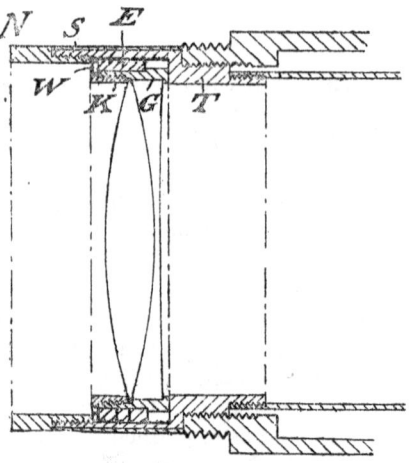

Fig 5A.

The front end of the telescope body (T) is recessed to form a seating for the eccentric ring (E). Within the ring (E) fits the other eccentric ring (G), its surface (H) being a good fit in (E), and its surface (O) bearing against the surface (F) in the telescope body. The surface (H) is not concentric with the optical axis of the object glass. A small screwed ring (K), screwed into (G), keeps the object glass in place. There are tommy holes for adjusting purposes around the rings (E) and (G), and slots (L and M) are cut in the body of the telescope, through which a tommy can reach the holes in (G) and (E) respectively.

When (G) has been placed in (E) the whole is inserted into the body of the telescope (Fig. 5A) and kept in position by a screwed ring (N) and washer (W).

It will be noticed that Fig. 5A shows the sections of the eccentric rings (E) and (G) to be slightly thicker below than above. If we revolve (E) through half a circle the ring (G) with the object glass and consequently the image formed at the focal point, will be lowered through a distance equal to the difference of thickness of the parts of the ring (E) shown in the section.

Similarly, if the ring (G) is revolved in (E), an up and down movement of the object glass will take place.

If we place the thickest section of either ring to one side, and the thinnest section to the other side and revolve it through half a circle the movement of the object glass will be to the right and left instead of up and down. When either ring is given a small movement so as to raise the object glass, it will also move it very slightly to the right or left, and *vice versa*.

Before collimating, the rings should be arranged so that one will give a vertical and the other a horizontal movement when turned through a comparatively small angle.

A thin German silver strip (S) is placed over the tommy holes (M) and (L) to prevent the eccentric rings being accidentally turned.

To Collimate (eccentric rings).

This can be done in conjunction with a collimator (see page 163), or as follows :—

Remove the ray-shade and German silver ring from the front end of the telescope so that the tommy holes in the eccentric rings can be seen through the slots (M, L) in the body. Slacken the screwed ring (N) about quarter of a turn so that the eccentric rings may be turned. Place the telescope in the brackets of the sight and after careful focussing, lay the tip of the pointer on a well defined distant point.

Revolve the telescope through half a circle and if the pointer appears to have moved off the distant point, bring them towards each other (vertically) half way by means of the range drum of the sight, and (horizontally) half way by means of the deflection scale. The remainder of the adjustment is done by turning the eccentric rings. It is as well to have two numbers working together to do this.

No. 1 keeps the telescope steady in the brackets of the sight, notes the position of the pointer with reference to the distant point, and directs the movements of No. 2.

No. 2 places tommies in the exposed holes in the eccentric rings. He revolves the outer, or front eccentric ring, allowing the inner one to move with it. This gives any large movements required. For small final movements he revolves the inner eccentric ring preventing the other one from moving.

When the tip of pointer is exactly on the distant point, the telescope is revolved through half a circle. If the tip of the pointer does not remain on the distant point, the process must be continued until it is found to keep on the distant point, whilst the telescope is being revolved through a complete circle.

It will sometimes be found that after moving the outer eccentric ring no further adjustment can be obtained by moving the inner eccentric ring, any movement of it appearing to make the adjustment worse. In such a case, without looking through the telescope, throw out the inner eccentric ring quarter of a turn, and start the collimation afresh.

In very rare cases it may be found that the collimation still cannot be corrected. This is due to the eccentric rings not having sufficient throw. The only remedy is to move the pointer in a horizontal or vertical direction having previously loosened the two screws which secure it. Only a very slight movement should be required.

After adjustment, the counter screw of the object glass cell adapter (N, Fig. 5) must be carefully tightened up, care being taken not to shift the eccentric rings. When the German silver ring and ray-shade have been replaced, the collimation should be again tested.

(2) Adjustable Diaphragm.

The diaphragm is usually mounted in front of the eyepiece, and has either a pointer attached to it by means of screws, or cross wires, which are pieces of spider's web, stuck on to it with lacquer. Graticules may be spider's web stuck on to the diaphragm, or fine lines engraved on a very thin piece of glass which is burnished into the diaphragm.

The diaphragms are held in the telescope in various ways, the most usual being shown in Fig. 6.

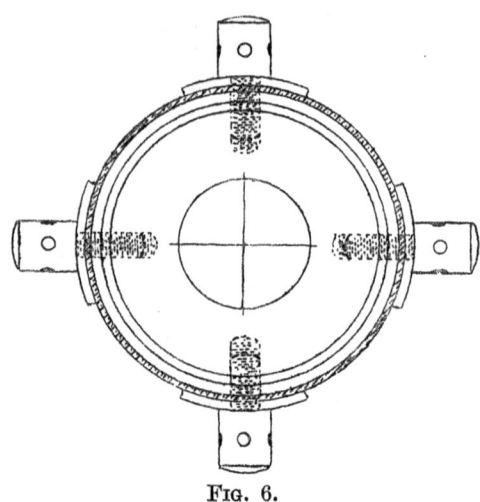

Fig. 6.

The diaphragm is adjusted by loosening one adjusting screw and screwing up the one opposite to it. The collimation should be tested after any movement of the adjusting screws.

The diaphragm used with some variable power telescopes is described on page 23.

Note.—It should be remembered that the pointer and cross wires are seen upside down through the eyepiece, and if they appear to be too low they require moving to a lower position and *vice versa*. This, however, does not apply to some telescopes of early manufacture, *e.g.*, the "Telescope Sighting No. 6 Mark I," where the pointer is immediately in front of the eye lens.

To Collimate (adjustable diaphragm).

This can be done in conjunction with a collimator (see page 163), or on a distant point, as follows.

Place the telescope in the brackets of the sight, and after careful focussing, lay the tip of the pointer, or intersection of the cross wires on a well defined distant point. Revolve the telescope through half a circle, and, if the pointer appears to have moved off the distant point bring it half way (up or down) towards it by means of the range drum of the sight, and the remainder by manipulating the adjusting screws, being careful to loosen one before tightening up the one opposite it. Revolve the telescope into its original position. If the collimation (vertically) is not yet correct, repeat the process until it is so.

Revolve the telescope in its bearings through quarter of a circle and adjust the horizontal collimation in a similar manner.

Check the adjustment by revolving the telescope through a complete circle and noting if the tip of the pointer or intersection of the cross wires keeps on the distant point.

Note.—It is very important that the adjusting screws should be screwed well home; but at the same time too much force must not be employed or the telescope body may become distorted. If much adjustment of the diaphragm is required all the adjusting screws should be slightly slackened at first.

TELESCOPES WITH ADJUSTABLE FOCUS FOR OBJECT GLASS.

(1) Most telescopes of high power, especially those which require to be very accurately focussed (*e.g.*, those for range-finders), have an arrangement by which the object glass can be moved forwards or backwards with reference to the pointer or cross wires.

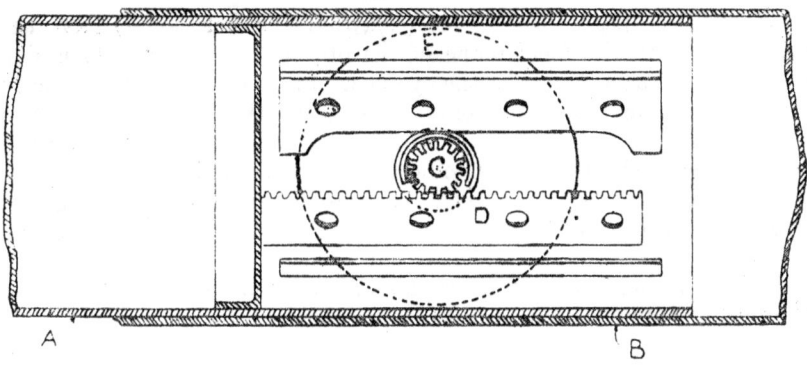

FIG. 7.

This is usually arranged for by having the object glass mounted in a focussing tube (A. Fig. 7), which slides in the telescope body (B), its movement being controlled by a pinion (C) mounted on a spindle passing through the body, which gears into a rack (D) on the focussing tube. Outside the body on the same spindle as the pinion, is mounted a milled head (E), by which the focussing gear is actuated.

If there is any play between the body and the focussing tube the collimation of the telescope will be upset. This is guarded against by slitting the front end of the body and so making it act as a spring bearing.

(2) In a few telescopes, *e.g.*, " Sighting No. 2 " and the " Sighting No. 6 Mark I," the object glass cell (A, Fig. 8) is mounted in a focussing

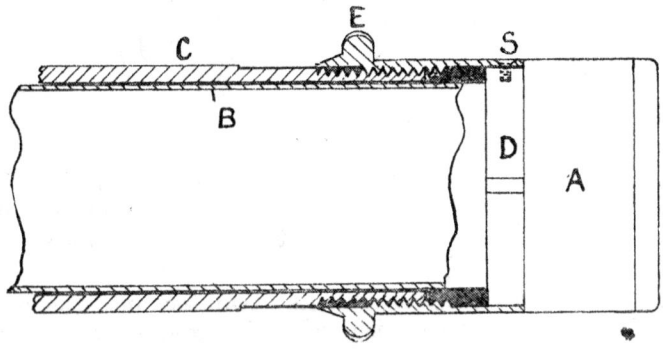

FIG. 8.

tube (B) which fits accurately in the body (C). A ring (D) encircles the focussing tube and can revolve around it, but cannot move backwards or forwards independently of it. Attached to the ring by screws (S) is a milled nut (E), which is threaded to screw on the body. When this nut is revolved, it and the ring (D) move backwards or forwards along the body and so alter the focus. A screw passing through the body and fitting into a longitudinal slot in the focussing tube, prevents the latter revolving, and so upsetting the collimation.

Telescopes with this pattern of object glass focussing are being converted to have a fixed focus object glass.

Telescopes with Fixed Object Glass.

Most telescopes of low power (*e.g.*, Sighting Telescopes) have the pointer fixed in the focal plane of the object glass. When focussing it is only necessary to adjust the eyepiece until the pointer is distinctly focussed, as the view will come to focus at the same time. This, however, only applies when the object laid on is at least 200 or 300 yards away. The telescopes could not be used for laying on objects a few yards away (*e.g.*, the target card of the apparatus training gun layers) unless the object glass were moved more forward in the telescope body.

Telescopes with a fixed focus should always be tested for parallax after being focussed (see page 6).

Focussing Arrangements of Eyepieces.

The following are the principal arrangements :—

(1) The eyepiece (A, Fig. 9) fits in a socket (B), which screws into the telescope, and can be moved backwards or forwards in it,

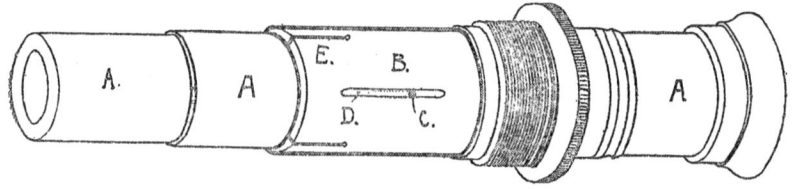

Fig. 9.

its movement being limited by a screw (C) fitting in a slot (D). The socket is slit in one or two places (E) and the portion between the slits slightly bent so as to act as a spring and prevent any play.

(2) The eyepiece (A, Fig. 10) fits accurately into the telescope body (B), and when it is revolved is forced to move backwards

or forwards by a sprial groove (C) cut in it coming in contact with a screw (D) passing through the body.

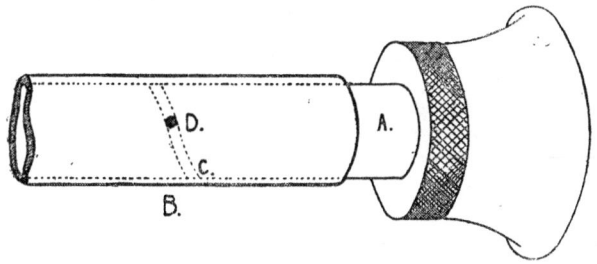

Fig. 10.

(3) The eyepiece (Fig. 11) is divided into two parts. The front portion or erector (A) is prevented from revolving by means

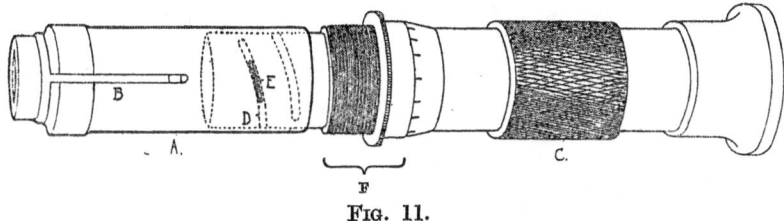

Fig. 11.

of a feather inside the telescope body fitting in a slot (B), it can, however, move forwards or backwards, and is forced to do so when the back portion of the eyepiece (C) is revolved, a groove (D) in the latter acting on a feather (E) attached to (A).

The rear portion of the eyepiece passes through a socket (F) screwed into the telescope body, and can be revolved in it, but cannot move forwards or backwards.

(4) The eye lens only is mounted on a screwed cell (A, Fig. 12) which fits into a screwed bush (B), attached to the body of

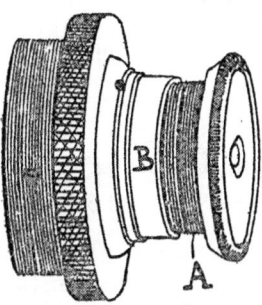

Fig. 12.

the telescope. When the eye lens cell is revolved it screws towards, or away from, the body. The cell or bush has longitudinal cuts through it. The portions between the cuts are pressed outwards or inwards to form springs and prevent undue play.

TELESCOPES, SIGHTING.

TELESCOPE, SIGHTING, No. 1.

This telescope is used with the automatic and rocking bar sights of most coast defence guns.

Magnification	3 diameters.
Field of view	10 degrees.
Clear aperture of object glass	1·5 inches.
Diameter of bearing collars	2·25 ,,
Length of ,, ,,	3·5 ,,

All Marks (except I and I*) have the following parts (see Plates I and II) in common, but other parts, which are only found in certain Marks, are described separately.

The brass body (A) on which are formed two gunmetal bearing collars (A_1, A_1) which are truly parallel throughout, of exactly the same diameter and concentric with the body. A feather fitted on the inside gears with a featherway in the sliding focussing bush (B) and prevents the latter from revolving when the telescope is being focussed.

The front of the body is threaded internally to take the object glass cell adapter (L), and externally to take the *ray-shade* (C).

The ray-shade is a long tube, which protects the object glass from the rain and keeps out extraneous light.

The rear end of the body is threaded internally to take the eyepiece (D).

The cap (E) is placed on the ray-shade when the telescope is not in use.

The eyepiece (D) consists of the following parts :—

*(1) Revolving focussing bush (F).

(2) Eyepiece proper (G) (with two lenses).

(3) Metal eyepiece cap (H).

*(4) Index bush (I).

*(5) Sliding focussing bush adapter (P).

*(6) Feather (K).

*(7) Sliding focussing bush (B).

(8) Erector (M) (with two lenses).

*Those parts marked * are not common to Marks I and I*.*

It is constructed on the principle described on page 13 (3). Figures numbered from 0 to 7 are engraved on the revolving focussing bush (except the Marks I and I* telescopes) and are read by an arrow engraved on the index bush. When the arrow is opposite 4 the telescope is in focus for a normal eye.

The removable dermatine eyeguard (N) is fitted to the eyepiece cap.

The object glass consists of two lenses separated by air only, and is prevented from revolving in the usual way.

[To face page 14.]   PLATE I.

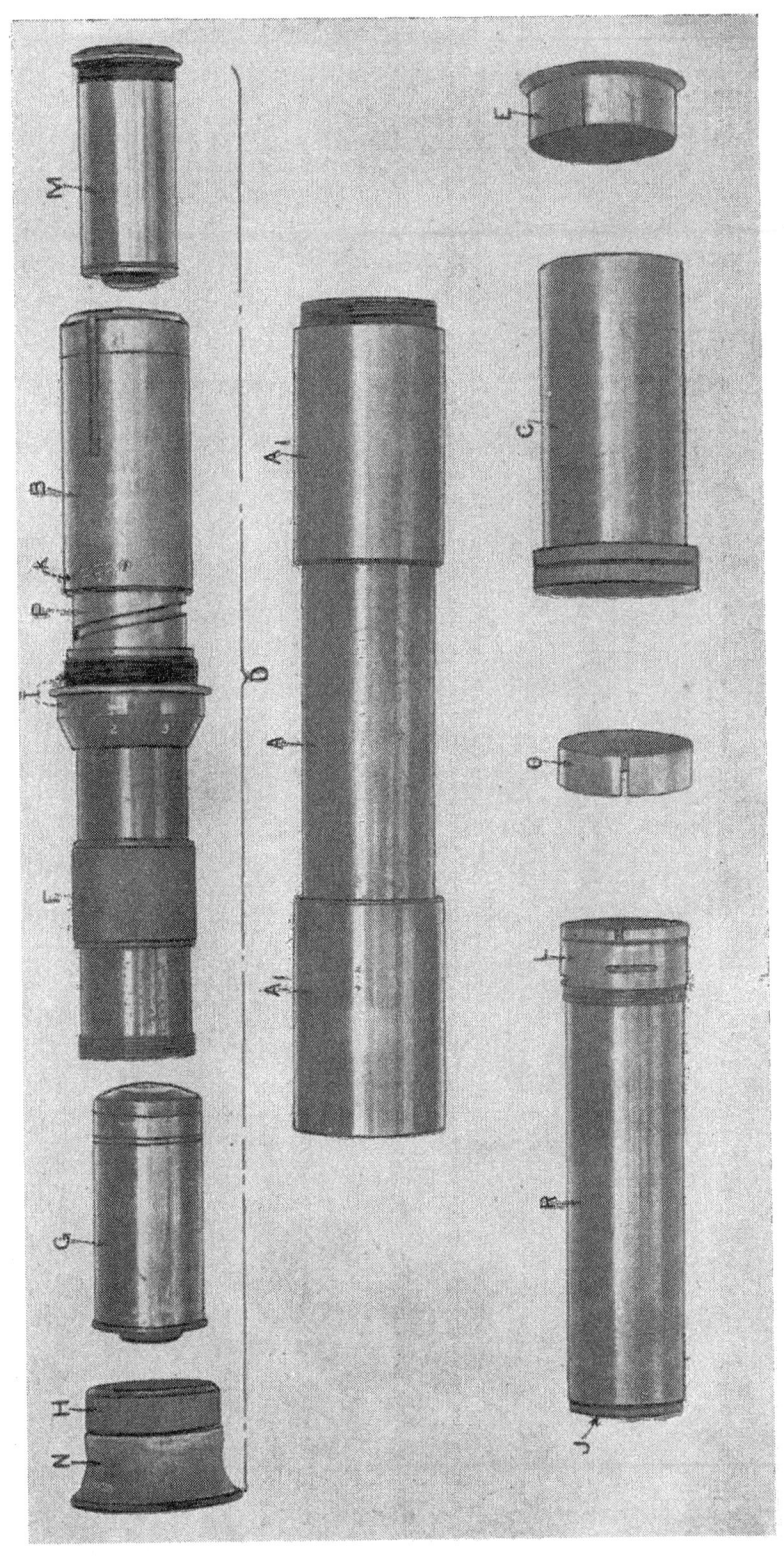

TELESCOPE, SIGHTING, NO. 1, MARK II. IN PARTS.

PLATE II.   [*To face page* 15.

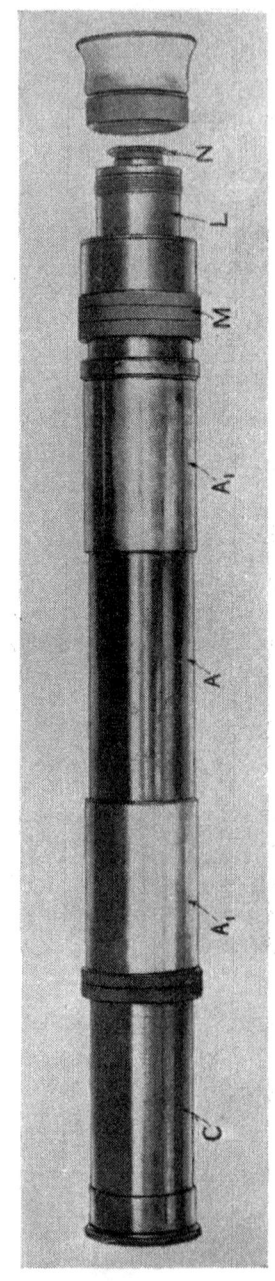

Telescope, Sighting, No. 1, Mark I*.

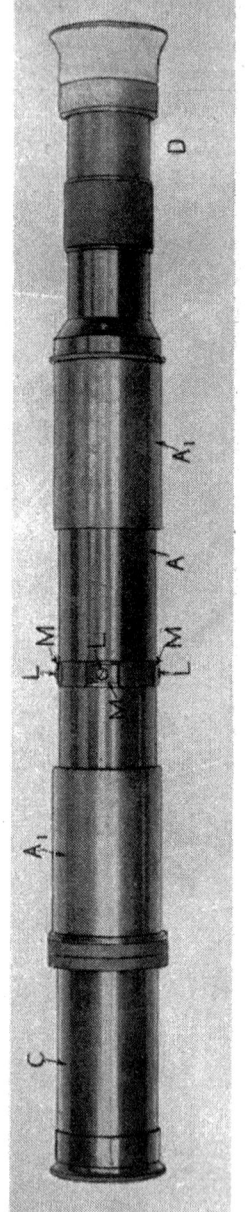

Telescope, Sighting, No. 1, Mark III.

The pointer (Fig. 13) has a diamoned-shaped head and is fixed

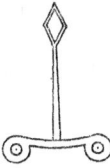

FIG. 13.

in the focal plane of the object glass (except with the Marks I and I*). When the pointer is focussed by the eyepiece, objects at ranges of 400 yards and beyond will also be in focus.

A wooden case with suitable fittings and a spring catch, or lock and key, is provided.

Mark II.
(Plate I.)

The pointer is attached by means of two screws to a diaphragm (J), which is screwed into the distance tube (R), at the front end of which is mounted the object glass in eccentric rings as described on page 7. The distance tube screws into the front of the body.

The weight of the telescope is 7 lbs. 4 ozs. and its length 24·25 inches.

Mark III.
(Plate II.)

The pointer is mounted on a diaphragm which is fixed to the body by means of four adjusting screws (L), the heads of which bear on thick washers (M). To prevent the pointer moving out of the focal plane of the object glass, the adjusting screws are made an accurate fit in the washers and the washers fit accurately in a groove cut round the body of the telescope.

The object glass is mounted in a cell which screws into the front end of the body.

The weight of the telescope is 7 lbs. 4 ozs. and its length 24 inches.
The external dimensions of the case are 27·2 × 5·4 × 4·65 inches.

Mark I*.
(Plate II.)

The pointer is attached to a diaphragm fitted between the eye and field lenses, and the object glass is mounted on eccentric rings as described on page 7.

The complete eyepiece (L) can slide axially in the telescope, and is kept in the rearmost position by a spiral spring beneath a knurled collar (M) which encircles it. The object of this arrangement was to prevent the telescope damaging the observer when the gun was fired, but with modern guns and mountings there is no likelihood of this.

The telescope is focussed by revolving the eye lens cell (N) in the manner described on page 13 (4). There is no scale for indicating the focus.

The weight of the telescope is 5 lbs. 12 ozs. and its length 23·15 inches.
The external dimensions of the case are 27 × 5·5 × 4·75 inches.

Mark I.

The Mark I, from which the Mark I* was converted, differs only in having a fixed eyeguard instead of a removable one.

TELESCOPE, SIGHTING, No. 2, MARK I.
(Plate III.)

This telescope is used with the 4·7-inch Q.F. gun on travelling carriage and the 6-inch B.L. Howitzer.

Magnification	5 diameters.
Field of view	5 degrees.
Effective aperture of object glass	1 inch.
Diameter of bearing collars	1·42 inches.
Over-all length	10 inches.
Weight	2 lbs.

It consists of the following parts :—

The body (A) on which are formed two bearing collars (A_1). The interior is accurately bored to form a seating for the draw tube. The front end is threaded externally to take the focussing ring (B) on the draw tube. The rear end is threaded internally to take the focussing bush adapter (D). Four holes are bored through it, through which pass the collimating screws, which hold the diaphragm with needle-shaped pointer in front of the eye lens. The heads of the collimating screws are covered over by a screwed ring (E).

The object glass consists of two lenses separated by air. It is mounted in a cell and kept in position by a counter cell. It is prevented from revolving in the usual way.

The draw tube fits accurately in the body and is prevented from revolving by a screw which passes through the body and fits into an elongated slot in the draw tube. The screw and elongated slot also limit the movement of the draw tube longitudinally. The object glass cell screws into the front end and a tube carrying the three front lenses of the eyepiece into the rear end. The screwed collar (B) can be revolved on it, but cannot move along it. When it is required to focus the object glass the screwed collar (B) is revolved, and, acting on the thread at the front end of the body, forces the draw tube in or out. An arrow on the focussing ring indicates when the object glass is adjusted for infinite focus.

The focussing bush adapter (D) screws into the rear end of the body, and is shaped to take a detachable dermatine eyeguard (not shown) if the telescope is of recent manufacture. Into it screws the focussing bush carrying the eye lens cell (G) which is revolved to focus the pointer, and which is prevented from unscrewing too far by a ring screwed into its front end.

The removable ray shade and shutter (H) protect the object glass.

Keep screws are provided where necessary to prevent parts becoming, unscrewed and lost.

To facilitate the focussing of these telescopes they will eventually be altered as follows :—

(1) The object glass fixed for infinite focus by passing screws through the draw tube, focussing ring and body, and so preventing any movement between these parts.

(2) Slackness in the screwed focussing bushes taken up by slitting them and making them act as springs.

[To face page 16.] PLATE III.

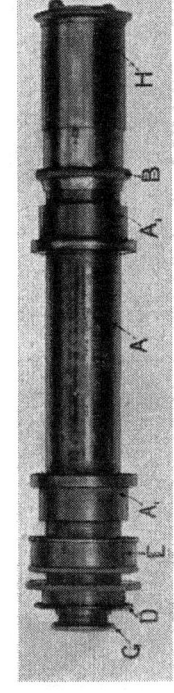

TELESCOPE, SIGHTING, NO. 2, MARK I.

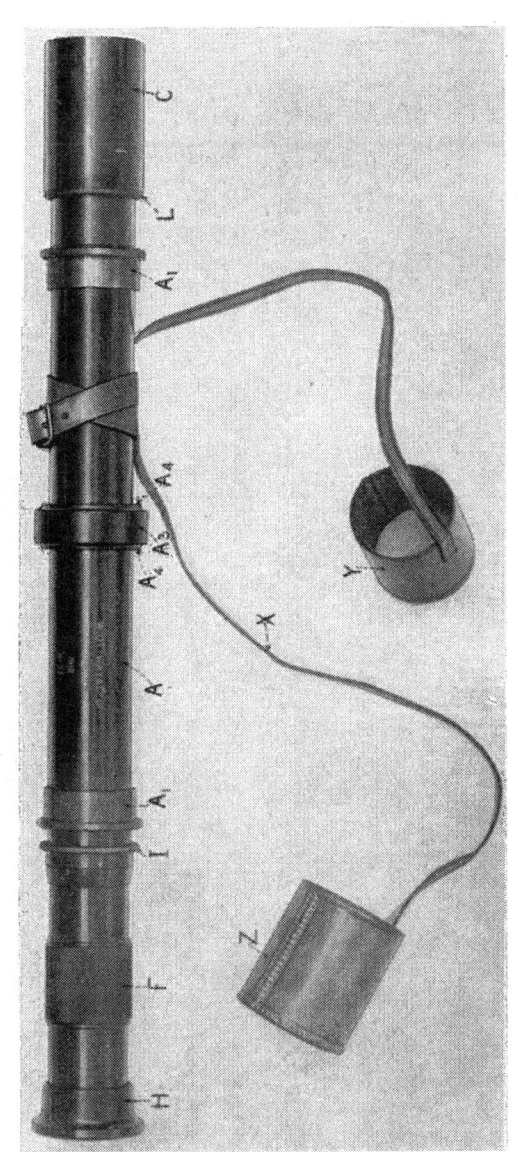

TELESCOPE, SIGHTING, NO. 4, MARK II.

PLATE IV.   [*To face page* 17.

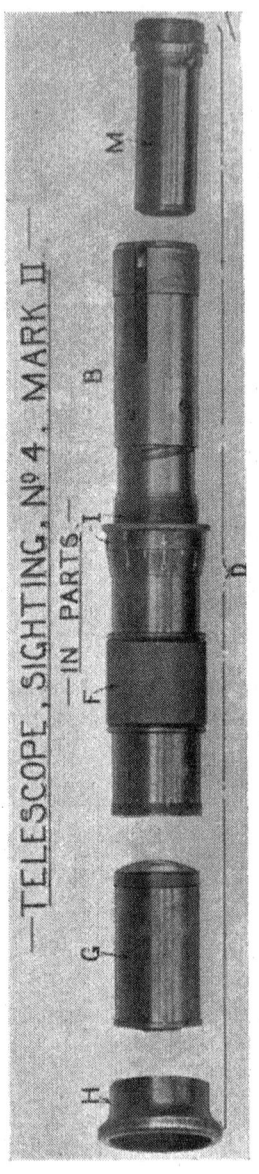

TELESCOPE, SIGHTING, Nº 4, MARK II.
—IN PARTS.—

Telescope, Sighting, No. 3.

This telescope is used with the automatic and rocking bar sights of most coast defence guns

Magnification	10 diameters.
Field of view	3·5 degrees.
Effective aperture of object glass	1·5 inches.
Diameter of bearing collars	2·25 ,,
Length ,, ,,	3·5 ,,
Over-all length	24·5 ,,
Weight	7 lbs. 4 ozs.

Marks I and II.

These are similar to the "Telescope, Sighting, No. 1," Marks II and III respectively, except as regards the optical properties and the shape of the pointer, which is shown in Fig. 14.

Fig. 14.

Telescope Sighting, No. 4.

(Plates III and IV.)

This telescope is used with the 13 and 18-pr. Q.F. guns.

Magnification	5¼ diameters.
Field of view	5·5 degrees.
Clear aperture of object glass	1·1 inches.
Diameter of bearing collars	1·47 ,,
Over-all length	18·25 ,,
Weight	2 lbs. 13 ozs.

The Marks I, II and III are generally similar and differ only in the arrangements for collimating. The Mark I has the object glass mounted in eccentric rings (see page 7 and the pointer attached to a diaphragm which is screwed into a distance tube in a manner similar to that already described for the No. 1, Mark II (page 15).

The Marks II and III have the pointer attached to a diaphragm, which is secured to the body by four collimating screws.

The Mark III is similar to the Mark II but several parts are made interchangeable.

The Marks II and III telescopes consists of the following parts :—

The body (A) has two bearing collars (A_1) formed on it, and two flanges (A_4) (near the centre) between which the collimating screws and thick washers are situated. The washers fit accurately between the flanges and so prevent the diaphragm from moving out of the focal plane of the object glass when the telescope is being collimated. The pointer attached to the diaphragm is needle-shaped. The heads of the collimating screws are kept covered over by the screw ring (A_3).

A pin (A_2) in the rear bearing collar fits into a hole in the rocking bar sight and prevents the telescope being revolved, the pointer in consequence is always in the same position and appears to point downwards.

The front end of the body is threaded internally to take the object glass cell adapter (K). This is shaped to act as a stop for the ring (L), which screws into the ray-shade (C) and cannot be slid off the telescope.

The object glass (E) is held in its cell (E_1) by the counter cell (E_2) and is prevented from revolving in the usual way.

The eyepiece (D) is similar to that described on page 13 (3). The eyecap (H) is made of brass and is not fitted with a dermatine eyeguard.

The leather sling (X) with caps (Y, Z) for the ray-shade and eyepiece is strapped to the body of the telescope.

TELESCOPE, SIGHTING, NO. 5.
(Plate V.)

This telescope is used with the 60-pr. B.L. gun.

Magnification	12 diameters.
Field of view	3 degrees.
Effective aperture of object glass	1·5 inches.
Diameter of bearing collars	1·685 ,,
Over-all length	22 inches.
Weight	3 lbs. 6 ozs.

The Marks I and II are generally similar, and differ only in the arrangement of the diaphragm and length of body. In the Mark I the diaphragm is very close to the rear bearing collar and is held in position by four capstan-headed screws, and there is no special arrangement to prevent the pointer on the diaphragm moving out of the focal plane of the object glass. With the Mark II, the diaphragm is farther to the rear, the four adjusting screws, which hold it, are accurately fitted through rectangular washers, which accurately fit into a groove running round the telescope body. In both Marks the diaphragm is fitted with a needle-shaped pointer.

The telescope consists of the following parts:—

The body (A) has two bearing collars (A_1) formed on it. Attached to it are two sighting vanes (B, B_1) which are kept up or down by means of flat steel springs (C). Beneath the vanes are open sights (D, D_1). The screws (H, H_1) are to prevent the vanes being pressed down too far. The front end of the body is threaded internally to take the object glass cell, and externally to take the *ray-shade* (E). The rear end is threaded internally to take the eyepiece (E_1) which is fitted with a detachable dermatine eyeguard (F).

A screwed ring (G) covers up the heads of the collimating screws.

The object glass consists of two lenses separated by air and is held in its cell by a counter cell. It is prevented from revolving in the usual way.

The eyepiece (E) is constructed on the principle described on page 12 (2) and is focussed by being turned.

To face page 18.] PLATE V.

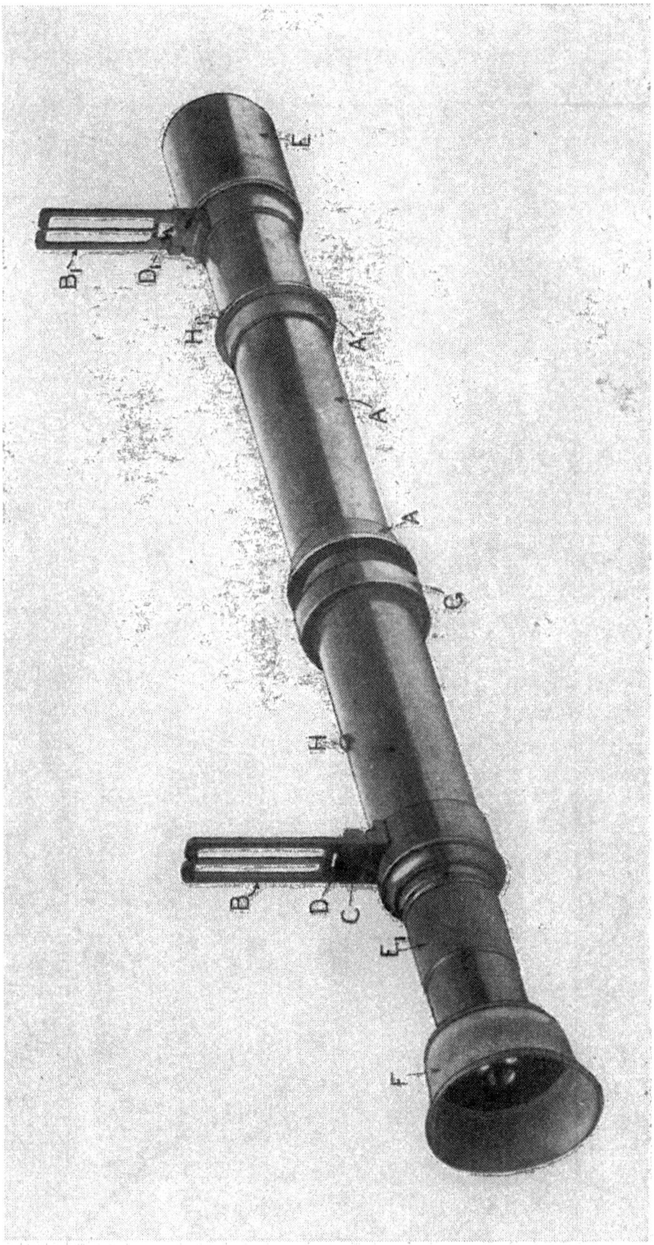

Telescope, Sighting, No. 5, Mark II.

PLATE VI.

[*To face page* 19.

TELESCOPE, SIGHTING, No. 6, MARK I.

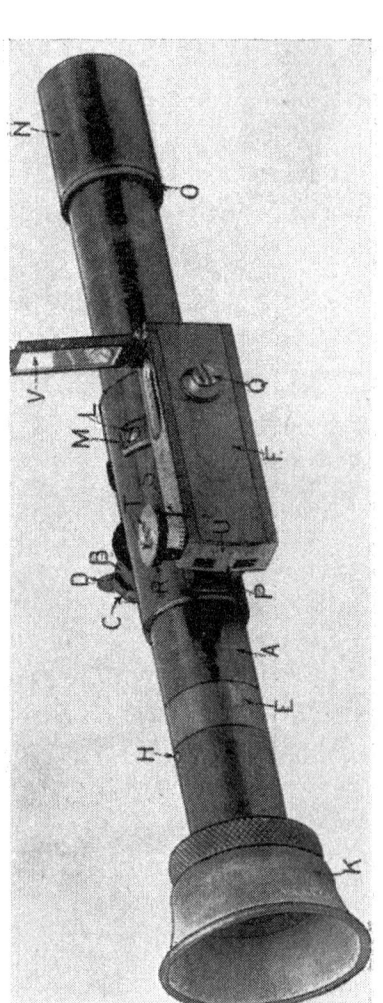

TELESCOPE, SIGHTING, No. 6, MARK III.

Telescope, Sighting, No. 6.

(Plate VI.)

This telescope is used with the 15-pr. B.L.C. and 15-pr. Q.F. guns.

Mark I.

This telescope is converted from the Mark IV Telescopic sight used with 12 and 15-pr. B.L. guns.

Magnification	5 diameters.
Field of view	5 degrees.
Effective aperture of object glass	1 inch.
Over-all length	9·5 inches.
Weight	2 lbs. 4 ozs.

It consists of the following parts :—

The body (A) which has formed on it a trunnion (B) (with washer (C) and nut (D)), and an accurately turned surface (E), which fit into the rocking bar sight. On the right is formed a seating for the clinometer level (F). The body is accurately bored to take the focussing tube which is prevented from revolving by a screwed stop which passes through the underside of the body and fits into a slot in it. The front end is externally threaded to take the focussing ring (G). The rear end is shaped to take the focussing bush adapter (K) and the diaphragm with needle-shaped pointer. The latter can be adjusted in a vertical plane by applying a forked screwdriver to a nut beneath the eyepiece. This nut (*a*, Fig. 15) acts on a screw (*s*) attached to the diaphragm

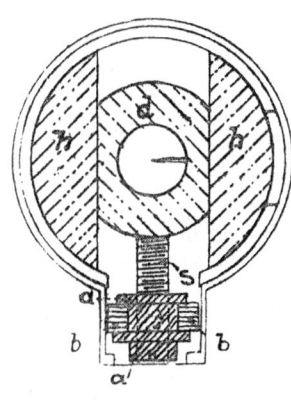

Fig. 15.

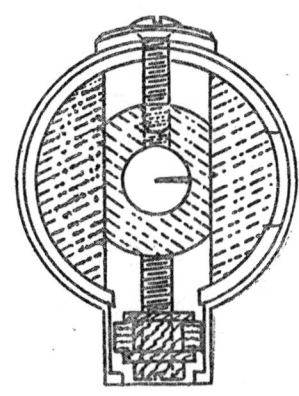

Fig. 15A.

(*d*), which slides in a dovetailed grooved holder (*h*), forcing it up or down. The lug bearing (*b*) in which the nut revolves is solid with the holder. The whole arrangement is held firmly in the body, which is slotted to receive the lug, by four screws. To prevent dust entering the telescope two suitable diaphragm shields are fitted.

There is no adjustment for the diaphragm in a horizontal plane.

The focussing tube extends for nearly the whole length of the body. At its front end is mounted, in a cell and secured by a counter cell, the object glass consisting of two lenses separated by air, and at the rear end the three front lenses of the eyepiece. A groove is cut near the front end into which fits a ring. Screws passing through the focussing ring (G) pass into this ring. When the focussing ring is revolved and screws backwards or forwards the focussing tube will also move backwards or forwards, but the stop screw prevents it revolving. (See page 11 (2).)

The eyelens is mounted in a cell (H) which can be slid in the focussing bush (J), but the cell should always be pressed well home. It is prevented from coming out of the telescope by a screwed collar at its front end. The focussing bush (J), is screw-threaded and the eyepiece is focussed by revolving it. The focussing bush adapter (K), which takes the focussing bush (J), is screwed into the body and secured by screws.

The ray-shade (L) *with shutter* (M) fits on the front end of the focussing tube and protects the object glass.

The clinometer level (F) consists of an arm, pivoted at (N), upon which is mounted a " Bubble, spirit glass " of either " B " " M " or special size. The front end of the arm has teeth cut upon it, which gear with a worm spindle having a milled head (O) attached to it. Beneath the latter is an adjustable minute skin (P) divided in two minute divisions, and graduated only at 0 and 30, so that it can be read in either direction. It can be adjusted when the two screws (Q) are slackened. The front end of the bubble arm has a degree scale plate (R) attached to it, reading from 0 to 6° elevation and 6° depression. It is read by the pointer (S) attached to the clinometer level. A flat spring pressing beneath the bubble arm takes up all play. Attached to the body is a hinged mirror (T) in which the reflection of the bubble can be seen, when it is not convenient to see the bubble direct.

To eliminate error due to looseness of fittings, backlash in the diaphragm, and to facilitate focussing, these telescopes will eventually be modified as follows :—

(a) Slackness in the screwed focussing bushes taken up by slitting them and making them act as springs.

(b) The degree scale plate and pointer riveted in position.

(c) The object glass fixed for infinite focus by passing screws through the focussing tube, focussing ring and body, and so preventing any movement between these parts.

(d) Play in the diaphragm eliminated by a countersunk headed screw which passes through the telescope body into the diaphragm diametrically opposite the diaphragm screw (see fig. 15A).

Case.

A padded leather case is provided.

Mark II.

The Mark II is not a converted telescope. It was made of practically the same size as the Mark I so that it would fit into the same case. Its optical properties are superior. Its construction is the same as the Mark III, but it is considerably smaller. It is not fitted with a dermatine eyeguard. In the clinometer level a " Bubble, spirit glass A " is used, but these will be eventually replaced by " L " bubbles.

Magnification	..	..	..	..	5 diameters.
Field of view	..	..	..	..	5 degrees.
Effective aperture of object glass			..		1 inch.
Over-all length	..	..	..	..	10 inches.
Weight	..	..	..	..	2 lbs. 4 ozs.

Mark III.
(Plate VI.)

Magnification	..	..	..	..	5 diameters.
Field of view	..	..	..	..	5 degrees.
Effective aperture of object glass			..		1 inch.
Over-all length	..	..	..	..	13·5 inches.
Weight	..	..	..	..	Varying from 2 lbs. 11 ozs. to 3 lbs. 4 ozs.

The telescope consists of the following parts :—

The body (A) which has formed on it a trunnion (B) (with washer (C) and winged nut (D)), and an accurately turned surface (E) which fit into the rocking bar sight. On the right is formed a seating for the clinometer level (F).

At the front end is mounted, in a cell and kept in position by a counter cell, the object glass, which consists of two lenses separated by air. A screw prevents the object glass cell becoming detached from the body. The rear end is accurately bored to take the eyepiece.

The eyepiece is constructed on the principle described on page 12 (2). The screw (H) prevents it becoming detached from the telescope and acts as a guide for the focussing arrangement. It is fitted with a detachable dermatine eyeguard (K).

The diaphragm (Fig. 16) is fitted with a needle-shaped pointer and is supported by four collimating screws (L), the heads of which

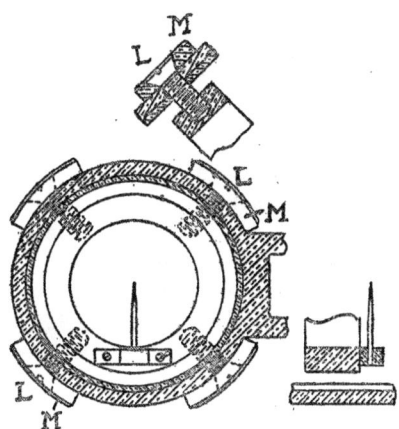

Fig. 16.

bear on washers (M). The pointer is fixed in the focal plane of the object glass.

The ray-shade (N) is held on the telescope by the screwed ring (O). It can be slid backwards or forwards over the object glass cell adapter.

The clinometer level (F) consists of an arm (P) pivoted at (Q) upon which is mounted a " Bubble, spirit glass A."* The rear end of the arm has teeth cut upon it, into which gears a worm spindle having attached to it the milled head (R) and a skin (S). The skin is divided every two minutes and is marked only at 0 and 30, so that it can be read in either direction. It can be adjusted when the screws (T) are slackened. A spring acting beneath the arm takes up all backlash.

A degree scale (U) reading from 0 to 6° elevation and 6° depression is engraved on the body and read by a reader on the bubble arm (P).

Attached to the body is a hinged mirror (V) in which the reflection of the bubble can be seen when it is not convenient to see the bubble direct.

Box.

A box is provided for carrying the telescope.

Mark IV.

The Mark IV is generally similar to the Mark III, differing from it only as follows :—

(1) The graduated ring on the micrometer head is higher and has two minute scales engraved on it. The scale for elevation being black on brass, and that for depression white on black.

(2) The bubble in the clinometer level is a " Bubble, spirit, glass L."

TELESCOPE, SIGHTING, No. 7 (VARIABLE POWER).

(Plate VII.)

This telescope is used with the automatic and rocking bar sights of 9·2-inch B.L. guns, and will gradually replace the Nos. 1 and 3.

Magnification	Varying from 5 to 21 diameters.
Field of view	Varying from 6° to 1° 15'.
Effective aperture of object glass	1·8 inches.
Diameter of bearing collars	2·25 ,,
Over-all length	31·5 ,,
Weight	8·25 lbs.

Owing to different makers having patents for the method by which the power can be varied, and the telescope collimated, the construction of this telescope is not always the same. It is, however, usually constructed to either the Ross or Ottway design.

Externally the different patterns are very similar. The body (A) (Plate VII) is made of steel truly turned for its entire length to fit into the sight. The pointer, which is shaped as shown in Fig. 17, is

FIG. 17.

---

* These will eventually be replaced by L bubbles.

To face page 22.] PLATE VII.

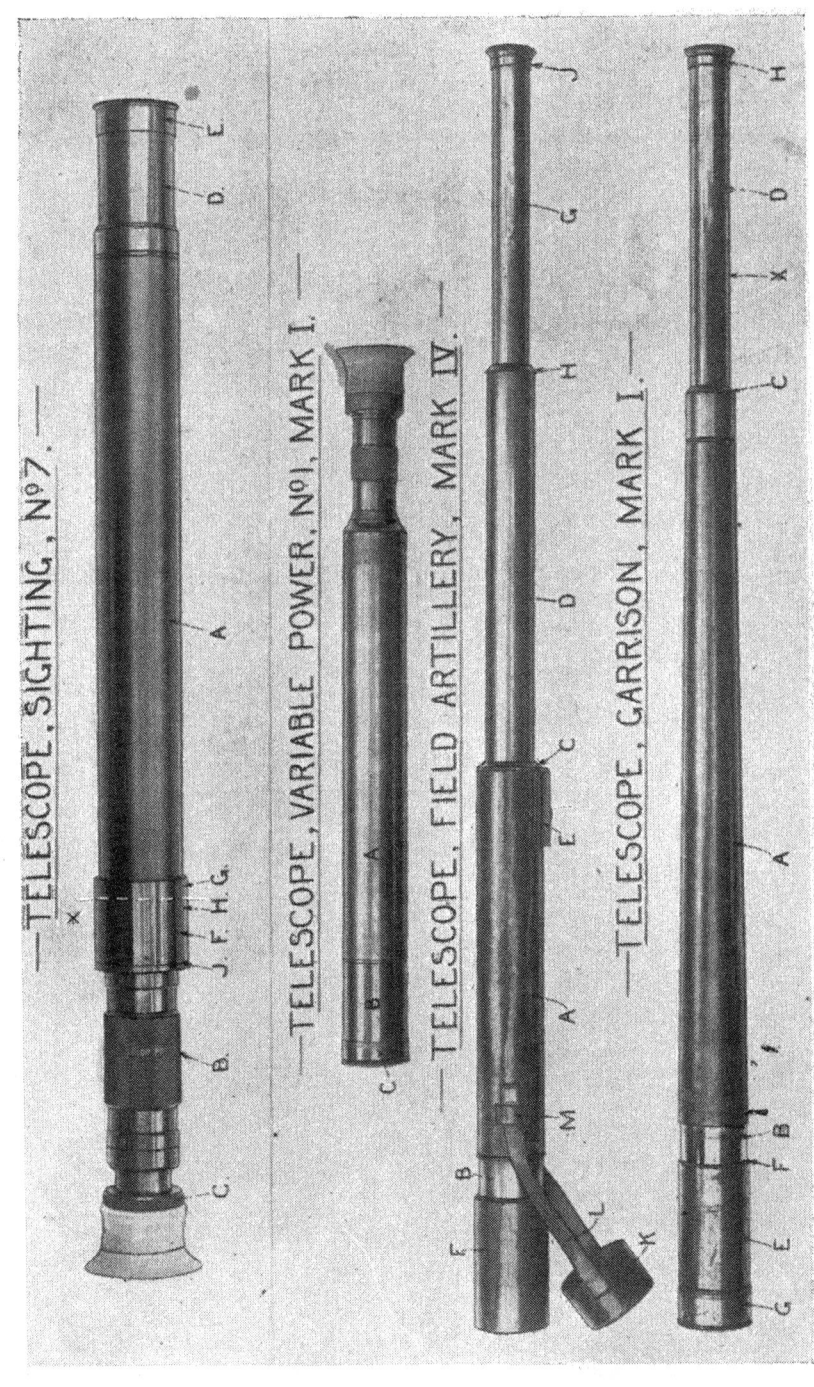

fixed in the focal plane of the object glass or glasses, which do not move. The power is varied by revolving the milled portion (B), and the pointer is focussed by revolving the eyepiece cap (C), which is fitted with a detachable dermatine eyeguard.

The object glass is protected by a long ray-shade (D) and cap (E).

When using the telescope the power should be varied until the object laid on is most distinctly seen. If the light alters it may be advisable to alter the power of the telescope. Whenever the power is altered the telescope should be very carefully tested for focus, especially if the iris diaphragm is in use.

It may often be found convenient to use the low power, with its large field of view, for picking up a target, and then to change the power for laying on it.

Ross Pattern.

(Plate VII.)

The object glass consists of two lenses separated by air, which are kept in their cell by a counter cell and prevented from revolving in the usual way. The object glass cell screws into the front end of the body.

A second object glass is burnished in a cell, and the latter is screwed into the "bush connecting eyepiece to body" (F), which screws on to the rear end of the steel tube and is secured there by the keep screw (G). Its approximate position is shown by the dotted line (X). Inside (F) there is a flange against which the diaphragm with pointer (Fig. 18) is held by four collimating screws. The rim of the diaphragm

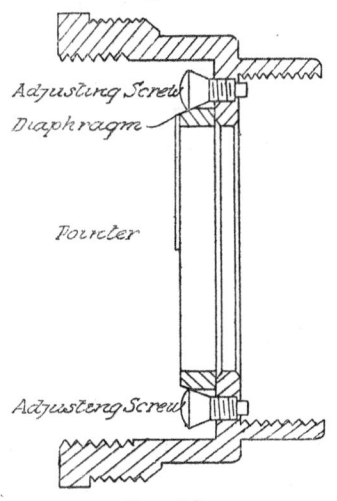

Fig. 18.

and the heads of the screws are coned, so that if a screw is slackened and the one opposite to it is tightened up, the diaphragm will be forced towards the former.

When the telescope is being collimated it is necessary to remove the eyepiece to get at the collimating screws. This is done by removing the set screw (J) and unscrewing the rear portion of the eyepiece.

The three lenses of the eyepiece are mounted as follows. (Plate VIII.)

The erector, which consists of a single lens (J), is mounted in a tube having the stud (B) secured to it by the small screws (s, s) projecting from it.

The other two lenses forming a Ramsden eyepiece are mounted in the tube (A) which has a quick-motion thread cut on it and screws into the tube (A_1). The focus of the pointer and object depends upon the position of this tube (A), which has to be varied to suit different eyesights. The tube (A_1) has a stud (A_2), secured to it by the small screws (s, s), projecting from it.

The two tubes holding the erector (J) and the Ramsden eyepiece, are free to slide inside a tube (C), the front end (C_1) of which is enlarged and threaded to screw into the body of the telescope, in which it is prevented from revolving by a set screw. This tube (C) has two slots (C_2) cut along it (shown in dotted lines), in which the studs (B and A_2) fit, thus preventing the tubes carrying the lenses from revolving.

The tube (C) fits into an outer tube (D), which can be revolved about it, but is prevented from moving longitudinally. In this tube are cut two spiral cam grooves (E and F) in which the studs (B and A_2) work. The tube is covered over by the tube (G), the outer surface of which is milled, and to which it is rigidly attached by screws passing through the holes (H, H_1, V, V_1).

When (G) is turned it also turns (D), and the cam grooves acting on the studs force the tubes carrying the Ramsden eyepiece and erector towards or away from one another, thus varying the power of the telescope and at the same time keeping it in focus.

Ottway Pattern.

The principle of this pattern is the same as that of the Telescope, Variable Power, No. 1, described on page 25.

CASE.

A wooden case with internal fittings for the telescope and a compartment for a spare dermatine eyeguard is provided. It is fitted with a spring catch, two hooks and eyes and a carrying strap.

Weight .. .. .. 9.25 lbs.
Approximate dimensions .. 38 × $5\frac{3}{4}$ × $4\frac{1}{2}$ inches.

TELESCOPE, SIGHTING, No. 8.

This telescope is a conversion of the Telescope, Sighting, No. 1, or No. 3, arranged to focus at very short distances. It is used with the "Apparatus, training gunlayers." As the conversion is fully described in List of Changes no details are given here.

TELESCOPE, VARIABLE POWER, No. 1, MARK I.

This telescope is used for observing the fire of Siege Artillery.

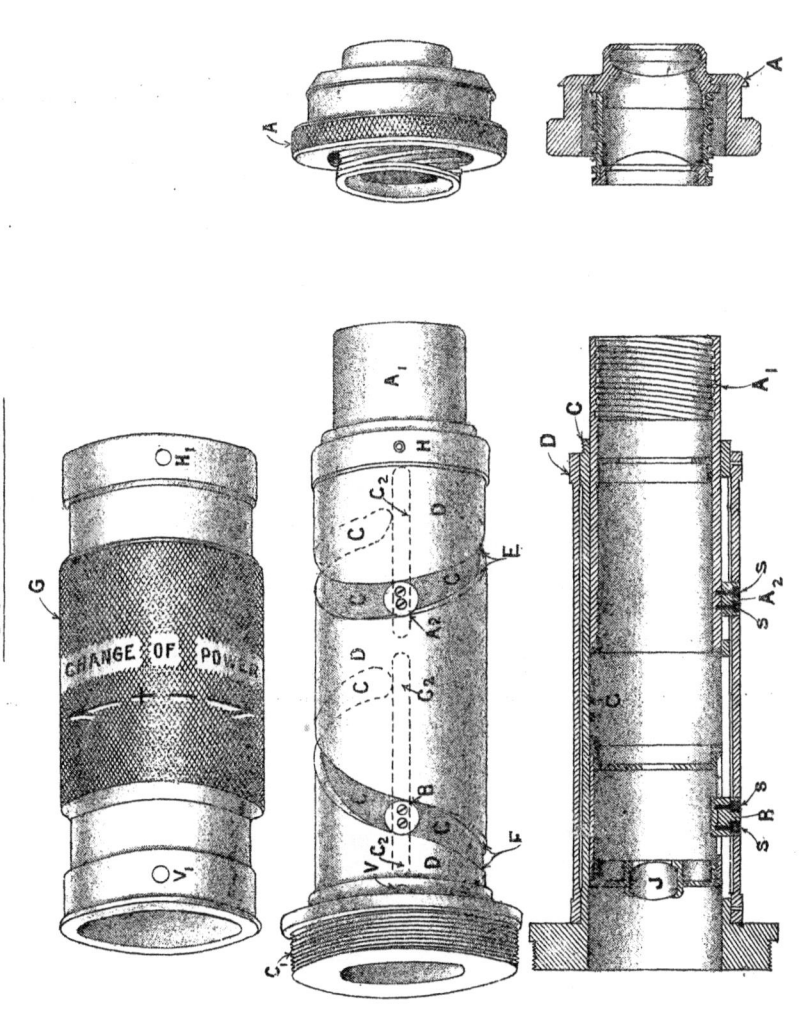

To face page 24. Plate VIII.

ARRANGEMENT FOR VARYING POWER, Nº 7. SIGHTING TELESCOPE.
ROSS PATTERN.

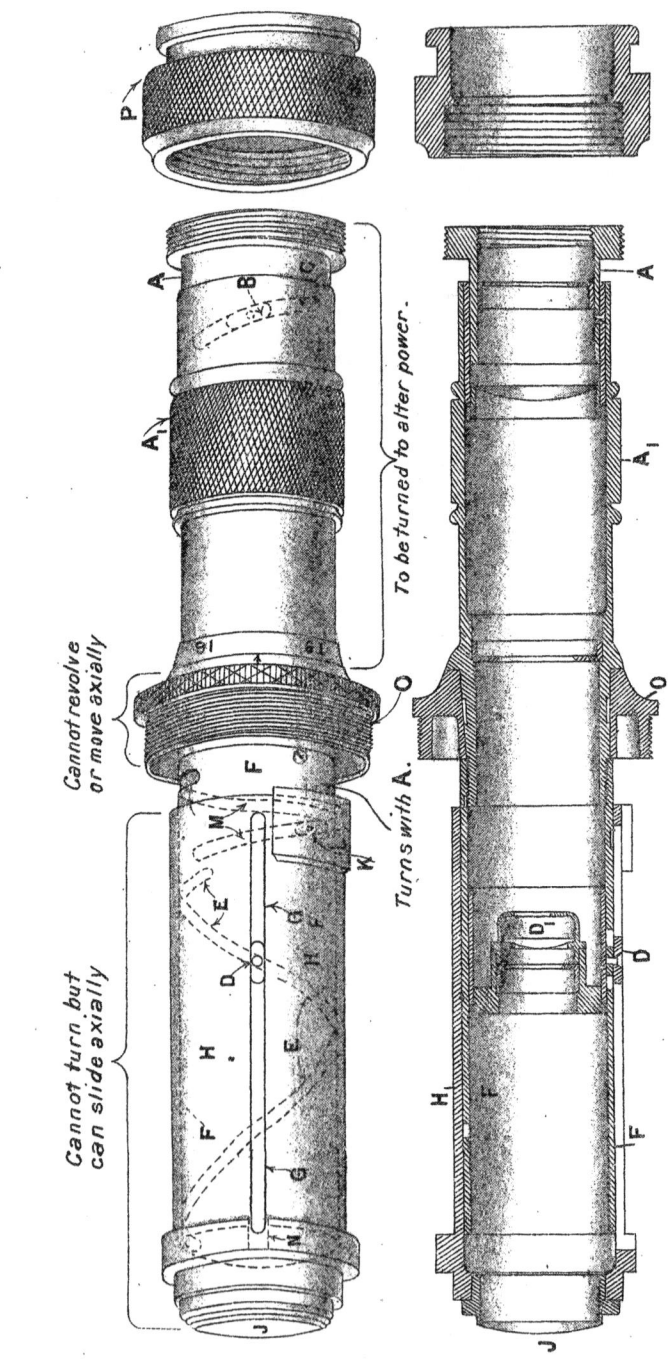

Magnification	Varying from 7 to 21 diameters.
Field of view	Varying from 4° 30' to 1° 30'.
Effective aperture of object glass	2 inches.
Weight	9½ lbs.
Length	About 30 inches.

Owing to different makers having patents for the method of varying the power and collimating arrangements, the telescopes are not always of the same design, but they are usually of either the Ross or Ottway pattern. The Ross pattern is similar to that described for the "Telescope, Sighting, No. 7," on page 23, differing from it only in small details. The Ottway pattern is described below.

Graticules are engraved on a glass diaphragm mounted in front of the eyepiece. They are 1', 10', 30', 60' and 90' on either side of the axis, the 10' and 60' ones being thicker than the remainder. They extend 34' above and below a line which cuts them at right angles (Fig. 19).

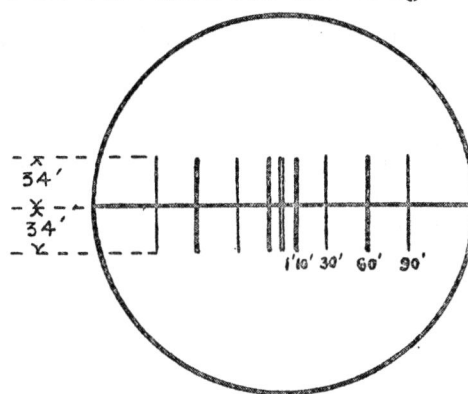

FIG. 19.

For method of use, focussing, &c., which is similar to that described for the Telescope, Sighting, No. 7, see page 22.

CASE.

A wooden case with spring catch, two hooks and eyes and a carrying strap is provided.

Ottway Pattern.

(Plates VII and IX.)

The telescope consists of the following parts:—

The body (A) is a brass tube, the front end of which is threaded internally to take the adapter which carries the object glass (which consists of two lenses). The object glass is mounted in eccentric cells for collimating purposes, as described on page 7.

It is threaded externally to take the ray-shade (B) which is provided with a cap (C).

The diaphragm with graticules is attached to a distance tube which keeps it in the focal plane of the object glass.

A feather is fitted inside the body in rear of the diaphragm and engages with a groove (N) (Plate IX) at the front end of the eyepiece, and prevents the tube (H) from turning.

The eyepiece (Plate IX) contains four lenses. The two rear ones form a Huygens eyepiece and are mounted in a tube (A) which accurately fits in another tube (A_1). The eyelens and its cell are not shown. The latter screws into the tube (A). When (A) is revolved for focussing, it is forced in or out of (A_1) by a feather (B) acting on a groove (C) (shown in dotted lines).

One (D_1) of the two lenses of the erector is mounted in a tube, the movement of which, when the power of the telescope is being altered, is controlled by a double feather (D), one part of which slides in a groove (E) cut round the tube (F), and the other part slides along a straight groove (G) in the tube (H) which cannot revolve. This lens is thus forced straight to the front or rear when the power is being changed.

The front lens (J) is mounted in the tube (H), and its movement is controlled by a feather (K) on the plate (L), which fits in a groove (M) in the tube (F). (L) is rigidly fixed to (H).

The tube (H) is prevented from turning by the feather inside the telescope body sliding in the groove (N), which is shown in dotted lines underneath the front of it. When the power is being altered by turning (A), the tube (H) carrying the front lens (J) will therefore be forced straight to the front or rear, and its movement combined with that of (D_1) will keep the telescope in focus.

The eyepiece adapter (O), which screws into the rear end of the body of the telescope, acts as a bearing for the eyepiece to revolve in. An arrow engraved on it, read in conjunction with figures on the eyepiece, indicates the magnification or power that the telescope is set for.

The eyecap (P) screws on to the eyepiece and holds a detachable dermatine eyeguard.

STAND, VARIABLE POWER TELESCOPE, No. 1, MARK I.
(Plate X.)

The stand consists of the following parts :—

Three steel legs (A) which are attached to the base plate by coned pivots (B). Each pivot is prevented from revolving by a small feather which fits in a groove in the legs, and is held in position by a washer, nut, keep nut and split pin. Each leg consists of an upper limb or tube (A) having a leg hinge (C) accurately fitted into its upper end and secured by three screws, a clamping arrangement (D) at its lower end, and a lower limb or tube (E) which slides in the upper limb and has a stop fitted at its upper end and a pointed shoe (F) at its lower end.

A securing strap (G) is attached to one leg.

The base plate (H) is a casting with lugs (J) for the legs. It is centrally bored to take the main pivot (K) of the revolving plate. On one side it takes the milled headed clamp spindle (L). This spindle has an eccentric cut on it, which when it is turned forces a clamp block into a V groove in the revolving plate, and so prevents it from revolving. The clamp spindle is fitted in bearings and kept in position by a washer and nut.

The revolving plate (M) has the main pivot attached to it by three screws. A V groove is cut round its rim to take the clamp block.

The main pivot (K) passes through the revolving plate, and is held to it by three screws. One end passes through the base plate and is held by a washer and nut. The top of the main pivot is formed to

To face page 26.] PLATE X.

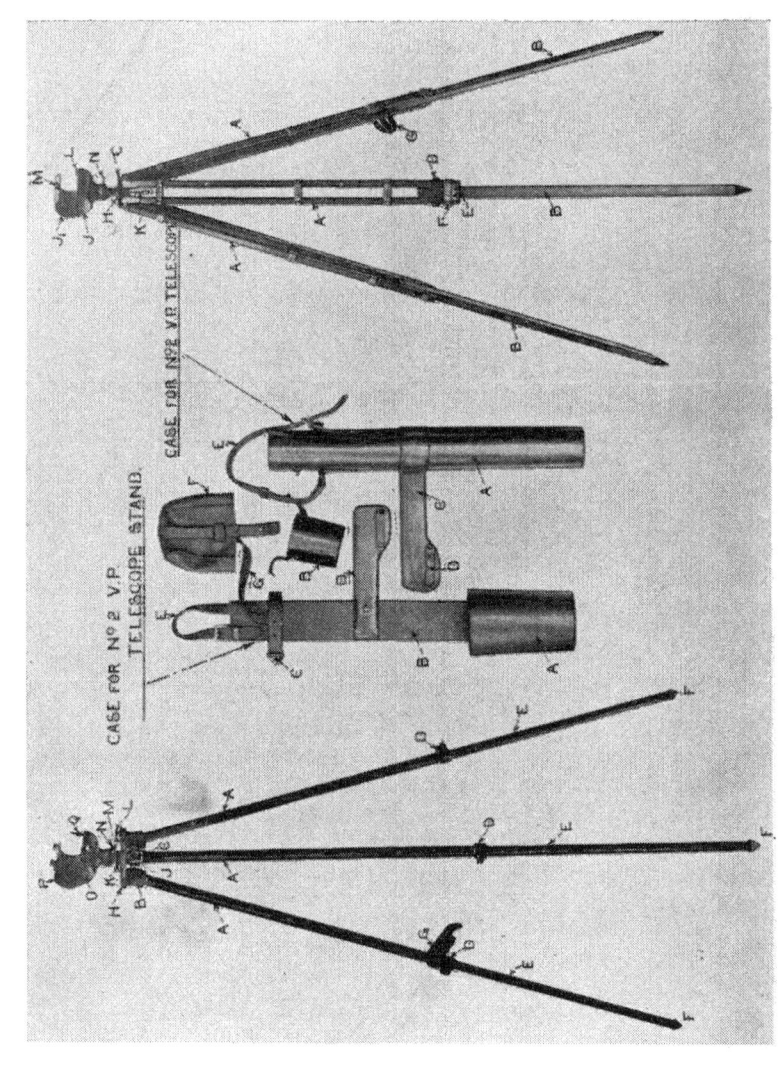

take the socket hinge bolt, which can be clamped up by the winged nut (N) and washer. The bolt is prevented from revolving by a steel pin and groove.

The hinged telescope socket (O) is shaped to take the telescope. The cover (P) can be clamped down on the telescope by two thumb nuts (Q).

The weight of the stand is 22 lbs.

TELESCOPE, VARIABLE POWER, No. 2, MARK I.

This telescope is used by Heavy Artillery for observing. It is similar to the Variable Power No. 1, but it is not fitted with graticules.

It is provided with two leather end caps joined together by a strap. These fit over the ends of the telescope, protect the eyepiece and facilitate the removal of the telescope from its leather case.

CASE, VARIABLE POWER TELESCOPE, No. 2, MARK I.

(Plate X.)

The case consists of a leather bucket (A), which with its leather cap (B) entirely enclose the telescope.

A flap (C) enclosing a piece of steel, projects from its centre and has a loop (D) riveted to it, through which the surcingle passes. A suspending strap (E) is attached to the case by a brass D ring, its other end passing through a buckle.

The weight of the case is 3 lbs. 2 ozs.

STAND, VARIABLE POWER TELESCOPE, No. 2, MARK I.

(Plate X.)

The stand consists of the following parts :—

Three jointed ash legs (A B) which are attached to the lugs in the base plate (C) by bolts with nuts, washers and keep pins. The lower portions (B) can slide a short distance between the side pieces of the upper portions (A), the two parts being held together by bolts (D) which are fixed in (A) and pass through the slots in (B).

Small brass plates (E) fixed by screws to (B) prevent the latter folding back when they are in contact with other plates (F) attached to (A). When setting up the stand the lower portions (B) are swung round until they are in prolongation of (A) and are then forced upwards until the plates (E) and (F) are in contact.

A securing strap (G) is attached to one leg.

The base plate (C) has lugs formed on it to take the legs, a distance piece being inserted in each lug. It is bored cylindrically to take the pivot (H).

The pivot (H) is attached to the base plate by two nuts and a washer. Its upper end is forked to form a hinge for the telescope socket (J).

An anchoring hook (K) is screwed into the pivot. By attaching a heavy weight to this hook the stand can be made very steady in rough weather.

The telescope socket (J) with its cover (J_1) is shaped to take the telescope, which can be firmly clamped in position by a nut (L) and lug (M). The telescope socket is held to the pivot (H) by a bolt which can be tightened up by the winged nut (N).

The weight of the stand is $11\frac{1}{3}$ lbs.

Case for No. 2 Variable Power Telescope Stand.
(Plate X.)

The case consists of the following parts :—

A leather bucket (A) to take the legs of the stand, which are held to the *backstrap* (B) by the *securing strap* (C).

A flap (D), which has a steel strengthening piece sewn in it and is secured to the backstrap by sewing and a copper rivet.

A suspending strap (E).

A cover (F) to fit over the head of the stand, attached to the backstrap by the strap (G).

The weight of the case is 3 lbs.

Telescope, Field Artillery.
(Plate VII.)

This telescope was introduced for observing purposes for the use of Field Artillery and General Staff.

Magnification	35 diameters.
Field of view	55 minutes.
Effective aperture of object glass	2·3 inches.
Weight	5 lbs. 4 ozs.
Length extended	49 inches.
„ closed	22 „

Mark IV.

This telescope consists of the following parts :—

The body (A) which is a brass tube covered with brown leather. Screwed rings are fixed to it, one of which takes the tube (B) carrying the object glass and the other the spring box (C) through which the front draw tube (D) slides.

An attachment (E) which fits into the top of the Stand, Field Artillery Telescope, is secured to it by six screws.

The object glass consists of two lenses, separated by air, which are kept in their cell by a counter cell and prevented from revolving in the usual way. The object glass cell screws into the tube (B) which is so shaped that the leather covered ray-shade (F) can be slid along it, but cannot become detached.

Two draw tubes (D, G), which pass through spring boxes (C, H) to prevent play. Each spring box consists of a brass tube, the front end of which is threaded, and the rear end carefully turned to fit accurately into the tube into which it is screwed. The centre of the tube is cut through longitudinally in four places, the portions between the cuts being pressed in, so as to form springs, which bear upon the draw tube passing through it.

The rear draw tube holds the eyepiece lenses, the two erector lenses being screwed in the front end and the two lenses of the eyepiece proper being held in the rear end by the cap (J).

A fine wire mounted on a diaphragm, is placed immediately in front of the eyelens, and can be used in either a horizontal position (for obtaining angles of sight) or a vertical position (for obtaining battery angles). When used for the former purpose the clinometer level on the stand must be adjusted so that when the line of sight is horizontal and the scales are set to zero the bubble is in the centre of its run.

The cap (J) is provided with a shutter, pivoted on a screw, for protecting the eyelens when the telescope is not in use.

A leather cap (K) is provided to cover the object glass. It is attached to the telescope by two straps (L) having thickened ends which pass through guides (M).

The telescope is used on the same stand as the No. 1 director (see page 41.)

The earlier Marks are obsolescent.

CASE.

A leather case is provided for carrying the telescope on a saddle.

TELESCOPE, GARRISON, MARK I.
(Plate VII.)

This telescope was introduced for observing purposes for Coast Defences.

Magnification	35 diameters.
Field of view	55 minutes.
Effective aperture of object glass	2·3 inches.
Weight	5 lbs. 4 ozs.
Length extended	4 feet 4 inches.
,, closed	37 inches.

The telescope consists of the following parts :—

The body (A), which is a coned brass tube covered with leather. Two screwed rings are fixed to it, one of which screws into the tube (B) which carries the object glass, and the other takes the spring box (C) through which the draw tube (D) slides.

The object glass consists of two lenses separated by air, which are held in the object glass cell by a counter cell and prevented from revolving in the usual way. The object glass cell screws into the tube (B), along which the ray-shade (E) can be slid. The ray-shade is prevented from becoming detached by the screwed ring (F) coming in contact with a projection on (B). A metal cap (G) protects the object glass when the telescope is not in use.

The spring box (C) consists of a tube, one end of which is threaded to screw into the body. It has four longitudinal cuts in it, the portions between the cuts being slightly bent inwards to act as springs against the draw tube and prevent play.

The draw tube (D) is made in two pieces which screw together near its centre at (X), and so allow of the erector lenses being removed. It carries the usual four lenses; the two lenses of the eyepiece proper are kept in the draw tube by the eyecap (H) which is provided with a shutter pivoted on a screw.

STAND.

A tripod stand is provided for holding the telescope. It has three mahogany legs, which unscrew near their centre. The legs have chains attached to them, which, when tightened by the legs being splayed, make the stand very rigid. The legs are pivoted to a plate on which is mounted a baize lined carrier for the telescope. The carrier is arranged to elevate and traverse as required.

CASE.

A wooden case is provided to take both the telescope and stand (with the legs in halves). It is provided with a spring catch, two hooks and eyes, two leather handles and two securing straps.

STEREOSCOPIC TELESCOPE.
(Plates XI and XII.)

This telescope is employed for observing purposes with all batteries having 9·2-inch B.L. guns.

Magnification	.. 10 diameters.
Field of View	.. 4 degrees.
Effective aperture of object glasses ..	.. 1·625 inches.
Weight of instrument in case ..	.. 30 lbs.
Interocular distance	.. From 54 to 74 mm.
Length when fully extended	.. 30 inches.

The telescope consists of the following parts :—

Two steel arms (A, A) with gunmetal fittings to hold the prisms, lenses, &c. They are hinged together at (B) and can be clamped in any desired position by the clamping screw (C).

Two scales for indicating interocular distances in millimetres are engraved on the hinge cap (D), one being used when the arms are nearly vertical, and the telescope is being used behind cover, and the other when the arms are nearly horizontal, and the greatest stereoscopic effect is being obtained.

Two bearings are formed on the hinge, which rest on the top of the carrier (E). One of them can be clamped to the carrier by a winged nut (F) being screwed down on a cap square (G).

Each arm (Fig. 20) has a single reflecting prism (Z) mounted at

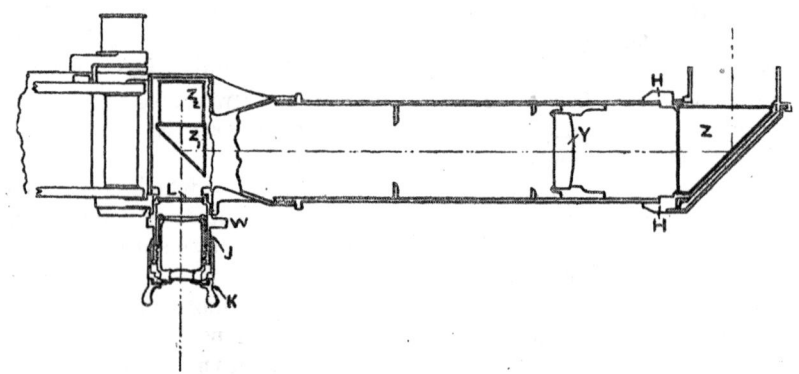

FIG. 20.

one end in the prism head (H); behind this is mounted, in the steel tube, an achromatic object glass (Y) consisting of two lenses. At the other end are mounted, at right angles to one another, two prisms, one of which (Z_1) receives light from the end prism and reflects it at right angles into a double reflecting prism (Z_2), which reflects it into the eyepiece (J).

[*To face page* 30.]   PLATE XI.

Stereoscopic Telescope.

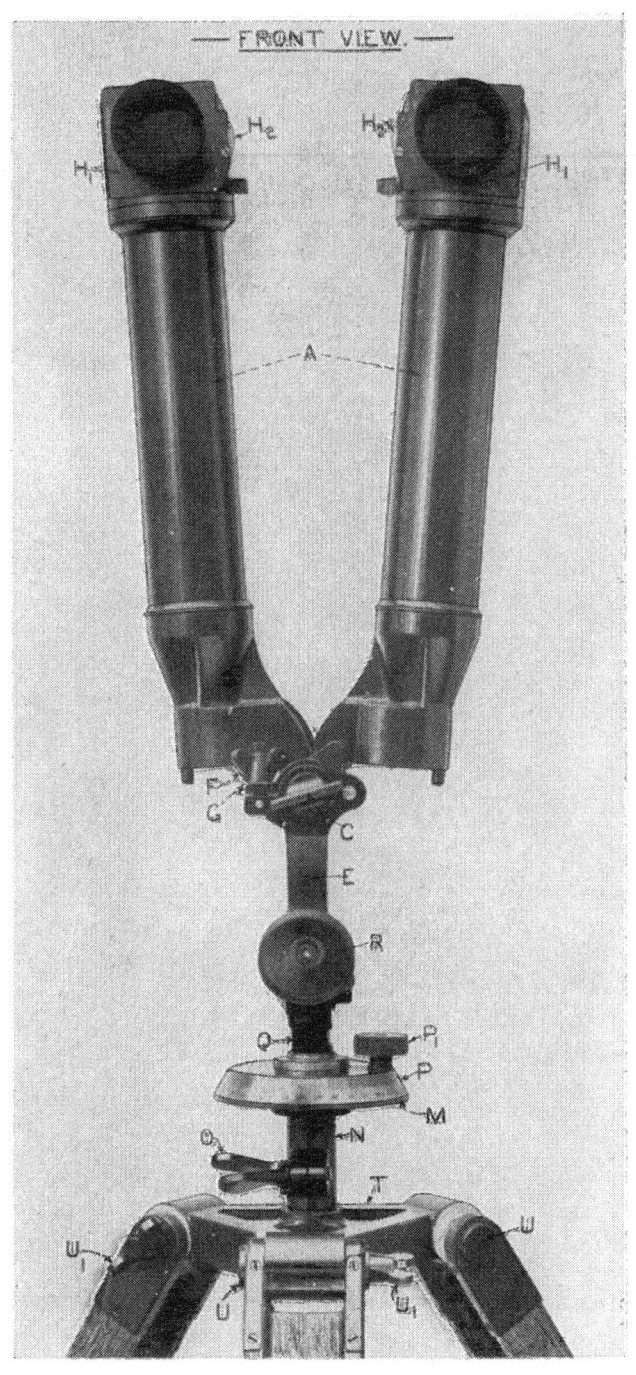

PLATE XII.   [*To face page* 31.

STEREOSCOPIC TELESCOPE.—REAR VIEW.—

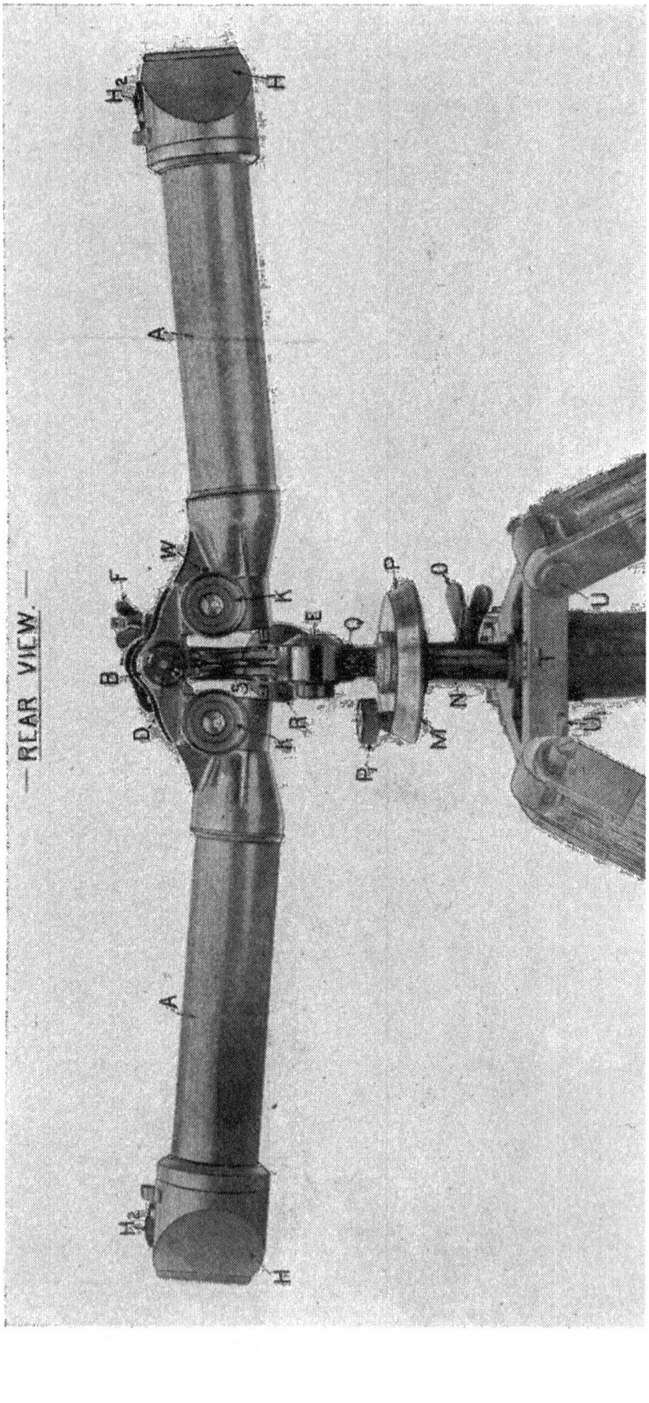

The eyepiece contains two lenses, one of which is acromatic, and is focussed by being revolved. A scale of diopters* is engraved on it and is read by a line on the eyepiece adapter. It is fitted with a vulcanite eyecap (K).

The right eyepiece is provided with a glass diaphragm (L) having engraved on it two horizontal lines 2 minutes apart, and three vertical ones 30 minutes apart (Fig. 21). The diaphragm can be revolved by the lever (W) so as to bring the vertical graticules vertical in both the upright and extended positions of the arms.

The end prisms are partially protected by covers (H₁) (Plate XI) which can be slid away from the bodies when the catches (H₂) are pressed in. The faces of the prisms are then fully exposed and can be easily cleaned.

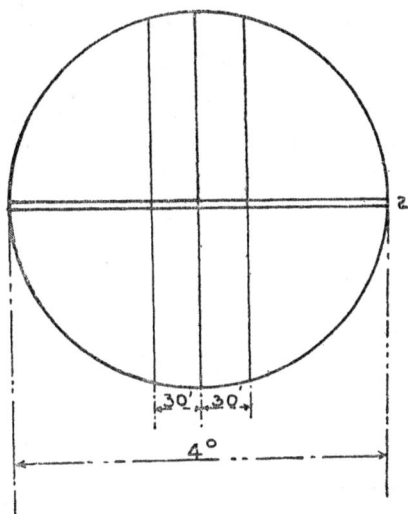

Fig. 21.

The carrier (E) (Plates XI and XII) consists of a plate (M), graduated in single degrees of training, from 0 to 360°, to which is attached the socket (N) which fits over a pivot projecting from the stand. The side of the socket is cut through and can be clamped to the stand by the winged nut (O).

The other plate (P), having a reader for the training scale engraved on it, can be clamped to it by the milled headed nut (P₁).

Attached to the upper plate (P) is a fitting (Q) containing a worm wheel, into which gears a worm spindle having attached to it the

---

* A diopter is the unit of refractive power of a lens, having a focal length of 1 metre. A person who requires a concave spectacle lens of 1 diopter for seeing distant objects distinctly would have to set the diopter scale of a telescope or binocular to − 1 diopter, or, if he required a convex lens, to + 1 diopter.

The diopter numbers are obtained by dividing 100 centimetres (1 metre) by the focal length of the lens, measured in centimetres, thus:—

A 2 diopter lens is the same as one having a focal length of 50 cm.
,, 4 ,, ,, ,, ,, ,, 25 ,,
,, 5 ,, ,, ,, ,, ,, 20 ,,

milled head (R), by which the telescope can be elevated or depressed. The worm spindle is supported in the fitting (S), which is shaped to take the telescope.

When orienting the telescope the milled headed nut (P_1) should be slackened and the training of the datum set on the plate (M). (P_1) is then tightened and (O) slackened, and the telescope swung round until the centre graticule is in line with the datum. (O) is then tightened up, and (P_1) slackened.

Box.

The wooden box has fittings to take the telescope, carrier, adjuncts, spare parts and cleaning material, as follows:—

Two ray-shades, which fit over the end windows.

Four moderating lenses, or coloured glasses, which fit over the eyepieces. They are used in a very bright light, and it is claimed that they are superior to iris diaphragms.

A spare vulcanite eyecap.

A chamois leather and camel hair brush for cleaning purposes.

The box is fitted with a spring catch, two stout hooks and studs, two carrying handles and a carrying strap.

Stand.

The stand consists of an aluminium frame (T) having a vertical brass pivot centrally fitted to take the socket (N) of the carrier. To this can be fitted either three long or three short ash legs. The legs have hinge pins (U) passing through them which can be clamped to the frame by the winged nuts (U_1). Care must be taken when moving the stand that the legs do not become detached, as the hinge pins are liable to come out of the slots in the aluminium frame.

The long legs have sliding portions, which allow of the height being increased, and the lower ends are fitted with brass shoes having spikes which can be forced into the ground. A strap for binding the legs together is attached to one leg.

The short legs, which are only 16 inches long, are employed when it is desired to rest the telescope on a parapet.

The weight of the stand with long legs is $10\frac{1}{4}$ lbs., and with short legs $4\frac{3}{4}$ lbs.

CHAPTER II.

BINOCULARS.

Service Binoculars are constructed upon two different systems, viz., the Galilean and the Prismatic.

The following are the principal binoculars in the Service :—

GALILEAN.

Name.	Magnification.	Field of View.	Apparent Field, or Magnification × Field.	Approximate Weight including Case, &c.	Remarks.
Binocular, Mk. III	3	4° 30′	13½°	2 lbs. 4 ozs.	
Binocular, Mk. IV	5	3° 15′	16¼°	2 lbs. 1 oz.	
Binocular, Mk. V	5	3° 15′	16¼°	2 lbs. 1 oz.	Not hinged. Made in three widths.
Binocular, Night, Mk. I	4	4°	16°	3 lbs. 7½ ozs.	

PRISMATIC.

Name.	Magnification.	Field of View.	Apparent Field, or Magnification × Field.	Approximate Weight including Case, &c.	Remarks.
Binocular, Prismatic, No. 1	8	4½°	36°	1 lb. 15 ozs.	For Siege Artillery, fitted with graticules.
Binocular, Prismatic, No. 2, Mk. I	6	8° 24′	50·4°	2 lbs. 14 ozs.	Has much larger object glasses than No. 3.
Binocular, Prismatic, No. 2, Mk. II	6	8° 24′	50·4°	2 lbs. 14 ozs.	Same as No. 2, Mk. I, but is fitted with graticules.
Binocular, Prismatic, No. 3, Mk. I	6	8° Ross pattern. / 6° 50′ Zeiss pattern.	48° / 41°	2 lbs. 13 ozs.	Is a cheaper and smaller glass than No. 2, and does not give so much brilliancy.
Binocular, Prismatic, No. 3, Mk. II	6	,,	,,	2 lbs. 13 oz.	Same as No. 3, Mk. I, but is fitted with graticules.

Binoculars can be compared with one another in a similar manner to telescopes (see page 2).

DETAILS OF CONSTRUCTION.

GALILEAN.

As all the binoculars constructed on this principle differ from one another only in size, material, optical data and small details, it is proposed to give here a general description, and to give details of the different natures later on.

Each binocular (Fig. 1 and Plate XIII) consists of the following parts:—

BINOCULAR, MARK V.

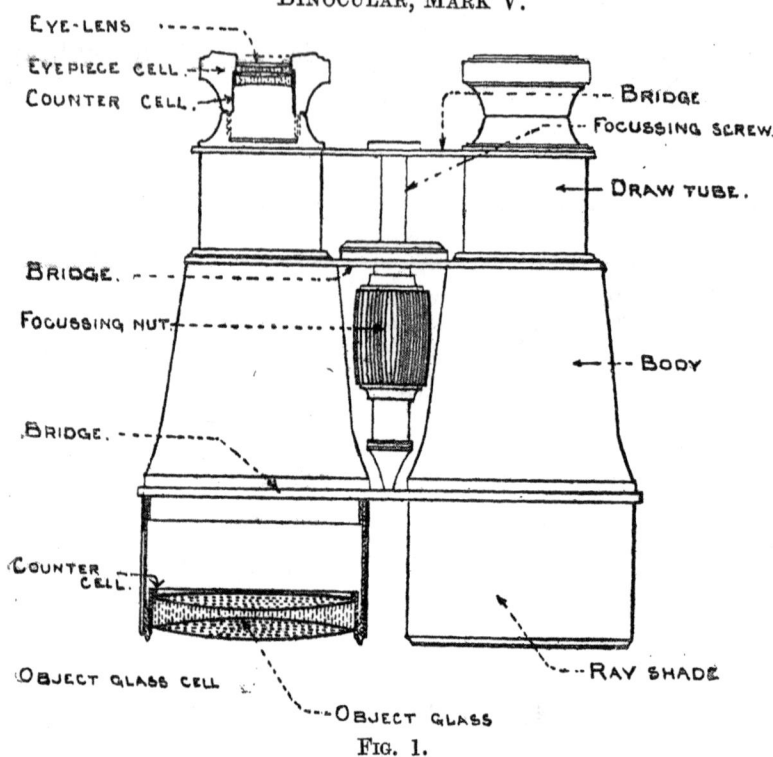

FIG. 1.

Two bodies or barrels joined together by two bridges, which in some cases form hinges.

Two object glasses which are secured in object glass cells by means of counter cells. Each object glass is composed of two or three lenses cemented together with Canada balsam. The more lenses used the more achromatic the binocular will be.

Two ray-shades, whose object is to keep out extraneous light and prevent drops of rain settling on the object glasses. They may be fixed or sliding.

Two draw tubes, which slide in the bodies and are joined together by a bridge. The joints between the draw tubes and bodies are packed with cloth to prevent undue play.

Two eye lenses, which are kept in the eyepiece cells by means of counter cells. Each eye lens consists of one or three lenses cemented together in a similar manner to the object glasses.

A focussing gear, which consists of a focussing screw, one end of which is fixed to the bridge between the draw tubes and prevented from turning, the other end being threaded and gearing into a tube having a female thread. This tube has a milled focussing nut attached to it, and is fitted into bearings in the two bridges which connect the bodies together. When the focussing nut is turned, the focussing screw, which carries the bridge, draw tubes, eyepieces, &c., is forced towards or away from the object glasses.

PLATE XIII. [*To face page* 35.

BINOCULAR, MARK IV.   BINOCULAR, MARK V.

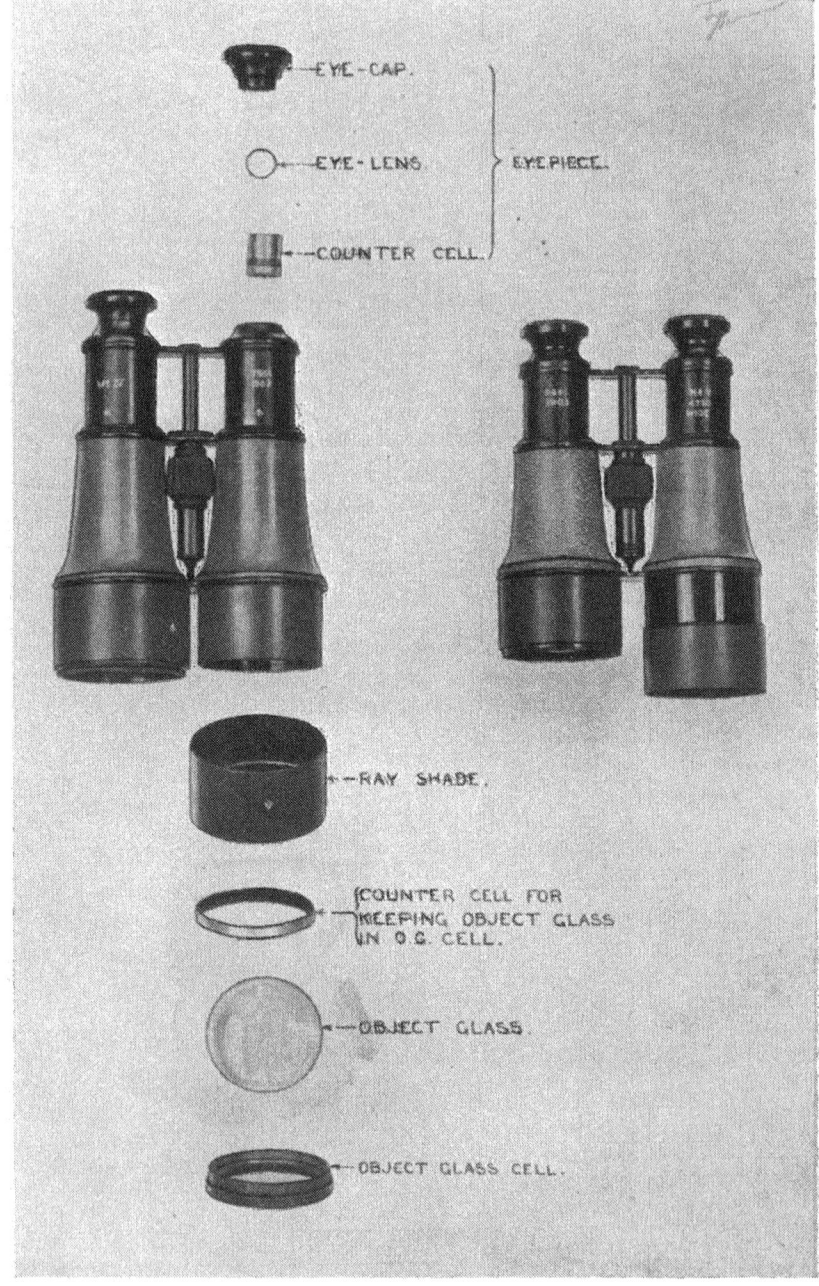

Each binocular is provided with a leather case with shoulder strap. Most cases are also fitted for wearing on a belt.

In Plate XIII are shown the different lenses, cells, &c., of a **Mark IV** binocular, with their correct names.

As the two halves are focussed simultaneously, no allowance can be made for one eye of the observer being of a different focus to the other.

As the rays of light from an object do not come to a focus within the binoculars, it is impossible to fit them with cross wires or graticules.

Owing to their construction they have a relatively small field of view and low magnification as compared with prismatic binoculars; but they give very brilliant illumination, which, however, is not equal over the entire field.

BINOCULAR, MARK III.

Magnification, 3 diameters.
Field of view, 4° 30'.
Weight without case, 1 lb. 8 ozs.
Effective aperture of object glasses, 1·75 inches.
Hinged, allowing of interocular distances of from $2\frac{1}{4}$ to $2\frac{5}{8}$ inches.

Each object glass is composed of three lenses, and each eye lens of three lenses.

Bodies, &c., made of brass, and covered with black leather.
Ray-shades are adjustable and covered with black leather.

BINOCULAR, MARK IV.
(Plate XIII.)

Magnification, 5 diameters.
Field of view, 3° 15'.
Weight without case, 1 lb. 2 ozs.
Effective aperture of object glass, 2 inches.
Fixed interocular distance of $2\frac{1}{2}$ inches.

Each object glass is composed of two or three lenses, and each eye lens is composed of one or three lenses.

Bodies, made of German silver, covered with brown leather, bridges, eyepiece sockets, and focussing gear made of hard brass, all other parts of aluminium.

Adjustable ray-shades.

BINOCULAR, MARK V.
(Plate XIII.)

Magnification, 5 diameters.
Field of view, 3° 15'.
Weight without case, 1 lb. 1 oz.
Effective aperture of object glasses, $1\frac{3}{4}$ inches.
Made in three widths having fixed interocular distances of $2\frac{1}{4}$, $2\frac{7}{16}$ and $2\frac{3}{5}$ inches.

Each object glass and eye lens is composed of three lenses.

Bodies are made of German silver and covered with pig skin, Bridges, cells, sockets, screw threads and focussing gear are of hard brass, and other parts of aluminium alloy.

Adjustable ray shades.

BINOCULAR, NIGHT, MARK I.
(Plate XIV.)

Magnification, 4 diameters.
Field of view, 4°.
Weight without case, 2 lbs. 4 ozs.   Effective aperture of object glasses, 2 inches.

Hinged, allowing of interocular distances of from 60 to 70 millimetres (2·36 to 2·76 inches).

All parts made of brass, the body being covered with pigskin.
Fixed ray-shades.
Each object glass consists of two lenses and each eye lens of one.
Hinged ray-shades, are fitted to each eyepiece to keep out extraneous light.

PRISMATIC.
(Plates XIV, XV and XVI.)

The optical principle of prismatic binoculars is the same as that of terrestrial telescopes except that the two lenses of the erector are omitted, and two prisms substituted in their place. The functions of the two prisms are :—

(1) To enable a long focus object glass to be used in a short body.
(2) To keep the image erect.

The prisms are right angle ones, and two reflecting surfaces of each are utilised. They are mounted (Fig. 2) with their large flat surfaces in parallel planes; but with the side of one in a plane at right angles to the side of the other.

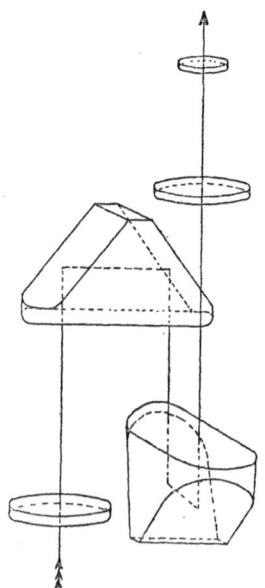

Fig. 2.

PLATE XIV.

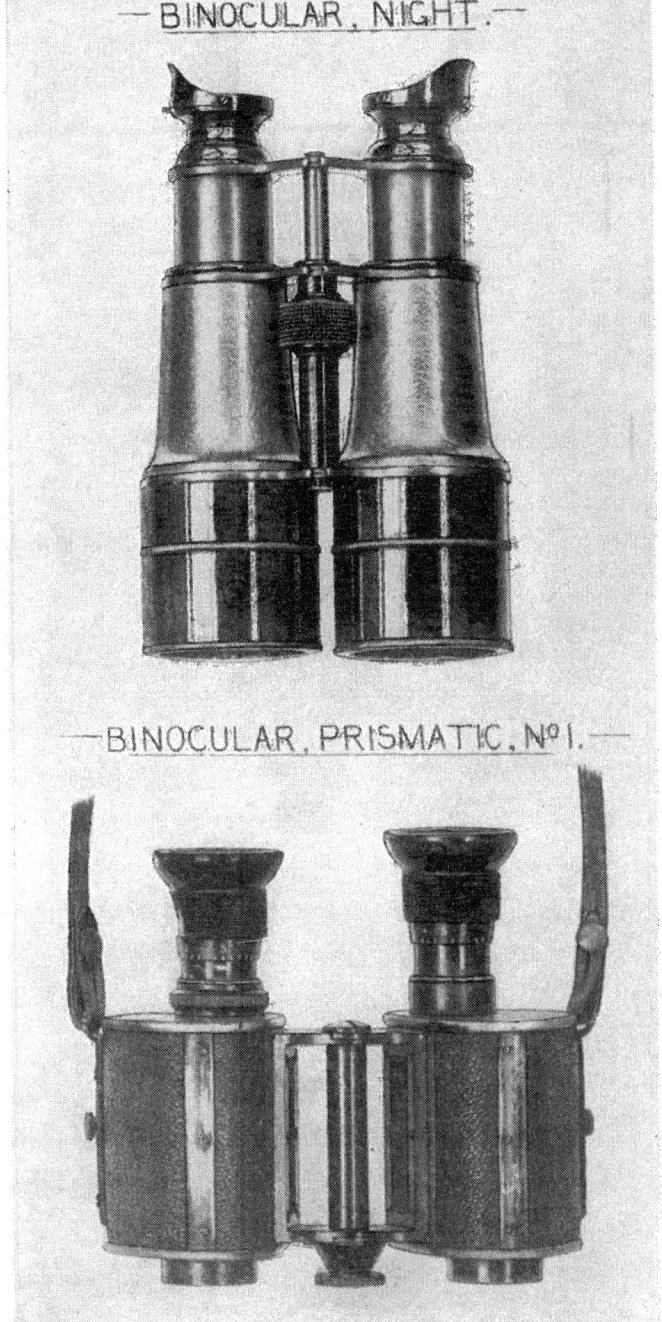

One prism will consequently reverse an image "right for left," and the other "up for down," thus correcting the effect of the object glass which inverts the image in both directions. The eyepiece magnifies the image but does not invert it. The distance that a ray of light has to travel between a fixed object glass and an eyepiece can be varied by altering the distance between the two prisms.

Cross wires or graticules can be placed in front of one eyepiece in the focal plane of the object glass.

All modern prismatic binoculars are constructed to give increased stereoscopic effect. This is effected by placing the object glasses as far apart as possible. If the eyepieces are 60 millimetres apart and the object glasses are 120 millimetres apart, the stereoscopic effect would be twice as much as if the eyepieces and object glasses were in line with one another. The stereoscopic effect also varies with the magnification, and, if the binoculars mentioned above had a magnification of 6 diameters, the stereoscopic effect would be 12 times as great as that obtained by the unaided eyes, and objects at a considerable distance would appear to stand out in relief.

All the Service prismatic binoculars, with the exception of the No. 1, have the following points in common :—

The bodies are castings of aluminium alloy, shaped internally to form seatings for the prisms, which are kept in position by means of springs pressing upon them. The exterior of the bodies is coated with hard ebonite moulded to look like leather.

The object glasses consist of two lenses cemented together with Canada balsam. They are mounted in eccentric rings so that during manufacture the optical axis of each half of the binocular can be brought parallel to the axis of the hinges. The eccentric rings are similar to those used with some sighting telescopes (see page 7).

The eyepiece contains two lenses. The one nearest to the eye is achromatic, being made in two pieces cemented together, and the other one is a single lens.

The bodies are hinged together, so as to allow for varying interocular distances, which are indicated by a scale of millimetres on the rear hinge cap. In some cases the hinges are part of the body castings, and in others they are part of the front and rear cover plates.

The eyepiece adapters are made of brass and are screwed into the bodies. Each eyepiece can be focussed independently by revolving the diopter collar adapter, which screws the tube holding the two eye lenses, in or out of the eyepiece adapter. The revolving portions have scales of diopters (page 31) marked on them, which are read by an index on the fixed portion.

When the interocular distance and the focus of each eye are once known, any binocular set to read them will be in correct adjustment for the user.

Ebonite eyecaps are screwed on to the eyepieces. They are so shaped that they prevent extraneous light getting into the user's eyes, and at the same time keep his eyes at the correct distance from the eye lenses.

At each end of the bodies are fitted brass cover plates.

All joints between the different parts are filled with packing, so as to make the binoculars watertight. They should never be taken to pieces, excepting by Artificers who are qualified to do so.

Plate XV shows a No. 2, Mark I, binocular in pieces, with the names of the various parts.

A leather neck sling is attached to the binoculars, and fixed to this is a rain guard, which can be placed over the eyepieces in wet weather, when the binoculars are out of their cases, but not in actual use. These parts should be attached as shown in Plate XVI, or the binoculars will not fit in their cases.

Suitable brown leather cases with shoulder straps are provided. They are also fitted with loops to pass over the waist belt.

BINOCULAR, PRISMATIC, No. 1, MARK I.
(Plate XIV.)

Magnification, 8 diameters.

Field of view, 4° 30'.

Weight without case, 1 lb. 1 oz.

Effective aperture of object glasses, 0·75 inch.

Distance apart of axes of object glasses, when eyepieces are set at 62 millimetres apart, is 76 millimetres.

Hinged, allowing of interocular distance of from 56 to 70 millimetres (2·2 to 2·75 inches).

Body made of aluminium alloy covered with black morocco leather, other metal parts of brass, eyecaps of ebonite.

Object glass is composed of two lenses, balsamed together, and the eyepiece contains two lenses, one of which is achromatic.

Each eyepiece can be focussed separately, and has a scale of diopters engraved on it.

A scale of interocular distances is engraved on the rear hinge cap, but it is not numbered.

A glass diaphragm with graticules engraved on it (Fig. 3) is mounted in front of the right eyepiece.

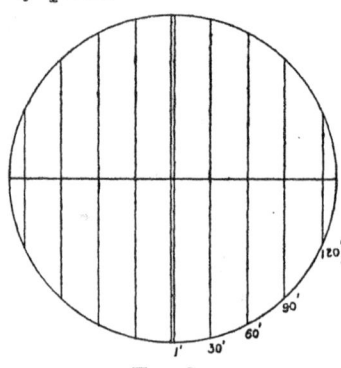

Fig. 3.

It can be revolved so that the graticules may be used either horizontally or vertically. The graticules are 1, 30, 60, 90 and 120 minutes to the right and left of the centre, and a line crosses them at right angles.

A neck sling is attached to the rear cover plates.

A brown leather case with shoulder strap is provided.

These binoculars are obsolescent.

PLATE XV.

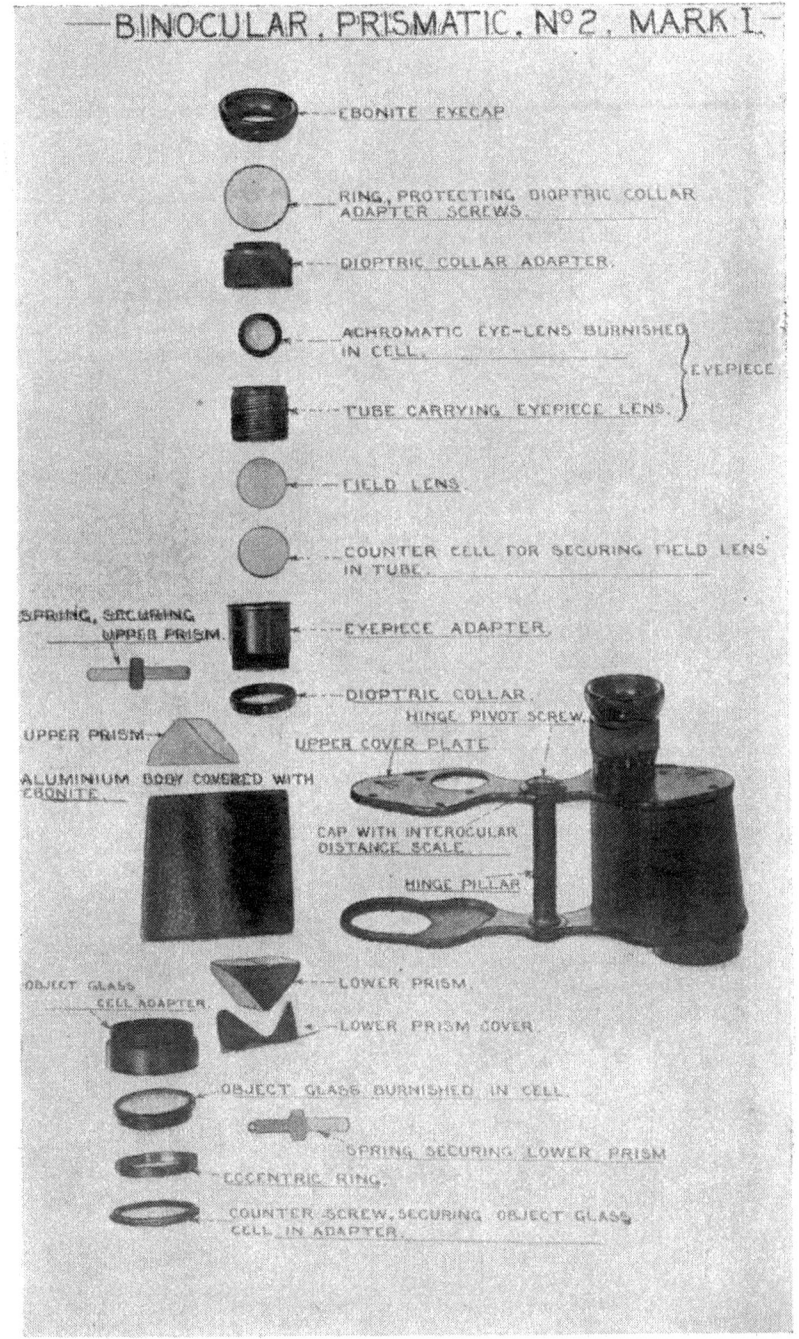

PLATE XVI. [*To face page* 39.

BINOCULARS, PRISMATIC, No. 2, MARK I.

ZEISS PATTERN. ROSS PATTERN.

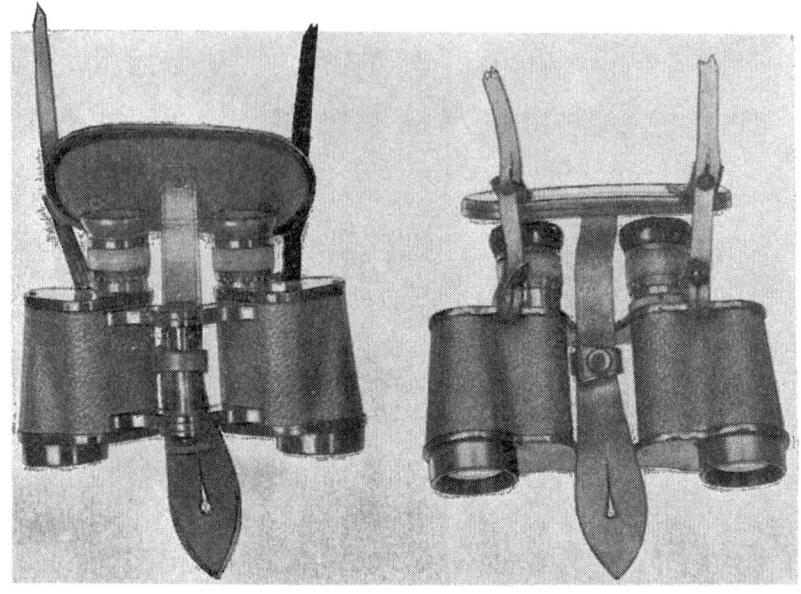

BINOCULARS, PRISMATIC, No. 3, MARK I.

ZEISS PATTERN. ROSS PATTERN.

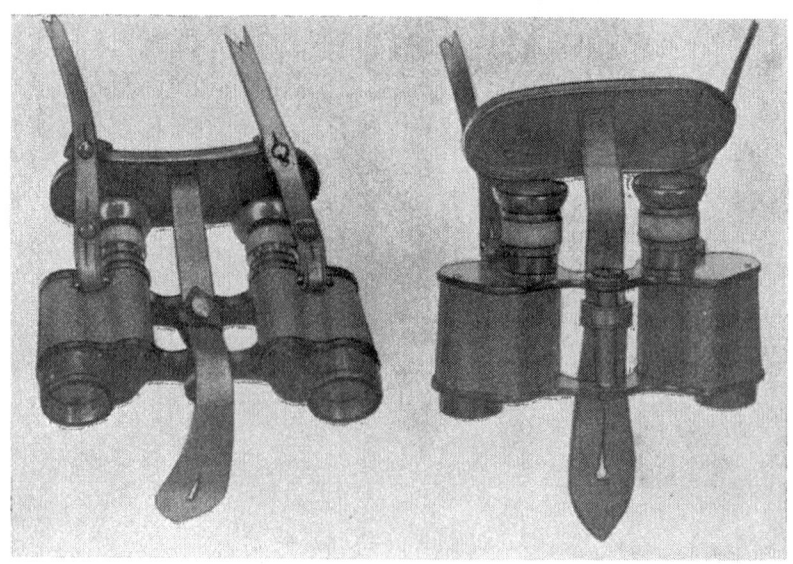

BINOCULAR, PRISMATIC, No. 2, MARK I.

(Plate XVI.)

Magnification, 6 diameters.
Field of view, 8° 24′.
Weight without case, 1 lb. 8 oz.
Effective aperture of object glass, 1·2 inches.
Distance apart of axes of object glasses, when eyepieces are set for 62 millimetres interocular distance, is 127 millimetres.

Hinged, allowing of interocular distances of from 54 to 74 millimetres (2·15 to 2·92 inches).

The binoculars vary slightly in construction; makers being allowed to manufacture to the designs they consider best. They must, however, comply with the details given above.

The principal differences are that those made by Ross have the hinges formed from the cover plates, whereas those made by Zeiss have the hinges formed on projections from the aluminium bodies.

There were two patterns of case, one of which takes the Zeiss pattern binocular, and the other which takes the Ross pattern binocular. but recently a case, which will take any pattern, has been introduced.

BINOCULAR, PRISMATIC, No. 2, MARK II.

This binocular is similar to the No. 2, Mark I, except that the right eyepiece is fitted with a glass diaphragm having graticules engraved on it.

The graticules are shown in Fig. 4. The length of the centre

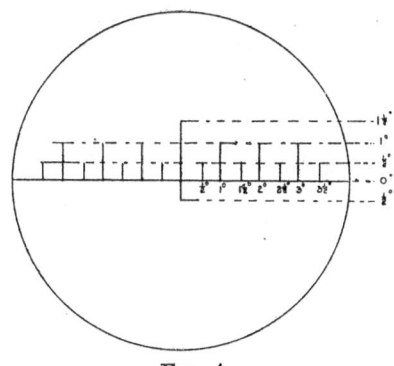

Fig. 4.

graticule is 1½° above and ½° below the horizontal line. The other graticules are ½° apart and are alternately ½° and 1° high. By their means the height of burst of a shell and its distance right and left of the target can be measured.

If the diaphragm requires cleaning, one of the small keep screws in the cover plate, or in the milled collar should be removed, and the eyepiece with or without the diaphragm unscrewed. Small pieces of dirt can then be removed by blowing on the diaphragm or rubbing it very gently with a fine piece of linen or camel's hair brush.

A section of the right eyepiece and diaphragm is shown in Fig. 5. It is of the upmost importance that, when the diaphragm is being cleaned, the diaphragm adapter should not be turned, or the distance of the diaphragm from the object glass will be altered, with the result that the graticules and view will not come in focus simultaneously.

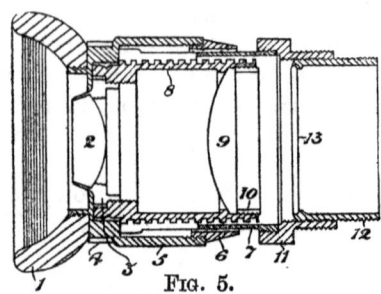

Fig. 5.

(1) Ebonite eyecap.
(2) Eye lens (achromatic).
(3) Eye lens cell.
(4) Ring protecting diopter collar adapter screws.
(5) Diopter collar adapter.
(6) Diopter collar.
(7) Eyepiece adapter.
(8) Tube carrying eyepiece lenses.
(9) Field lens.
(10) Counter cell for securing field lens in tube.
(11) Milled collar carrying diaphragm adapter.
(12) Diaphragm adapter.
(13) Glass diaphragm.

BINOCULAR, PRISMATIC, No. 3, MARK I.
(Plate XVI.)

Magnification, 6 diameters.
Field of view, 8° (Ross) or 6° 20′ (Zeiss).
Weight without case 1 lb. 6 ozs. or less.
Effective aperture of object glasses, 0·85 inch.
Distance apart of object glasses, when eyepieces are set for 62 millimetres interocular distance, is 114 millimetres.
Hinged, allowing of interocular distances of from 54 to 74 millimetres (2·13 to 2·92 inches).

The binoculars vary slightly in construction; makers being allowed to manufacture to the designs they consider best. They must, however, comply with the details given above. The Zeiss pattern, although it has a smaller field than the Ross pattern, has greater brilliancy.

The principal differences are that those made by some makers have the hinges formed from the cover plates, whereas those made by other makers have the hinges formed on projections from the aluminium bodies.

There is only one pattern of case, which is suitable for all makes.

BINOCULAR, PRISMATIC, No. 3, MARK II.

This binocular is similar to the No. 3, Mark I, but is fitted with graticules similar to those in the No. 2, Mark II (Fig. 4).

PLATE XVII. [To face page 41.

DIRECTOR, No. 1, MARK II ON STAND, TELESCOPE, FIELD ARTILLERY, MARK I

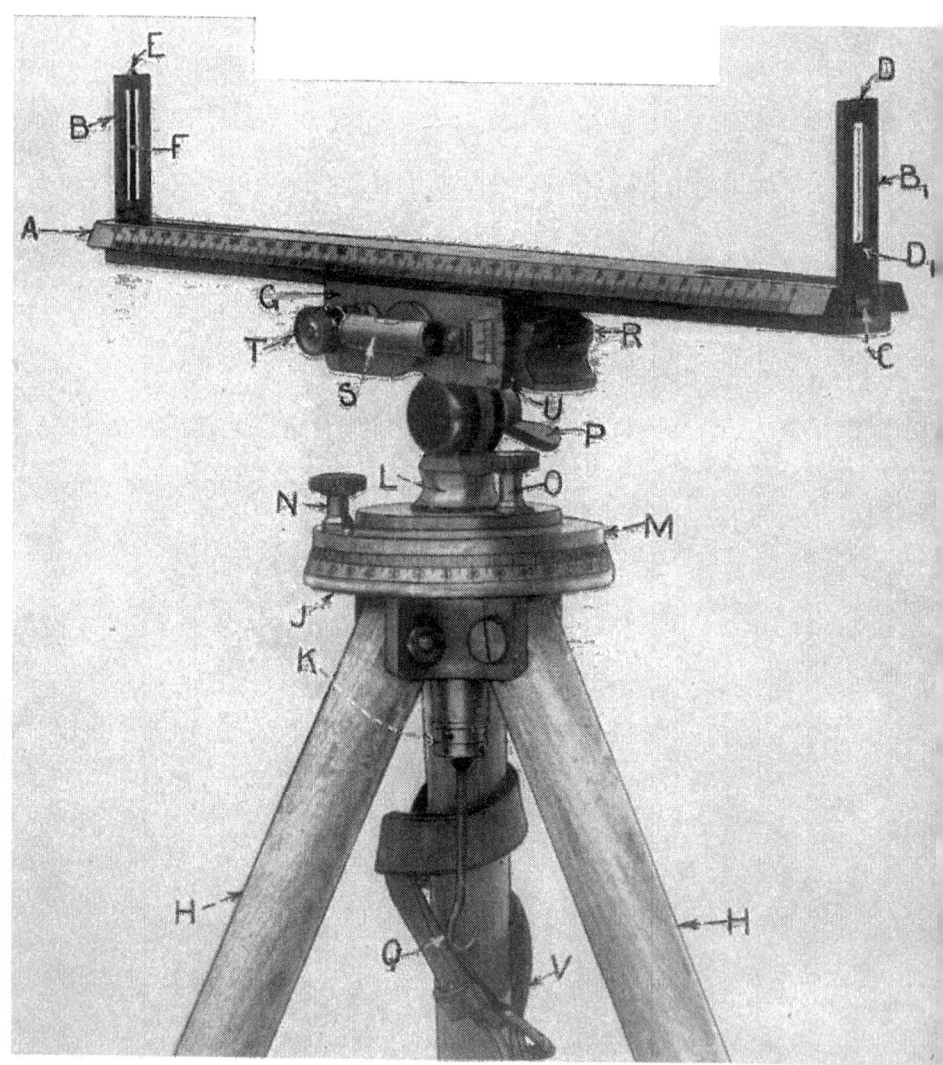

CHAPTER III.

DIRECTORS AND STORES USED WITH THEM.

The following instruments are described in this chapter:—

Director, No. 1, and Stand, Field Artillery Telescope.
Director, No. 2, and Stand.
Director, No. 3, and Stand.
Apparatus observation of fire and stand.
Slide Rules.
Field Plotters.

DIRECTOR, No. 1, MARK II.
(Plate XVII.)

The director consists of a boxwood rule (A) with a folding sighting vane (B. B_1) at each end. These vanes are kept vertical, or folded down by means of springs (C). The rear vane has two notches (D. D_1) cut in it, which are used in conjunction with a tip (E) or wire (F) in the front vane when measuring angles in a horizontal plane. When finding angles of sight a point midway between the edges at the top of the upper notch (D) and the tip of the front vane are laid on the target. Attached to the underside of the director is a fitting which engages with the carrier (G) on the top of the "Stand, Telescope, Field Artillery."

The sides of the director are bevelled, and one has a scale of inches, and the other of "6 inches to 1 mile" marked on them.

The director is carried in a pocket on the side of the "Case, Stand, Telescope, Field Artillery."

STAND, TELESCOPE, FIELD ARTILLERY, MARK I.
(Plate XVII.)

This stand is used in conjunction with the Director, No. 1, described above, or the "Telescope, Field Artillery" (page 28).

The three ash legs (H) are circular in section, and have ferrule joints, so that the stand can be used with either short or long legs as may be most convenient. Brass chains are attached to the legs and to one another and prevent undue splay, and make the stand more rigid when they are taut. The legs are pivoted to three lugs on the circular base plate (J). The nuts on the pivots should always be well tightened up to prevent undue shake. The base plate is graduated from 0° to 180° "Right" and "Left." In the latest stands "Right" graduations are white on a black background and "Left" are black on brass. In the base plate are formed a socket for the pivot (L) and a bearing for the index plate (M).

The index plate has an arrow engraved on it for reading angles off the base plate, and it can be clamped to the base plate by means of the milled headed screw (N).

The pivot (L) can be clamped to the index plate by means of the milled headed screw (O). To the top of it is pivoted the carrier (G), which can be elevated or depressed, and clamped by means of the butterfly nut (P). To the lower end of the pivot is screwed a hook (Q) from which a weight may be suspended and so steady the stand in rough weather.

The carrier (G) is shaped to take the projection beneath the director or telescope, a stop and spring catch (R) preventing any end play. It may sometimes be found necessary to bend in slightly the sides of this seating, so that the director fits into it without side play.

On the left of the carrier is pivoted an arm to which is attached a " Bubble spirit glass " in a case (S). On one end of the arm, teeth are cut, which gear with a pinion on the same shaft as the milled head (T); and on the other end is engraved a reader and vernier which are used in conjunction with the degree scale (U). The bubble casing is clamped to the arm by three screws, so that it can be adjusted. When the top notch and tip on the vanes of the director, or the horizontal wire in the telescope, are laid on a distant point in the same horizontal plane, the bubble should be in the centre of its run, when the reader is at zero. For the method of obtaining a point in the same horizontal plane, see page 174.

For transport, the detachable portions of the legs are strapped outside the upper portions by means of straps (V) and the whole dropped into a leather bucket (Case, stand, telescope, Field Artillery) which can be attached to the saddle on the off side.

Angle of Sight Instruments, Marks I and II, (see page 160) *can be used with this stand.*

DIRECTOR, No. 2, MARK I.
(Plates XVIII and XIX.)

This instrument consists of the following parts :—

The telescope (A), which is of the ordinary terrestial pattern, having a magnification of 15 diameters and a field of view of $2° 10'$.*

In front of the eyepiece is fixed, by collimating screws (B), a diaphragm, with spider's web graticules attached to it. One web is horizontal; the others are vertical, one being on the axis of the telescope, and the remainder 5, 10, 20, 30, 40, 50 and 60 minutes to either side of it. (Fig. 1.)

In rear of the diaphragm is a socket (C) for the 4-volt lamp (see page 168) by which the graticules can be illuminated. A screwed plug is kept in this socket when the lamp is not in place.

The graticules are focussed by revolving the eyepiece (D) and the view by turning the milled head (E).

Folding vanes (F F_1) are provided for picking up an object, and for use in place of the telescope in thick weather. A dermatine eyeguard (G) is attached to the eyepiece.

A clinometer level (H) is provided for taking angles of sight. A " Bubble B " is attached to an arm pivoted at (I). One end of this arm has a toothed arc cut on it, into which gears a worm, to the upper end of which is attached a micrometer head (J). A German silver spring beneath the arm prevents any play. The micrometer is divided in divisions of $2'$ but only numbered 0 and 30, so that it can be read in

---

* A second eyepiece, having a magnification of 8 diameters and a field of view of about $3\frac{3}{4}°$, has recently been approved.

To face page 42.]   PLATE XVIII.

DIRECTOR, No. 2, MARK I.

PLATE XIX. [*To face page* 43.

DIRECTOR, NO. 2, MARK I.

either direction in conjunction with the degree scale (K). The reader

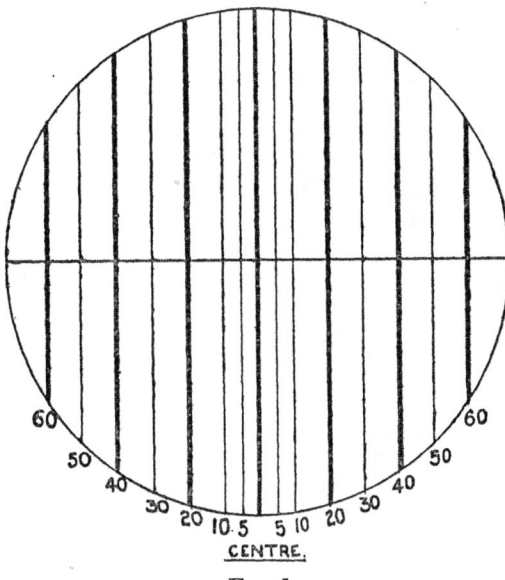

Fig. 1.

for the degree scale (which reads from 5° elevation to 5° depression) is on the end of the bubble arm.

The skin of the micrometer can be turned independently of the worm, when two small screws on the top of the milled head are loosened. This adjustment is necessary to enable the scales to be set to read zero, when the horizontal wire of the telescope is laid on an object in the same horizontal plane and the bubble is in the centre of its run. A mirror (L) is pivoted above the level. The reflection of the bubble can be seen in this when it is not convenient to see the bubble direct. The object glass is protected by a removable ray-shade (M) with shutter (N).

The trunnions of the telescope rest in bearings at the top of the "Telescope support" (O). Two crosses are marked near the trunnions, and come opposite two similar ones on the clips (P), when the telescope is in its correct position. The clips can be clamped down on the trunnions so as to give the necessary friction, by means of the milled nuts (Q). A lug (R) projecting from one side of the telescope support is pressed against a slow motion screw (S) by means of a spiral spring connected to the under sides of the telescope support and the graduated plate (T). By means of this slow motion screw the direction of the telescope can be altered without altering the reading of the graduated plate. The slow motion fitting allows of about $2\frac{1}{2}°$ traverse to the right and left of the central position of the lug, which is indicated when an arrow on the telescope support is in line with a line on the graduated plate.

The graduated plate (T) is graduated in single degrees, and numbered every 10° from 0 to 180 "Right" and "Left." The right graduations are filled with white on a black background, and the left are black on brass. A "Bubble, spirit, circular, cased" (U) is attached to it for levelling purposes.

The rim of the plate has 360 teeth cut on it, each representing one degree of traverse. A worm spindle or tangent screw engages with these teeth.

The body (X) is a gunmetal casting. Beneath it is a projection which fits into a socket at the top of the stand. It is threaded internally to take the attachment bolt (Y) of the stand, and two holes are bored in it, into which fit two steel pins projecting from the gunmetal bush. On one side of the body is situated the *traversing gear*. This consists principally of a tangent screw or worm spindle (V) which gears with the teeth on the rim of the graduated plate. On the end of this worm is fixed a micrometer head consisting of a milled head and an adjustable skin (Z). The latter has two scales on it to agree with the "Right" and "Left" degree scales, and is graduated every 5 minutes. When two screws on the face of the milled head are slackened the skin can be revolved independently of the milled head.

The bearing of the worm is pivoted at one end so that the worm can be put in or out of gear with the teeth on the graduated plate. This is effected by means of the lever (Z_1) having a small cam cut on it, which engages with a screw (Z_2) projecting from the worm spindle bearing. A German silver spring tends to press the worm in gear with the teeth.

A pivot projecting up from the centre of the body fits into sockets in the graduated plate and the telescope support.

The cover (X_1) protects the teeth of the graduated plate and the traversing gear, and has an arrow engraved on it, by which the degree graduations are read.

The weight of the director is 7 lbs.

A mahogany case with a spring catch and suitable fittings is provided to hold the director. Its weight is 6 lbs. 2 ozs.

Stand, No. 2 Director, Mark I.

The stand consists of the following parts :—

Three tubular steel telescopic legs, the lower portions of which slide into the upper portions, and can be clamped in any position by means of gunmetal rings. Mild steel shoes are fitted at the lower end of each leg, and gunmetal hinge pieces at the top of them.

The base plate has three projections formed on it. These are recessed to take the hinge pieces of the legs. The *hinge bolts*, which are tapered, have feathers formed on them to prevent them turning. The base plate is centrally bored to take the projection beneath the director. In this socket there is an *attachment bolt* (Y) which screws into the director and clamps it down on to the stand. To increase the friction there is also a *gunmetal bush* having two steel pins which fit into the director.

A leather securing strap for binding the legs together when not in use.

The weight of the stand is $12\frac{3}{4}$ lbs.

To make these stands more rigid they will eventually be modified as follows :—

    (1) The upper part of the leg will be screwed on to the hinge piece and further secured with a set screw.

    (2) The junction between the upper and lower portions of the leg will be made more rigid by means of a coned stop ring

[*To face page* 44.]   PLATE XX.

DIRECTOR, NO. 3, MARK I ON MARK I STAND.

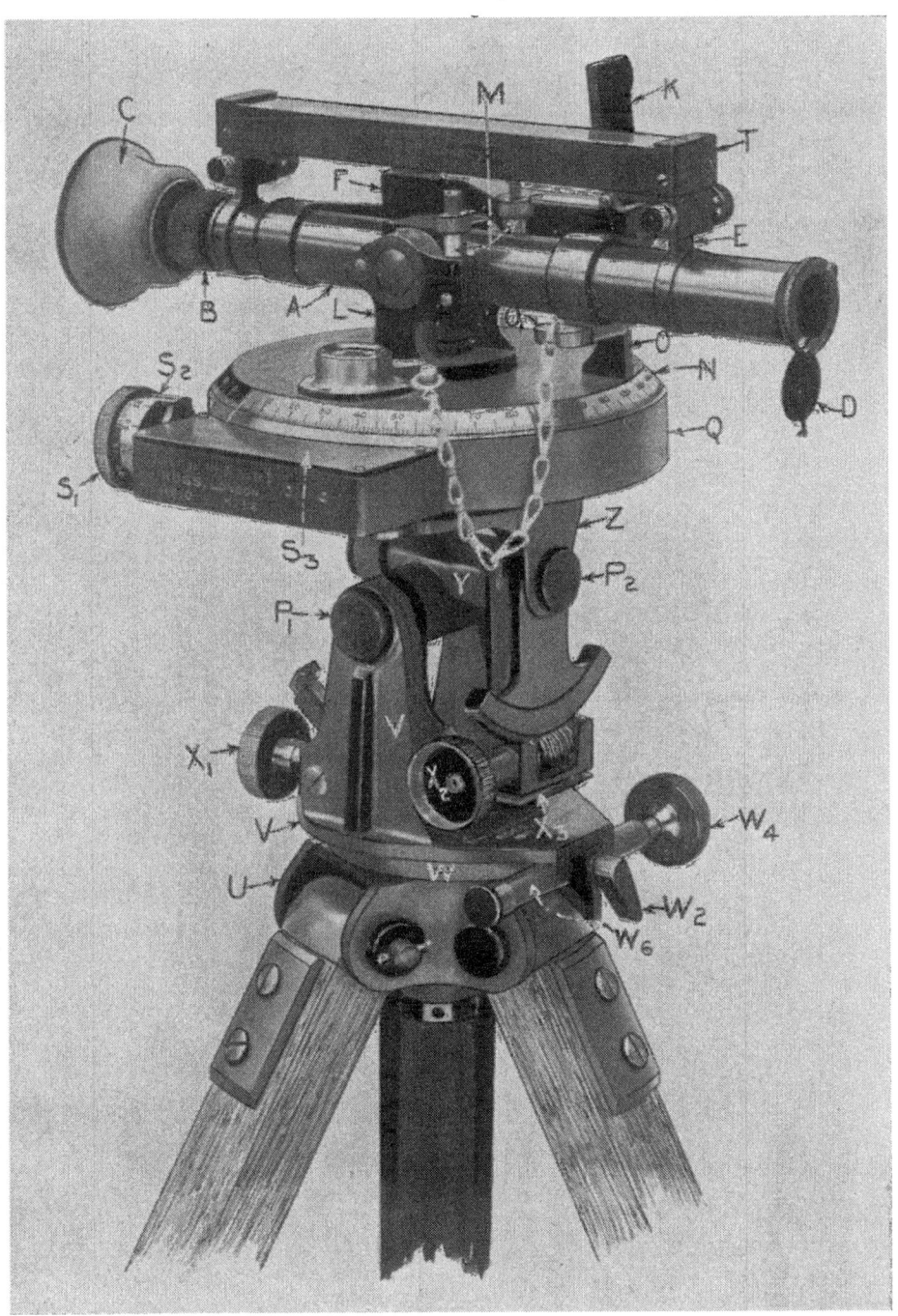

PLATE XXI. [*To face page* 43.

DIRECTOR, No. 3, MARK I ON MARK I STAND.

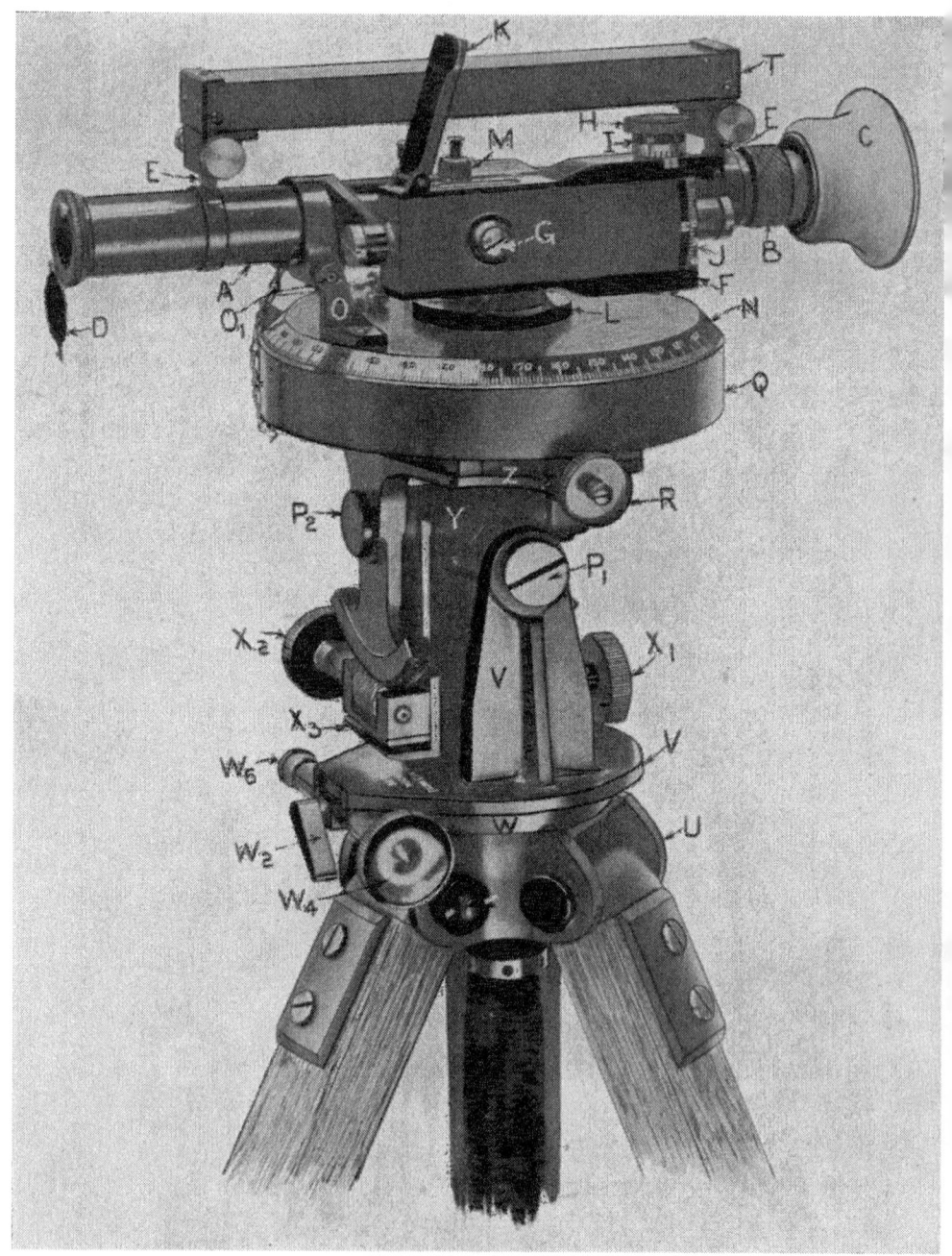

fixed in the upper portion which will engage with a corresponding cone on the lower portion.

To obtain the full benefit of (2) the lower portion of the leg should be pulled out as far as it will go.

DIRECTOR, No. 3, MARK I.
(Plates XX and XXI.)

This director was designed for measuring horizontal angles and angles of sight very accurately; and also for ascertaining angles of sight from a battery, when it is situated some distance from it, and to one flank.

It consists of the following parts :—

The telescope (A), which is of the ordinary terrestrial pattern and has a magnification of 6 diameters and a field of view of 4° 20'. In front of the eyepiece is fixed a diaphragm having cross wires, of spider's web, mounted on it.

The cross wires and view can be simultaneously focussed by revolving the eyepiece (B).

It is fitted with a dermatine eyeguard (C), shutter (D), and open sights (E) for rough laying. Two projections are formed on the left of it for supporting the clinometer level (F).

The clinometer level (F) is supported on two trunnions, so that when taking angles of sight it can always be placed in a vertical plane. It consists principally of a case, in which is pivoted at (G) an arm, on which a "Bubble, spirit glass A" is mounted. One end of the arm has a toothed arc cut on it, into which gears a worm spindle. To the upper end of the latter is attached a micrometer head (H). Beneath the milled portion of the micrometer head is an adjustable skin I, which is sub-divided to read every 2 minutes, and numbered every 10 minutes. The figures are black on brass for elevation and white on black for depression. When two small screws on the upper face of the head are slackened, the skin can be revolved independently of the head, and set to the required reading (when being adjusted). The scale is read by means of an arrow on the case.

The end of the bubble arm beneath the micrometer head has an arrow engraved upon it, by means of which a degree scale (J) (graduated from 10° elevation to 10° depression) on the case can be read. A German silver spring fitted to the under side of the bubble arm takes up all play.

A hinged mirror (K) is pivoted above the bubble, so that the reflection of the bubble can be seen in it, when the bubble itself cannot be conveniently seen.

The telescope support (L), which has bearings for the trunnions of the telescope. Caps are provided, which can be clamped down on to the trunnions by means of the two nuts (M).

The caps have crosses engraved upon them, which correspond with one on the telescope when the latter is in its correct position.

It is rigidly attached by screws to the degree scale plate (N).

The degree scale plate (N) is a metal casting. There are teeth cut round its rim, which engage with the worm of the traversing gear. It is graduated in single degrees from 0° to 180° "Right" and "Left," the right graduations being filled white on black, and the left black on brass.

A small bracket (O) is attached to it. When a coned pin (O_1) passes through a hole in this bracket and a corresponding one in the telescope the axis of the telescope will be at right angles to the vertical axis of the instrument, and in a plane parallel to those in which are situated the axes of the cross levelling pivots of the stand (P_1, P_2). This arrangement is known as the *pin stop.*

A "Bubble spirit, circular, cased" is attached to the top of the plate, and is used for levelling the instrument, when it is being used as an ordinary director.

The body (Q), which is a metal casting. To it is attached a pivot for the degree scale plate. On its under surface it has two projections, which fit into the top of the stand, and another one against which the nut (R) on the stand presses. A recess is formed on one side to receive the traversing gear.

The traversing gear, which consists principally of a worm spindle, which engages with the teeth on the graduated plate. This is mounted in a bearing upon which a flat German silver spring acts, and tends to press the worm into the teeth of the degree scale plate.

On one end of the worm spindle is mounted a micrometer head consisting of a milled portion (S_1), which revolves with the spindle, and an adjustable skin (S_2) which is divided and numbered every 5 minutes. The numbering is white on black and black on brass to agree with the degree graduations. The skin can be unclamped by slackening the two small screws on the top of the micrometer head. A small cover plate (S_3) upon which the reader of the degree scale is engraved, fits over the traversing gear.

When it is required to traverse the telescope and degree scale plate rapidly, the micrometer head is forced outwards until the worm disengages from the teeth.

The compass (T), which is of the ordinary surveying pattern, is kept in a mahogany box in the director case, when not required for use. It has two sockets beneath it, which fit over the open sights of the telescope. Two adjusting screws with keep nuts fit into one side of these sockets, and by means of them the needle can be adjusted so as to be parallel to the axis of the telescope, when the latter is pointing to the magnetic north. Two milled headed screws are fitted on the opposite side of the sockets, and by means of these the compass can be clamped to, and released from the telescope without upsetting the adjustment of the compass. The compasses of all directors which are likely to be used in conjunction with one another should be adjusted so that the needles are central when the axes of the telescopes are parallel.

The weight of the director with telescope is 5·5 lbs.

CASE.

A leather case with shoulder strap is provided for carrying the No. 3 director. It is lined with felt, and has a fitting for the flat part of the body (near the traversing gear) to rest upon *Great care must be taken to see that the weight of the director is not taken by the micrometer head. Before inserting the instrument in the case, insert the stop pin in the bracket (O) and telescope, and set the horizontal degree scale to 180°. When in the case the object glass end of the telescope should be near the compass.*

The weight of the case is 3 lbs.

The cases will eventually be converted to be carried on the saddle (see fig. 2).

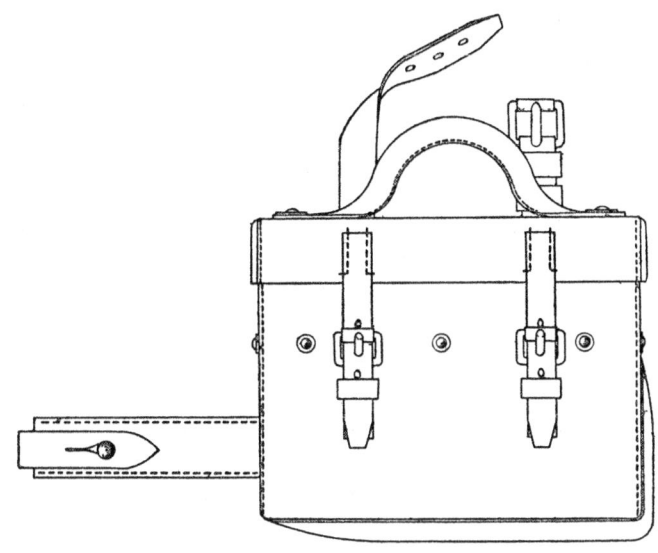

Fig. 2.

Stand for No. 3 Director, Mark I.

Stands should always be used with the directors with which they were issued, and which bear the same numbers, or inaccurate results may be obtained. If, however, it is necessary to use a director with a stand having a different number, the test laid down on page 51 must be gone through, and the reader of the scale on the degree scale plate altered if necessary. If this is not done the director will not find angles of sight from a distant battery correctly, but it will still be accurate for all other purposes.

The stand (Plates XX and XXI) has three ash legs, with tubular brass extensions, which can be clamped at any desired height by three winged nuts. The lower ends of the legs are pointed. A strap is attached to one leg, for binding them together when travelling.

The upper ends of the legs are fitted with metal castings through which hinge pins pass and fix them to the base plate (U).

The base plate (U) is centrally bored to receive the pivot (V), and turned on the outside to take the clamping ring (W).

Clamping ring (Fig. 3). The clamping ring (W) has a projection (W_1) upon it, through which passes a clamping screw with a lever head (W_2). In front of the screw is a metal block (W_3). When the screw is screwed home it presses this block against the base plate (U) and prevents the clamping ring from turning. The upper part of the stand is prevented from turning independently of the clamping ring (except when the slow motion screw is turned) by the slow motion

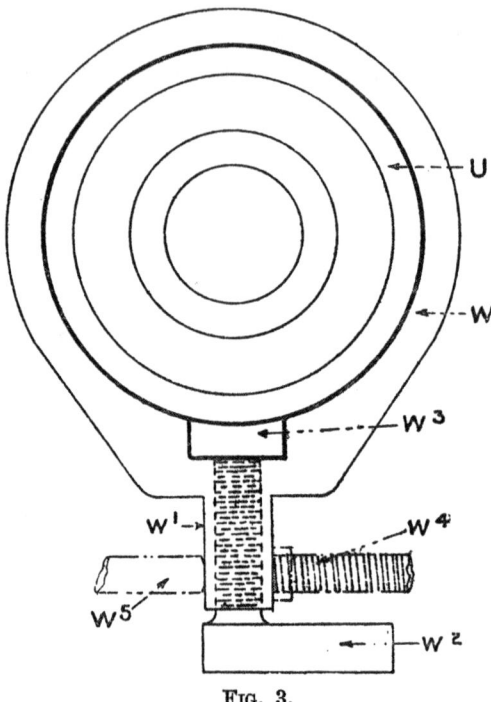

FIG. 3.

screw (W_4), and a plunger (W_5) in a spring casing (W_6), which press against the projection on the ring.

When the clamping screw (W_2) is partially unscrewed the clamping ring and upper part of the stand can be freely revolved.

The pivot (V) is a gunmetal casting. The lower portion is coned, and fits in the seating in the base plate (U). There are two projections on the top of it, which are bored to take the hinge pin (P_1) of the "bracket, supporting carrier" (Y). To one of these projections is attached a bearing in which is mounted one of the cross-levelling worm spindles (X_1). The worm on this engages with an arc on the "bracket, supporting carrier," and is kept in gear by means of a flat German silver spring. A projection on one side takes the slow motion screw (W_4) and spring casing with cap (W_6), which contains a spiral German silver spring and a plunger. The slow motion traversing gear allows of a total movement of about 6°.

The bracket supporting carrier (Y) is a gunmetal casting in which are bored two sockets at right angles to one another. The lower socket contains the hinge pin, by which it is attached to the pivot, and the upper one the hinge pin which attaches it to the carrier (Z).

A toothed arc is attached to it and gears with the worm (X_1) on the pivot. By its means the top of the stand can be tilted from the horizontal to the front or rear. Two sets of arrows on the carrier and bracket and on the carrier and pivot should be made to coincide when the instrument is being set up.

PLATE XXII. [*To face page* 49.

Mark II Stand for No. 3 Director.

The carrier (Z), has its upper surface shaped to take the director, the sliding surfaces being inclined to one another so that there shall be no shake between the director and stand. A screw with nut (R) is pivoted in front of the carrier. When the director is in place the nut, which butts against a projection on the director, is screwed home, and keeps the latter in place. The nut must not be screwed up unnecessarily tightly, or it may be found difficult to disconnect the director from the stand.

The weight of the stand is 11 lbs.

Mark II.

The Mark II stand (Plate XXII) is generally similar to the Mark I, but some of the parts are made stronger, and small parts are prevented from becoming unscrewed and lost. The principal modifications are :—

(1) Slightly larger base plate (U).
(2) Strengthened traversing screw (W_4).
(3) Stronger spring case with more powerful spring (W_6).
(4) Stronger clamping screw (W_2) with stop screw (A) fitted to prevent it becoming detached.

Mark I*.

When the weak parts of a Mark I stand are removed, and a plate, with the strengthened parts mounted on it, is fitted to it, the stand is known as Mark I*.

Case, Stand, Director, No. 3, Mark I.

This case (Fig. 4) consists of the following parts :—

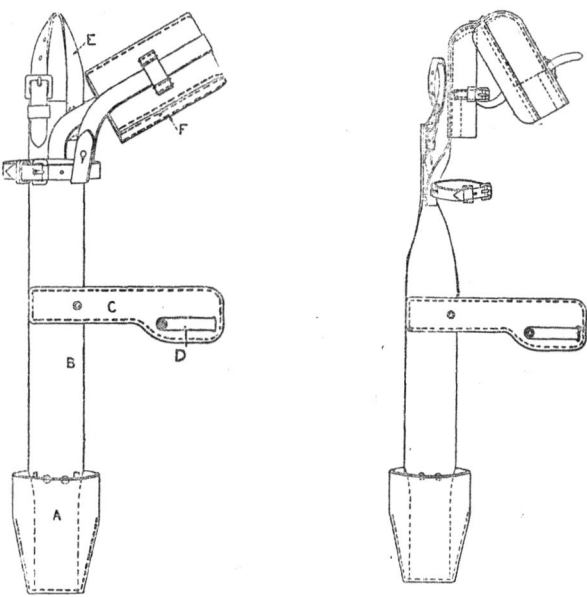

Fig. 4.   Fig. 4A.

A leather bucket (A) having a steel plate riveted in the bottom.

A leather backstrap (B) secured to the bucket, having a flap (C) in which is fitted a steel strengthening plate, and a strap (D).

An adjustable suspending strap (E).

A leather cover (F) to fit over the head of the stand.

Its weight is 3·5 lbs.

CASE, STAND, DIRECTOR, No. 3, MARK II.

This is similar to the Mark I, except that the bucket and cover are ·5 inches shorter.

Its weight is 3·25 lbs.

CASE, STAND, DIRECTOR, No. 3, MARK III AND MARK I*.

The Mark III (Fig. 4A) differs from the Mark I in the following particulars :—

The top cover is riveted to the back strap and is formed in two parts, which are hinged at the top, to facilitate the removal of the stand.

The interior of the top cover is fitted with leather-covered cork fittings, which clamp the legs of the stand and form a more rigid protection to the mechanism of the stand head. When placing the stand in the case the slow motion clamp should be slackened and brought in line with the uppermost leg.

The bucket is $1\frac{1}{2}$ inches shorter.

The approximate weight of the case is $4\frac{1}{4}$ lbs.

Mark I cases converted to resemble the Mark III are known as Mark I*.

GENERAL REMARKS ON THE No. 3 DIRECTOR AND STAND.

In order that the director may correctly find the angle of sight from a battery some distance away from it, it is necessary that it and its stand should be very accurately constructed and pass the tests detailed below. Those marked with a star (*) should be checked occasionally and the necessary adjustments made, if they are not found to be correct. All are applied to the instrument before it is passed into the service, and should be applied again after a new bubble or cross wires have been fitted, any large repair carried out, or if a director is used with a stand having a different number.

The general principle of obtaining the angle of sight from the battery is that—

(1) The telescope is fixed parallel to the degree scale plate by inserting the pin stop (O) (Plate XX).

(2) The degree scale plate is brought into the plane in which are situated the director, the battery and the target. This is done by means of the cross levelling screws on the stand.

(3) The telescope is traversed into a vertical plane parallel to that in which are situated the battery and the target. The axis of the telescope being therefore in the same plane as the battery and target, and also in a plane parallel to a line between the battery and the target will be parallel to the line from the battery to the target (i.e., the line of sight). The horizontal angle at which the telescope should be set is ascertained by solving the triangle (T O B), the base and two base angles of which are known, by means of a field plotter and a simple calculation.

(4) The bubble of the clinometer level is brought to the centre of its run, and the angle between the horizontal and the axis of the telescope (which is parallel to the line of sight from the battery) is read off. This angle is the angle of sight from the battery to the target.

As the degree scale plate cannot be tilted more than a certain amount, the director cannot ascertain angles of sight when the plane, in which the director, battery and target are situated, is inclined more than that amount to the horizontal. Thus, suppose that the battery, director and target are in line with one another, but at different heights, it would be necessary to tilt the degree scale into a vertical plane, which cannot be done.

TESTS.

The director, having been secured to its stand and the pin stop inserted, proceed as follows :—

*(a) Set all scales to zero. Lay the horizontal wire in the telescope on a distant point known to be in the same horizontal plane. (For method of obtaining such a point, see page 174.) The bubble of the clinometer level should be found to be in the centre of its run. If it is not so, it must be brought there by means of the micrometer screw (H), and the adjustable skin (I) shifted until it reads zero.

*(b) Set the clinometer level at zero and bring the bubble to the centre of its run. When the bubble casing is tilted to either side the bubble should remain in the centre of its run. If it does not do so, the glass bubble has not been fixed parallel to the trunnions of the clinometer level, and false angles of sight will be recorded.

(c) Remove the clinometer level, and insert in the trunnion holes a perfectly true circular rod, and hang on it two plumb bobs. Lay the cords of these in line with a distant object. The cross wires in the telescope should be found to be laid on the same distant object. If they are not so, the axis of the clinometer level is not parallel to the line of sight of the telescope.

*(d) With everything set at zero and the stop pin in position, bring the bubbles to the centres of their runs. Revolve the degree scale plate through exactly 180°. The bubble of the clinometer level should still be in the centre of its run. If it is not so the pin stop is not holding the telescope parallel to the degree scale plate.

(e) Set the horizontal scale at zero and level the instrument. Tilt it over on the axis parallel to the telescope by means of one of the cross levelling screws, keeping the clinometer level vertical. The bubble of the latter should remain in the centre of its run. If it does not do so, the reader of the horizontal scale is incorrectly marked. *This test should be applied if a director is used on a stand other than the one which was issued with it.* Repeat the same operation with the horizontal scale set at 90°, using the other cross levelling screw. If the bubble does not remain in the centre of its run it shows that the two pivots in the top of the stand are not at right angles to one another. This, however, is not likely to be the case unless the stand has been severely damaged.

DIRECTORS.

Instructions for Using No. 1 Director and Stand.

(1) Set up the stand so that the index plate is horizontal and with 180° towards the target, place the director in the carrier, and see that it is secured by the catch (R) (Plate XVII). Clamp the index plate (M) at zero, loosen screw (O) and lay on target or aiming posts, then clamp the pivot plate (L) by screw (O). On account of the play which occurs between director and carrier, the director should be moved horizontally by means of the pivot plate and not by the director.

(2) *To measure a horizontal angle.*—Method as in (2); " Instructions for Using No. 3 Director."

(3) *To measure vertical angles.*—Lay on the target for line and elevation, then turn milled head (T) until the bubble is in the centre of its run, the angle can be read in degrees, off the scale, and in one-third of a degree off the vernier.

(4) *To give individual angles to each gun.*—Method as in (5); " Instruc- for Using No. 3 Director."

(5) *When the battery angle is sent down to the Battery Director from the Observing Station.*—Method as in (6); " Instructions for Using No. 3 Director."

Instructions for Using No. 2 Director.

(1) Set up the stand to the height required and see that the gun-metal rings are securely clamped. Clamp the director to the stand by the attachment bolt (Y) (Plate XVIII).

Level the plate (T) so that the bubble is in the centre of its case (U). Raise the vanes (F, F_1) and focus the graticules by revolving the eyepiece, and the view by turning the milled head (E). Set the degree scale plate and micrometer head to zero using the lever (Z_1) if necessary.

(2) *To measure a horizontal angle.*—Slightly loosen attachment bolt (Y) and lay roughly on the target or aiming posts, with the vanes, then clamp bolt (Y) and complete the laying accurately through the telescope, using the slow motion screw. For further instructions see (2); " Instructions for Using No. 3 Director."

(3) *To measure vertical angles.*—Method as in (3); " Instructions for Using No. 3 Director."

(4) *To give individual angles to each gun.*—Method as in (5); "Instructions for Using No. 3 Director," except for Siege Artillery, when the method is as follows :—

Take the director about 200 yards, if possible, to the front or rear of the battery, set it up accurately on the Battery Commander's line, level it, set it to zero, except when it is between the Battery Commander's aiming posts and the target and is laid on the aiming posts, when it should be set at 180°, and unclamp. Then lay the telescope on the target or the aiming posts, and clamp and make a final adjustment if necessary by the slow motion screw (S). Disengage the degree scale plate and lay through the telescope on the dial sight of each gun, engage the traversing gear by the lever (Z_1), and make a final adjustment by the micrometer head of the worm spindle (V). Read the angle so found and send it down to the gun.

(5) *When the battery angle is sent down to the Battery Director from the Observing Station.*—Method as in (6); "Instructions for Using No. 3 Director."

(6) *Observation of fire.*—Method as in "Instructions for Using Apparatus Observation of Fire."

INSTRUCTIONS FOR USING No. 3 DIRECTOR.

(1) Set the degree scale plate at zero by pressing the micrometer head (S_1) (Plate XX) outwards, turning the plate until the zero is opposite the reader on the cover plate, the final adjustment being made by turning the micrometer head. Make the arrows on the carrier and brackets coincide, by turning the cross levelling screws (X_1) and (X_2).

Bring the circular bubble into the centre by moving the legs. Loosen the clamping screw (W_2).

Lay the sight in the direction of the target. Clamp the carrier and lay accurately on the target, or aiming posts, for elevation by means of the levelling screw (X_1), and for direction by the slow motion screw (W_4).

(2) *To measure a horizontal angle.*—With reference to an aiming point, the telescope being on the target or desired line of fire, disengage the degree scale plate which is at zero, by pressing the micrometer head outwards, swing the telescope on to the desired direction, making the final adjustment by the micrometer head.

If the aiming point is above the plane of the instrument it may be necessary to remove the stop pin (O_1), and incline the telescope. The angle in degrees and minutes is read off on the degree scale plate and the micrometer head.

White figures on "Black" are angles to the "Right."
Black figures on "Brass" are angles to the "Left."
A simple way of remembering the above is "White is Right."

In measuring the switch angle from one target to another it is obvious that the angle ordered will be right or left, according as the new target is right or left of the old one, irrespective of the markings on the degree scale plate.

(3) *To measure vertical angles.*—Set up the director as above and lay for elevation and line, turn the micrometer head (H) of the clinometer level till the bubble is in the centre of its run. The angle can then be read in degrees and minutes on the degree scale (J) and micrometer head (I).

(4) *To measure the angle of sight from battery to target when the observer is at a distant Observing Station.*—Set up the director. Lay on the target for elevation and line, then without touching the *lower*

elevating screw (X_1) measure the horizontal angle (T O B) (viz., target, observer, battery), as in (2), laying for elevation on (B) by the *upper levelling screw* (X_2), and for line by the micrometer head of the degree scale plate.

Set the degree scale plate to the apex angle by swinging the eyepiece towards the battery, *past the zero* to the amount of the apex angle. (The apex angle will have been obtained by plotter.) Level the clinometer level as in (3), the result will be the angle of sight from (B) (Battery) to (T) (Target).

(5) *To give individual angles to each gun.*—Set up the stand and director and lay on aiming posts, or target as in (1), disengage the degree scale plate and lay on the dial sight of each gun, laying back through the telescope, object glass-eyepiece, or foresight-backsight, and noting the angle for each gun thus read, and sending it to the battery. When using this method the director should be at least 80 yards from the guns.

(6) *When the battery angle is sent down to the Battery Director from the Observing Station.*—Set up the battery stand and director as in (1), and set the battery angle on the director as ordered, remembering " White is Right," lay on the observing station director roughly with the clamping screw (W_2) loose, then clamp and lay accurately with slow motion screw (W_4).

Disengage the degree scale plate and bring it to zero; the telescope will now be in the line of fire.

(7) *To use the compass as a director.*—Set up stand and director as in (1), fix the compass on the director, nick on the needle on the same side as the foresight of the telescope.

Lay on or in the direction of the target. Disengage the degree scale plate and swing the telescope till the nick of the compass needle is steady in the centre of the scale when it will be pointing north. Send the angle which is the angle between the North and the direction of the target, to the battery director + or − the allowance for displacement.

The battery director will proceed as follows :—

Set the arrow to the reading ordered, unclamp the carrier, swing it round till the nick of the compass needle is in the centre of the scale, clamp the carrier. Press the micrometer head outwards and swing the telescope round till the arrow is at zero; the telescope will now be in the line of fire.

APPARATUS, OBSERVATION OF FIRE—INSTRUMENT, MARK I.
(Plates XXIII and XXIV.)

This instrument consists of the following parts :—

The telescope (A) which is of the ordinary terrestrial pattern, having a magnification of between 14 and 16 diameters, and a field of view of 2°. It is provided with open sights (B, B) and a removable ray-shade with shutter (C). In front of the eyepiece is fixed on collimating screws (D) a diaphragm (Fig. 1) on which are mounted vertical spider's web graticules, one being on the centre line and the others 5, 10, 20, 30, 40, 50 and 60 minutes to either side of it, the 5, 10, 30 and 50 being thin, the remainder thick. There is also a horizontal graticule on the centre line.

[To face page 54.] PLATE XXIII.

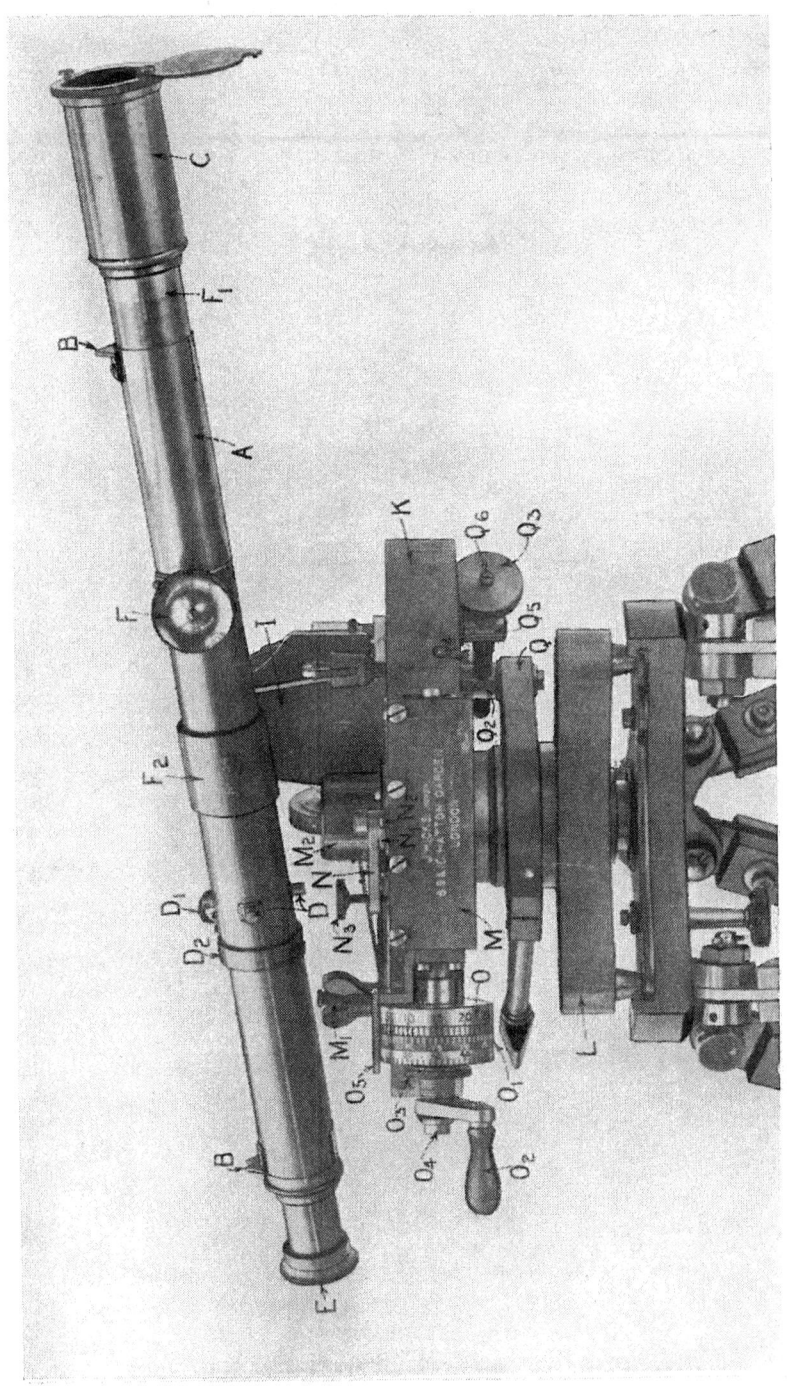

APPARATUS, OBSERVATION OF FIRE. INSTRUMENT.

PLATE XXIV. [*To face page* 55.

APPARATUS, OBSERVATION OF FIRE. INSTRUMENT.

In rear of the diaphragm is a socket for holding a 4-volt electric lamp (see page 166) for illuminating the graticules when required. A small ebonite screwed plug (D_1) is kept in the socket when the lamp is not in use.

The graticules can also be illuminated by light from a lamp entering the telescope through a slot which has a mica window. A revolving ring (D_2) covers this slot when it is not being used.

The graticules are focussed by pushing in or withdrawing the eyepiece (E), and the view is focussed by turning the milled head (F) which is mounted on a spindle, at the other end of which is a pinion, which gears in a rack on the focussing tube (F_1).

Near the centre of the telescope is rigidly attached a band (F_2), which projects to the left, forming a trunnion or coned pivot for the telescope. Beyond the cone is a square which fits accurately in a square hole in the elevating arc (G), and beyond this is a screw thread which engages with the nut (F_3). To remove the eyepiece from the telescope it must be pulled as far to the rear as it will go, and then turned slightly to the left, when it can be pulled straight out.

The elevating arc (G) moves with the telescope. On its lower surface are teeth which gear with the elevating screw (H). Each tooth represents 1°. The arc has a scale engraved on it from 30° depression to 30° elevation, the elevation being filled in black on brass and the depression white on a black background. A casing containing a " Bubble spirit glass B " is attached to the arc by two screws.

The telescope support (I) is attached to the main body by four screws. At the top is formed a coned socket for the pivot of the telescope. On the left side is pivoted at (I_1) a bearing (I_2) for the elevating screw. This bearing is always pressed upwards by a flat German silver spring (I_3), which ensures the elevating screw always being well home in the teeth of the elevating arc. The steel elevating screw (H) has shoulders formed on it, which, with a flat German silver spring (H_1), prevent any backlash. Its rear end is tapered to fit accurately into the brass milled headed disc (H_2). These two parts can be clamped together by tightening the screw (H_3). When adjusting the instrument, this screw can be loosened and the milled head turned independently of the elevating screw. On the rear face of the disc is engraved a scale of single minutes. This scale is read by a reader (J) on the main body. A reader for the scale on the elevating arc is attached to the bearing of the elevating screw.

The main body (K) consists of a heavy plate with a flange projecting downwards. To its under surface is fixed the main pivot which fits in a socket in the tripod stand (L). It is shaped to take the tangent box (M). On its upper surface are two screws (M_1) with winged nuts to take the sight arm, and a circular bubble for levelling. A special bubble was originally issued, but as these become unserviceable they will be replaced by a " Bubble, spirit, circular cased " or a " Bubble cased No. 1." A slide (M_3) with a spring fitting is provided to take the magnetic compass.

The tangent box (M) is pivoted at one end, a flat German silver spring tending to force the tangent screw into gear with the circular rack. A small lever (N) with a cam (N_1) cut on it, when moved outwards, acts on a stud (N_2) projecting from the tangent box, and can be made to overcome the spring and withdraw the tangent screw from the circular rack, when it is desired to traverse the main body quickly. The lever can be kept in the disengaged position by screwing the point of the screw (N_3) into a small hole beneath it.

The steel tangent screw is accurately fitted into its bearings in the tangent box, and end shake is prevented by a flat German silver spring.

The tangent screw projects well to one side, and fixed to it by a set screw is the fixed minute drum (O), beyond this it is circular to form a bearing for the loose minute drum (O_1), and beyond this it is squared to fit into a square hole in the handle (O_2).

The fixed minute drum (O) is graduated from 0 to 60 in single minutes, the graduations being black and agreeing with those on the circular rack. The loose minute drum has two scales, reading in opposite directions, engraved on it. The "Right" scale is white on black and the "Left" black on brass.

The handle (O_2) has a projection on it which is screw-threaded to take the milled nut (O_3). This nut can be screwed home against the loose drum (O_1) and so prevent it revolving independently of the fixed drum (O). The handle is kept in place by means of the screw and washer (O_4). Both drums are read by the reader (O_5).

The circular rack is a large plate having 360 teeth cut on its rim, each tooth representing 1 degree. A scale from 0 to 360 is engraved on its upper surface, and is read by the reader (P) on the main body. It is centrally bored to fit over the pivot formed on the top of the tripod stand (L).

The clamp piece (Q) consists of a metal ring which is cut through at one end. It fits over a bearing on the top of the tripod stand, beneath that for the circular rack. It can be clamped to, or allowed to move independently of, the tripod stand, by manipulating the thumb screw (Q_1).

Pivoted to the other end is an upright piece (Q_2) in which fits the slow motion screw (Q_3). This piece is cut through, and a small capstan headed screw (Q_4) can be made to take up all play between the piece and the slow motion screw.

The other end of the slow motion screw passes through a bearing piece (Q_5) attached to the circular rack, but which can move on its vertical axis. Its extreme end has a square formed on it, and on to this square fits the milled head, which is kept in position by a screw (Q_6).

A shoulder on the slow motion screw and another on the milled head prevent any backlash between the slow motion screw and its bearing, provided the screw (Q_6) is properly home.

The tripod stand (L) has three feet shaped to fit in to the top of the wooden stand. Its upper part is centrally bored to receive the main pivot (beneath the main body), and it has two bearings formed on it for the circular rack and the clamp piece.

The sight arm (Plate XXV) is a bar of T-section, about 30 inches in length. Two projections are formed on one side on which the winged nuts (M_1) bear when it is clamped to the main body. A folding vane is pivoted at each end, the rear one having three small

To face page 56.] PLATE XXV.

APPARATUS, OBSERVATION OF FIRE.

STAND. SIGHT ARM.

COMPASS.

peep holes bored through it, and the front one having a vertical wire fixed to it. It is used when for any reason (*e.g.*, thick weather) the telescope cannot be used.

The magnetic compass (Plate XXV) is a delicately pivoted magnetic needle contained in a metal box. Half the needle is bright and the other half blued. The blued half will point to the magnetic north. When the compass is in position on the instrument and the needle points to the two lines inside the box, the axis of the telescope should point to the magnetic north. A slide is formed beneath the box to fit over the slide (M_3) on the main body. When placed in its fitting in the wood case, it should be put in upside down, so that the needle cannot damage the point of the pivot.

The wood case has interior fittings for firmly holding the instrument, sight arm, compass, two screwdrivers, two adjusting tommies, spanner for tightening the screws of the " Base Plate," wooden box containing a spare webbed diaphragm, switch and resistance coil, and two 4-volt lamps. It is provided with two lifting handles, and the lid is kept down by a spring catch and two hooks and eyes.

To Place the Instrument in its Wood Case. (Fig. 5.)

Place the compass upside down in its fitting.

Set the vertical degree scale to 0° (to prevent the telescope becoming damaged by coming into contact with the lid).

Put the slow motion traversing gear out of action by moving the lever (N) outwards, and slacken the screw of the clamp piece (Q_1, Plate XXIV).

Lift up the instrument, the fingers being beneath the toothed rack (and on no account under the telescope), and lower it gently into the case, the object glass of the telescope being to the right, and the tangent box (A) (Fig. 5) fitting into its fitting (B). If it will not go completely

Fig. 5.

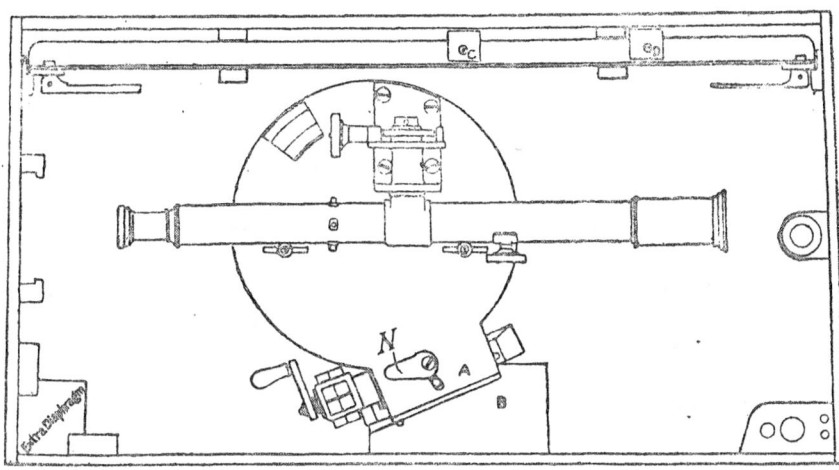

Instrument in Box.

down at once, see that the feet of the tripod stand and the clamping piece are not catching against anything.

Fold down the vanes of the sight arm, turn it on one side, so that the screws (C.D) are uppermost and the vanes towards the instrument, and place it in the fittings provided.

The weight of the apparatus with its adjuncts in the wood case is about 90 lbs., and the exterior dimensions of the case are $2'\ 8'' \times 1'\ 5\frac{1}{2}'' \times 11\frac{3}{4}''$.

APPARATUS, OBSERVATION OF FIRE—STAND TRIPOD.

This stand (Plate XXV) consists of three mahogany legs (A), pivoted to a metal plate (B). The plate has three recesses on its upper surface to receive the three feet of the instrument. Centrally pivoted above the plate is a locking plate (C) having three holes cut in it. The holes are so shaped that one end is large enough for the feet of the apparatus to pass through them, but the other end, when passed over the enlarged portion of the feet will not allow them to rise. The locking plate can be clamped down by means of the milled headed screw (G_1).

The pivots at the top of the legs can be clamped up by means of the capstan nuts (D).

Each leg has a metal fitting at its lower end, and pivoted to this is a hinged plate (E), the under side of which is roughened to prevent slipping. There is a hole in each plate through which a nail or spike may be hammered into the ground. A strap (F) for binding the legs together is secured to one leg.

A wood case with fittings for the stand, two carrying handles, a spring catch, and two hooks and eyes is provided.

Before inserting the stand in its case fold back the hinged plates on the feet and undo the strap.

Place one leg on the bottom fitting in the case and separate the two others, so that they rest on their respective fittings.

The weight of the stand in its case is about 70 lbs., and the external dimensions of the case are $4'\ 6\frac{1}{4}'' \times 11'' \times 12\frac{1}{2}''$.

METHOD OF USING THE OBSERVATION OF FIRE INSTRUMENTS BY DAY.

(1) The instruments are carried to the stations in their boxes, being previously carefully examined to see that they are in all respects complete and correct. Each observer on reaching his station will communicate his name and that of his station to the battery. He will note in writing all observations made, and all messages sent or received.

(2) Each battery should have its own separate system of observation, for which two instruments are required. Occasionally it may be necessary, when two or more batteries are firing at the same target, to place them under one pair of observers. In this case each of the observers must be in communication with each of the batteries, or with some central post, if such can be arranged, whence their messages can be rapidly conveyed to the batteries.

(3) Whenever possible, there should be two observers with each instrument. They should relieve each other frequently, and the one who is not observing with the instrument should observe with field glasses, and also keep a constant look-out for fresh targets, &c.

(4) The instruments are set up as follows :—

(a) Set up the tripod, roughly level.

(b) Place instrument on tripod, and secure it by the locking plate and clamp the latter.

(c)*Fix on the sighting arm, screwing up the fly nuts.

(d) Focus eyepiece until the graticules are clearly seen; then direct telescope on distant object and focus object glass till distant object is clearly defined. Check the focus (see page 6).

(e) Level the instrument by adjusting the legs till the bubble is in the centre of the glass, and secure the legs of the tripod to prevent their shifting.

(f) Set the instrument to zero, roughly with the drum out of gear and then exactly with the drum in gear, seeing that both the degree scale on the plate and the minute scale on the drum are at zero.

(g) Unclamp the bedplate, and lay the telescope or sighting arm (whichever is being used) roughly on the other instrument if visible, if not visible on the reference point; clamp it, and adjust it exactly on, by the slow motion screw. When the instrument is thus correctly layed, neither the clamp nor the slow motion screw must again be touched. Now take the angle to the "battery director," if visible, and also to the sub-base at the battery, and see that these readings are sent to the battery commander. Then put the drum out of gear and turn the instrument in the direction of the target.

(5) The observers will also be instructed in orienting the instrument when at zero on the other observer or reference point, to note the bearing of the instrument when the magnetic needle points north. This information is useful when night firing is to be carried out.

IF THE TARGET IS A SINGLE GUN, OR A WELL-DEFINED OBJECT.

(6) Lay the instrument roughly by hand on the target, looking over the sights on the telescope. Put the drum into gear and adjust exactly by drum and handle sending in the reading, in degrees and minutes to the battery, by telephone or signal, reading the degrees on the plate and the minutes on the drum (on the scale furthest from the handle). If the target is a disappearing gun, or a gun located by its flash, which is only seen at intervals, several observations should be taken before the instrument is finally set. In that case, the first reliable reading is sent in to the battery in degrees and minutes, and subsequent readings are sent in in minutes right or left of the first

---

* The sighting arm would be used in preference to the telescope for observing when the atmospheric conditions are such that a better view can be obtained by the naked eye than through the glass.

reading. The battery commander will communicate an angle at which the instrument is to be finally set. This is called the "clamping angle."

IF THE TARGET CONSISTS OF SEVERAL GUNS, OR OF MORE THAN ONE WELL-DEFINED OBJECT.

(7) Clamp the instrument on one of the guns, or objects, as in the case of a single gun, and send in the angle in degrees and minutes. Then send in readings for the other guns, or objects, in minutes right or left of the first reading. By this means the battery commander will be able to ensure that both observers are clamped on the same point. If the target consists of disappearing guns, or guns only located by their flash, the procedure will be as described below.

IF THE TELESCOPE IS BEING USED TO OBSERVE WITH.

(8) The minutes right and left of this angle at which shell are observed to burst are read by means of the graticules, and sent to the battery.

IF THE SIGHTING ARM IS BEING USED TO OBSERVE WITH.

(9) After the instrument has been set at the angle ordered, the adjustable part of the drum must be adjusted and clamped so that the zero on it corresponds with the number of minutes in the angle at which the instrument is set. The minutes right or left at which shell are observed to burst are then measured by traversing the sighting arm by drum and handle on to the burst, and reading the number of minutes on the adjustable drum (if the burst was to the right, reading on the white lines; if to the left, on the black lines), and sending in the number of minutes to the battery. After each observation the instrument must be traversed back to the original angle. When, in observing shell bursts, large angles, say 50', are read, there is a tendency to bring the zero on the drum back, by traversing through the last 10' of the degree. This alters, and causes an error of one degree in the angle, and can best be avoided by constantly checking the reading of the degree scale, to see that it corresponds with the original angle.

METHOD OF USING THE OBSERVATION OF FIRE INSTRUMENTS BY NIGHT.

(1) Instrumental observation can be carried on by night almost as easily as by day.

The flash of discharge or burst is observed, instead of the smoke; but owing to its instantaneous nature, the telescope and graticules alone can be used to observe with, as the time during which a flash is visible is too short to allow of the sighting arm being traversed on to it with sufficient accuracy.

(2) The graticules must be illuminated either by the electric lamp or by a bull's-eye lantern held to the small window of the telescope.

Observation at night may be required to be carried on under any of the following conditions :—

WHEN THE NIGHT FIRING FOLLOWS IMMEDIATELY ON THE DAY.

(3) In this case it is only necessary to illuminate the graticules and proceed as by day.

WHEN AFTER FIRING BY DAY, THE INSTRUMENTS HAVE BEEN TAKEN DOWN, AND MUST AT NIGHT BE SET UP AS BEFORE.

(4) The exact position of each leg of the tripods must be marked before they are taken down, by a peg being driven through the hole in the foot.

(5) In this case each instrument must be laid at zero as by day, and then set at the same angle as before. To lay at zero on the other instrument, the instrument must be lit up as may be most convenient ; but it is important that the method adopted should be such that it can be clearly and easily seen, and not liable to be confused with other lights.

(6) The "bearing" of the north point having been registered by day, this angle is set on the instrument and the base plate is revolved until the magnetic needle points north. The base plate is then clamped and the instrument set to zero when the telescope should be on the other observer ; but if several observing stations are close together, other means of identification will be necessary, such as different coloured lanterns, or lamp signalling.

(7) The inclination of the telescope by day, read in degrees on the arc on the left side and in minutes on the elevating wheel, should be carefully noted, so that time may not be wasted at night in getting the telescope to the proper elevation or depression.

(8) On Service, instruments should not, as a rule, be taken down, but once they have been correctly set up should be secured in position, and protected from weather by light waterproof covers that can be put on the instruments when they are not wanted for use.

WHEN THE OBSERVATION IS TO COMMENCE AT NIGHT.

(9) In this case the target must be a gun or guns whose flash is visible. The instruments must be marked by lights.

(10) If the target is a single gun, the observation is carried out as detailed for day observation.

(11) If the target consists of several guns, it is essential that both instruments should be clamped on the same gun.

To ensure this, the battery commander obtains readings to each gun from each observer, and is thus enabled to decide which two readings should refer to the same gun, and orders the observers to clamp accordingly.

(12) The procedure will then be as follows :—

The instrument, drum out of gear, is layed roughly, looking over the sights of the telescope, on one of the guns and the drum then put in gear.

Looking through the telescope it is adjusted by the drum and handle so that the target is in *or near* the centre of the field. The angle is then read and sent to the battery. The flashes of other guns are then read right or left of this angle by means of the graticules, and the observation of each *in minutes* is sent to the battery. The battery commander will, as soon as a sufficient number of observations have been received, send the angle at which the instrument is to be finally set. Shell bursts are then observed as before explained.

OTHER USES OF THE OBSERVATION OF FIRE INSTRUMENTS.

(1) The primary object of the observation of fire instruments is to observe fire, and for this purpose the main essential is that they should be clamped on the same point in the target. They can, however, also be used for finding the range and line of fire for the battery.

(2) In order to do this, it is necessary to determine:—
 (i.) The distance between the observers.
 (ii.) The distance of one of the observers from a director placed in front or rear of the battery—the latter for choice.
 (iii.) The clamping angle of each observer.
 (iv.) The apex angle. That is, the angle formed at the target by the intersection of the line of vision of each observer.
 (v.) The distance of each observer from the target.
 (vi.) The battery range.

These are worked out in the battery by a non-commissioned officer called the "plotter," in conjunction with and under the immediate supervision of the battery commander.

(3) It is important to note that the function of the instruments in obtaining these items of information is entirely distinct from their use for observing fire, for which none of this information is essential.

(4) The observations of the observers are called out to the plotter by telephonists or signallers who are in connection with them. In doing so, the observer from whom the observation comes and the number of round should always be stated before calling out the observation; for instance, "Right observer, 5th round, 40′ L," &c. Also, in order to prevent confusion from both telephonists calling out together, it is advisable to arrange for one particular observer's result to be called out first, the other telephonist waiting till this has been done; preferably, the "line observer's" results should be called out first.

(5) Any reliable information regarding the fall of the shot, which might assist the battery commander may be added by the observers to their reports of each round, such as "over and higher than the target" or "much short in valley below target."

APPARATUS, OBSERVATION OF FIRE—PLATE BASE.

The base plate (Fig. 6) is used, instead of the tripod stand, when the instrument is more or less permanently installed. It is cemented on to the top of a stone or concrete pedestal. It consists of a gunmetal body (A) having three radial grooves (B) cut in it to receive the feet of the instrument. A locking plate (C) is centrally pivoted on it, and held down by the clamping centre (D). Three holes (E) are cut in the locking plate and are of such a shape that the feet of the instrument can pass through one half, but not through the other. When the second halves are over the enlarged portion of the feet of the instrument, and the three screws (F) are screwed home by means of

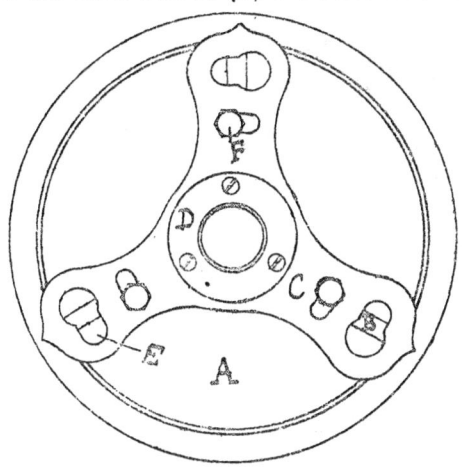

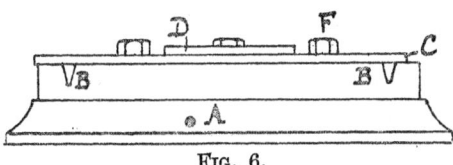

FIG. 6.

the spanner in the instrument case, the instrument is firmly fixed to the base plate.

APPARATUS, OBSERVATION OF FIRE—SLIDE RULE.

There are six Marks of this slide rule in the Service. They differ principally in—

(a) The material of which they are made, the earlier Marks being of boxwood and the later ones of aluminium.

(b) The number of yard graduations, the earlier Marks extending to 5,000 yards, the latter ones to 10,000 yards.

(c) The form of cursor and clamp.

It is proposed to describe the Mark VI only.

MARK VI.

This slide rule (Plate XXVI) consists of the following parts :—

The rule consists of two parallel bars of aluminium (A), the ends of which are held together by pieces of German silver (B) which encircle them.

One bar is marked on one side with figures from 1 to 1,000, the word "yards" being marked against the 1,000.

The other side of the other bar is similarly marked.

The slide (C), which slides freely between the two bars of the rule, has one side marked in a similar way to the rule, except that instead of "yards," "Minutes of Apex Angle or Battery Range in yards" is marked against the 1,000. The other side has a scale of sines from that of 1 minute to that of 90°. An "S" at the 90° graduation signifies sines.

The cursor (D) is a small German silver frame having on each side fine edges by which the rule and slide can be read. At the top there is a clamping screw (E) by which it can be fixed in any position, and at the same time clamp the slide and rule together.

The graduations are logarithmic, that is the distance of each graduation from the 1 on the left represents, to a certain scale, the logarithm of the number against the graduation. Supposing, for example, that the scale is "1 inch represents the logarithm of 10." The logarithm of—

2 is ·301
3 is ·477
6 is ·778
10 is 1·000

and the distance from the 1 on the slide rule to the 2, 3, 6 and 10 would be ·301, ·477, ·778 and 1 inch respectively.

The actual scale the slide rules are graduated to is "12·5 centimetres represent the log of 10." The distance of the 2 graduation from the 1 is therefore ·301 × 12·5, or 3·7625 centimetres, and of the 10 12·5 c.m.

The sine scale is calculated in a similar way, the sine of an angle (A B C) being merely a number representing the length of the side (A C) divided by the length of the side (A B), in a triangle (A B C) (Fig. 7) of which (A C B) is a right angle :—

$$\text{Sin ABC} = \frac{AC}{AB}$$

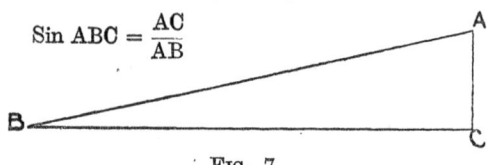

Fig. 7.

By manipulating the slide rule, numbers can be rapidly multiplied together, or divided by one another and proportional sums can be solved. Triangles can be solved by the formula—

$$\frac{a}{\text{Sine A}} = \frac{b}{\text{Sine B}} = \frac{c}{\text{Sine C}}$$

if the base and the two subtended angles, or two sides and the included angle are known.

As is well known, if it is desired to *multiply* two numbers together by logarithms, the logarithms of the two numbers are taken from a log table and *added* together, and the number whose logarithm is the sum of the two logarithms is also found in the log tables and is the number required. Thus, if it is required to *multiply* 2 by 3, the logarithms are found to be ·301 and ·477 (see above) which, *added together*, make ·778, which is the logarithm of 6.

This addition of the logarithms is done mechanically by the slide rule, and if we wish to multiply 2 by 3, we set the 1 on the slide under

PLATE XXVI.

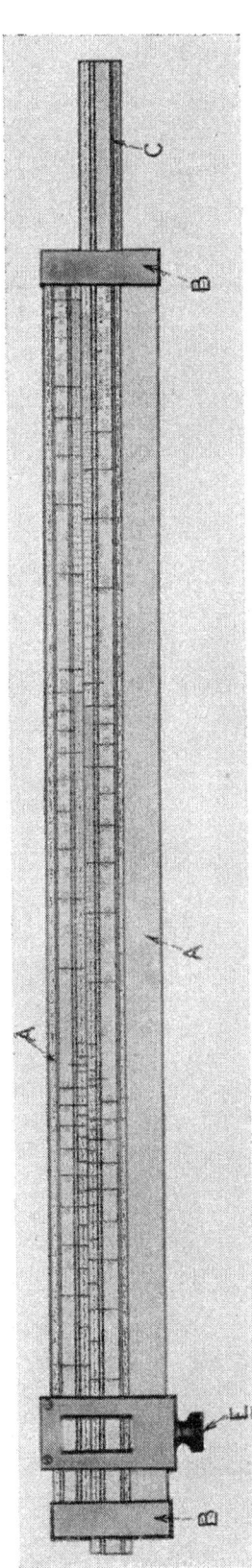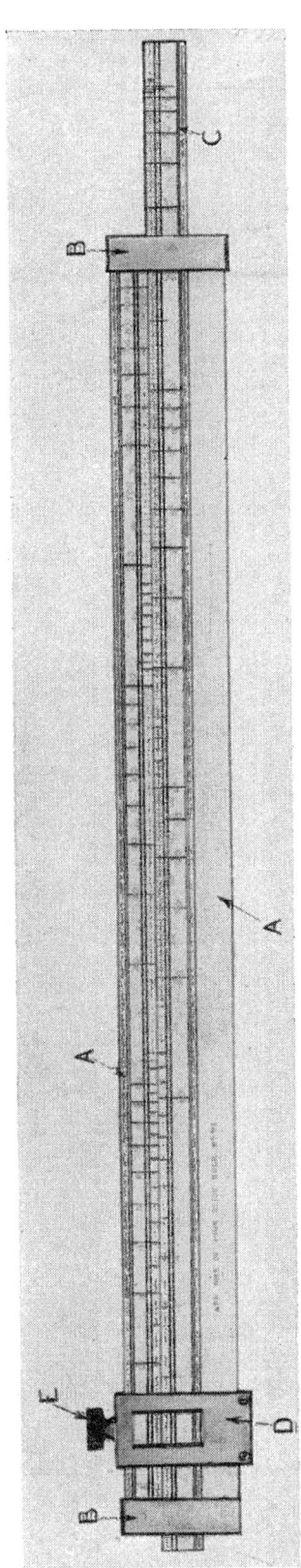

SLIDE RULE FOR APPARATUS, OBSERVATION OF FIRE.

the 2 on the rule and find above the 3 on the slide the number required, viz., 6. We have mechanically added the length of scale representing the logarithm of 2 to the length of scale representing the logarithm of 3, and found that the sum of these two lengths is the length of scale representing the logarithm of 6.

When the slide is set as above with the 1 under the 2, we can read off the product of any number multiplied by 2, thus above 2 is 4, above 5 is 10, above $5\frac{1}{2}$ is 11, and so on.

Setting the slide rule becomes exceedingly simple if one thinks of the problem as a proportional sum, and of the two lines between the numerators and denominators as a continuous line representing the line between the rule and the slide. Thus :

To multiply 2 by 3.

$$2 \times 3 = x \text{ or } \frac{2}{1} = \frac{x}{3}.$$

$$\left(\frac{2}{1} \quad \frac{x}{3}\right).$$

Set the 1 on the slide under the 2 on the rule, and over the 3 on the slide will be the answer x, or 6.

To divide 8 by 4.

$$\frac{8}{4} = x \text{ or } \frac{8}{4} = \frac{x}{1}.$$

$$\left(\frac{8}{4} \quad \frac{x}{1}\right).$$

Set the 4 on the slide under the 8 on the rule, and over the 1 on the slide will be the answer x, or 2.

Proportion.

$$\frac{8}{4} = \frac{6}{x}.$$

$$\left(\frac{8}{4} \quad \frac{6}{x}\right).$$

Set the 4 on the slide under the 8 on the rule, and under the 6 on the rule will be found the answer x, or 3.

A triangle can similarly be solved by the

$$\frac{h}{R} = \frac{m}{1146}$$

formula. Thus suppose " h," the height or base is 75 feet, " m " the apex angle is 55 minutes, and we wish to find the range in yards " R."

The proportional sum is

$$\frac{75}{R} = \frac{55}{1146}.$$

$$\left(\frac{75}{R} \quad \frac{55}{1146}\right).$$

Set the 1146 (marked with a red line) on the slide under 55 on the rule, and under the 75 on the rule will be found the answer R, or 1,563 yards.

To solve a triangle by the formula

$$\frac{a}{\text{Sine } A} = \frac{b}{\text{Sine } B} = \frac{c}{\text{Sine } C}.$$

(a) *When one side and the two subtended angles are known.*

In Fig. 8 suppose the base (B C (or a)) to be 750 yards, the angles (A B C) and (A C B) to be 73° and 87° respectively, and consequently

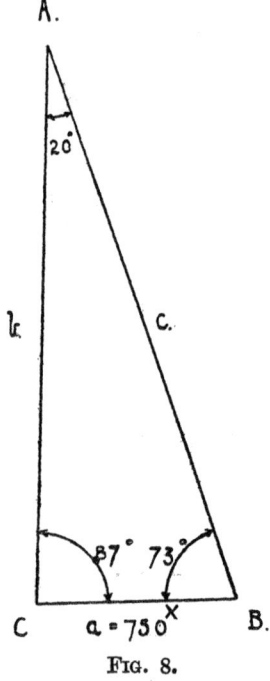

Fig. 8.

the apex angle (C A B (or A)) to be 20°, and that we want to know the ranges (B A (or c)) and (C A (or b)).

$$\frac{a}{\text{Sine } A} = \frac{b}{\text{Sine } B} = \frac{c}{\text{Sine } C}$$

$$\text{or } \frac{750^\times}{\text{Sine } 20°} = \frac{b}{\text{Sine } 73°} = \frac{c}{\text{Sine } 87°}.$$

$$\left(\frac{750}{\text{Sine } 20°} \quad \frac{b}{\text{Sine } 73°} \quad \frac{c}{\text{Sine } 87°}\right).$$

Set Sine 20 on the slide under 750 on the rule, above Sine 73° and Sine 87° we can read off the rule the ranges b and c, viz., 2,100 and 2,190 yards approximately.

Note.—If either of the angles (B or C) is greater than 90° subtract it from 180°, and take the sine of the remainder.

(b) *When two sides and the included angle are known.*

In a triangle suppose the angle (A) and sides (b and c) are known. Subtract the angle (A) from 180°; this gives the sum of the angles (B and C).

Mark (with cursors or otherwise) on the scale of numbers on the rule above the sine scale, the graduations representing the sides (b and c), and shift the slide about until the angles underneath the cursors or marks are together equal to the sum of the angles (B and C).

Now, under the side (b) will be the angle (B); under the side (c) will be the angle (C); and over the angle (A) will be the side (a).

If one of the angles (B or C) is greater than a right angle, this angle must be read backwards on the slide; that is 100° is read as 80° 110° as 70°, 122° as 58°, and so on.

It will be found that it is not possible to read the greater angle to much accuracy, as the divisions on the slide are so small. It is, therefore, best to read the smaller angle accurately, and subtract it from the sum of the two, in order to find the degrees and minutes in the greater angle.

In the case where the two sides and the included angle are known, the practical rule for working the slide rule so as to obtain accurate results is as follows :—

There are two cases.

(1) When the included angle is more than 90°. Set the exterior angle (which is equal to the two remaining angles of the triangle) under the longer side (or right hand mark on the rule), note the value of the angle under the left hand mark, shift the slide this number of degrees to the *right*, so that the reading under the right cursor is this number of degrees less than it was before; it will then be seen that the sum of the angles under the two cursors or marks is very nearly equal to the exterior angle, and a very slight further manipulation of the slide will obtain the required result.

(2) When the included angle is less than 90°. The sine of the exterior angle (or of the sum of the other two) is then equal to sine (180°—exterior angle). Set this angle under the longer side and proceed as before, but shift the slide to the *left* instead of to the right; and remember that the angle appearing under the right hand mark, is not the angle as it is read but its supplement.

Any triangle can be solved in this manner, but the more nearly equal the two given sides are, the greater will be the second movement of the slide in the final manipulation; and in the case of (2) when the sides are nearly equal, the angle under the right hand mark *is* the angle shown on the slide, and *not* its supplement.

If a field plotter is available, the slide rule is not required. It is merely an alternative method, which can be used failing the field plotter.

The following formulæ for use with the slide rule may be found useful for reference. They are arranged so that the required information is *always* found by reading *upwards* so as to avoid as far as possible mistakes caused by reading the rule wrongly.

Siege Artillery Formulæ.

(1) To FIND THE DISTANCE BETWEEN OBSERVERS.—Put subtended angle, in minutes, under sub-base, in feet, and look over 1,146 for answer in yards.

Or put subtended angle in degrees and minutes (using sine scale) under sub-base in yards and over 90° on sine scale, read distance between observers in yards.

The distance to the battery director is found in the same way.

(2) To FIND OBSERVERS RANGES.—Put apex angle, in degrees and minutes (using the sine scale) under distance between observers, in yards, and look over each base angle for the *opposite* observer's range.

(3) To FIND THE MINUTES IN THE 50 PER CENT. ZONES.—Put the " yards due to 5 minutes " under 5, and look over the yards in the zone.

(4) To FIND THE MINUTES DEFLECTION DUE TO DISPLACEMENT. Put the battery range under 1,146 and look over the displacement, in feet.

(5) To FIND THE DEFLECTION FOR DIFFERENCE OF LEVEL OF WHEELS.—Put 60 under the elevation due to range, in degrees and fractions, and look over the minutes difference of level.

(6) To CONVERT THE OBSERVATIONS TO BATTERY RANGE.—Put the battery range under the observer's range, and look over the observation sent in in minutes.

RULE, SLIDE, 10-INCH, MARK I.

This is a wooden slide rule surfaced with celluloid, and is shown in Plate XXVII.

On the front are engraved four scales, viz. :

A on the rule numbers from 1 to 100 ⎫ To a scale of " 12·5 centi-
B   „   slide   „   „ 1 to 100 ⎭ metres = 1."
C   „   slide   „   „ 1 to 10 ⎫ To a scale of " 25 centi-
D   „   rule   „   „ 1 to 10 ⎭ metres = 1."

The scales are used in the same way as the yard scales on the slide rule for the Apparatus, observation of fire. When great accuracy is required the C and D scales are used as the divisions are twice as large as those on the A and B scales. Squares and square roots of numbers can be read off at once, using the A and D scales. Thus, it will be noticed that the 2, 4, 8, &c., on the D scale are immediately beneath their squares, viz., 4, 16, 64, &c., on the A scale.

The reverse side of the slide has three scales on it marked as follows:

(S) Which is sine scale similar to that on the slide rule used with the apparatus, observation of fire, except that it does not read below 34'.

(L) Which is a scale of logarithms, by which the logarithms of any number can be ascertained, but is it not required for service purposes.

(T) Which is a scale of tangents.

PLATE XXVII.

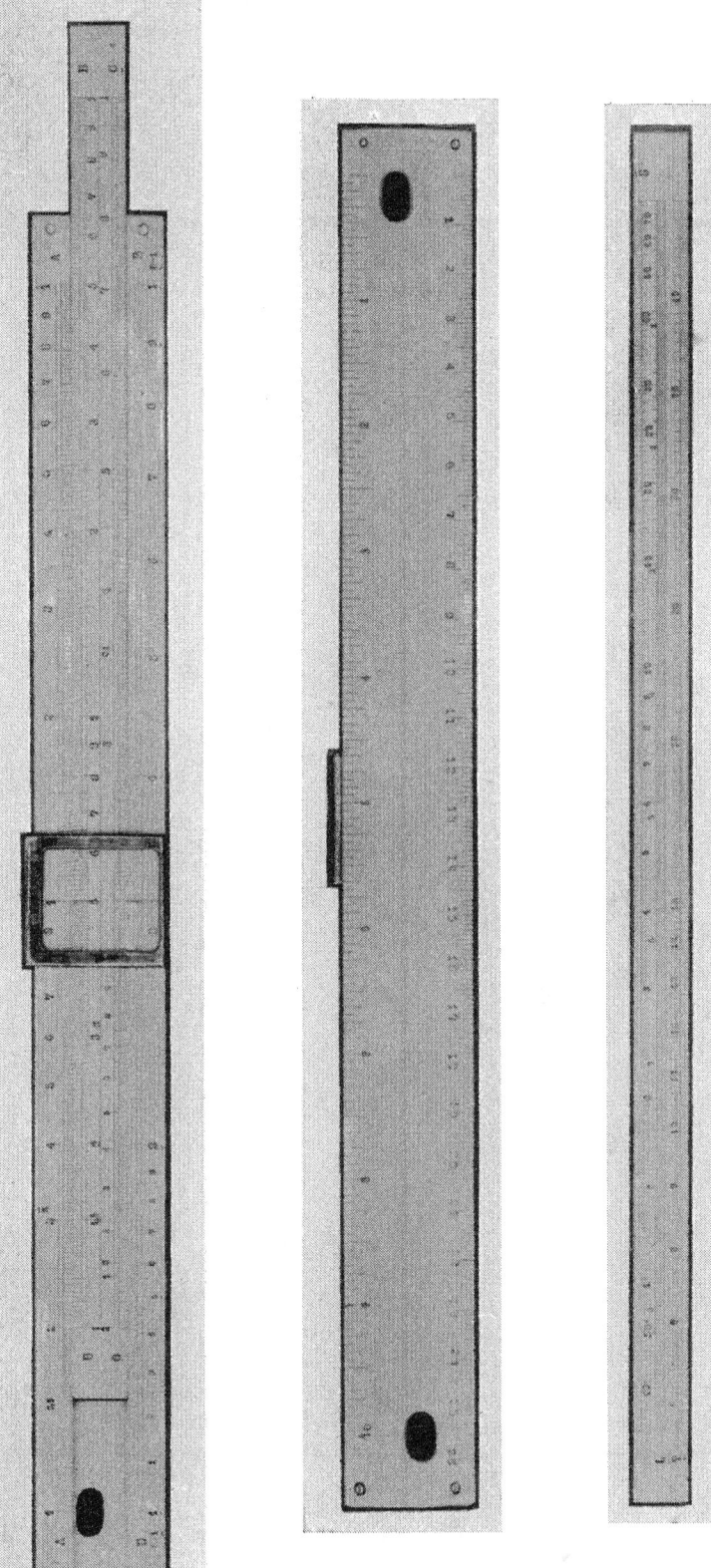

RULE, SLIDE, 10 INCH, MARK I.

When the S scale is used for solving triangles, it is placed beneath the A scale and used in conjunction with it.

When it is required to find the sine or tangent of an angle the A, B, C and D scales are to the front, and the angle whose sine or tangent is required is set opposite a reader in one of the small windows at the back of the rule, the tangent being read off the A, B, C or D scales.

To Find the Tangent of an Angle.

Set the angle on the T scale against the reader in the window on the left of the back of the rule. Thus, suppose that the tangent of 45° is required. Set the 45° opposite the reader. The right hand 1 of the C scale will be found to be over the left hand 1 of the D scale, and this indicates that $\tan 45° = \frac{1}{1}$ or 1.

Similarly if we wish to find the tangent of 11° 18', we set that number opposite the reader in the window, and find the right hand 1 of the C scale over the 5 on the D scale, which indicates that $\tan 11° 18' = \frac{1}{5}$. Similarly the tangent of any angle between 45° and 5° 44', whose tangent is $\frac{1}{10}$, can be found.

The tangents and sines of smaller angles are practically the same, and can be read off the sine scale.

To find the Sine of an Angle.

The angle on the sine scale is set opposite the reader in the right-hand window, and the left hand 1 of the B scale over the number on the A scale represents the sine. Thus, when set for sine 90° the sine is found to be $\frac{1}{1}$ or 1, when set for 5° 44' the sine is $\frac{1}{10}$, and when for 34'. the sine is $\frac{1}{100}$ and so on.

The cursor is a small aluminium frame into which is fixed a piece of glass having a thin line engraved on it. This line is used for reading the scales. Slide rules have recently been provided with a second cursor.

On the back of the rule are engraved scales of inches and centimetres.

A cardboard case is supplied for holding the slide rule.

Field Plotters.

There are four Marks of field plotters in the service. They differ from one another in the following details:

(1) Material.—Marks I and II are made of brass, Marks III and IV of nickel plated steel.

(2) Length of scales, Marks I and II.—Arms read from 1,200 to 4,500 yards and base from 0 to 3,000. Marks III, Arms read from 1,800 to 5,400 yards and Mark IV. arms read from 2,100 to 6,500 yards. Marks III and IV base reads from 0 to 3,500 yards.

(3) In the Marks 1, II and III the base is clamped by means of two screws, but the Mark IV has only one.

(4) Scale.—Marks I, II and III are 450 yards to 1 inch. Mark IV 550 yards to 1 inch.

Field plotters are used for mechanically solving triangles. If the base, range from one end of it to the target and the included angle are known, and the plotter is set to read them on one side, the range from the other end of the base, and the included angle can be read off from the other side.

PLOTTER, FIELD, MARK IV.

This plotter (Plates XXVIII, and XXIX.) is composed of two nickel plated steel plates (A.B) a portion of each being a semi-circle around which are engraved degree graduations from 0° to 180°.

The plates have each a parallel slide (C.D) formed on the left side, in which fits the guide plate (E.E$_1$) from the other plate, so keeping the slides parallel. One guide plate has a screw with a nut (F) attached to it, by means of which the two plates can be clamped to read any required base.

Each slide is graduated to read bases of from 0 to 3,500 yards in divisions of 50 yards, and a reader (G.G$_1$) is engraved to the right of the semi-circle.

Centrally pivoted to each semi-circle is a steel arm (H.H$_1$) having ranges of from 2,100 to 6,500 yards in divisions of 50 yards engraved on it. A reader (J.J$_1$) for the degree scale on the semi-circle is engraved on each arm.

The two arms are prevented from moving independently by means of a double arm clamp. This consists of two small brass guides (K.K$_1$), which can be slid along the arms, a screw passing through them. On the screw are mounted the two clamping nuts (L.L$_1$) and the washers, &c., necessary to prevent undue friction or play.

On the brass plates are engraved arrows for reading the scales on the arms.

The weight of the plotter is about 2 lb. 2 oz.

A leather case with shoulder strap, lined with chamois leather is provided for carrying the plotter. Its weight is about 2 lb.

TO USE THE PLOTTER.

The operations in using the instrument are as follows, and should be performed in the order given:

1. Slightly loosen all clamps.
2. Set the base to the distance from the battery (B) to the observer (O).
3. Move the double clamp along the upper range arm to the distance from (O) to the target (T) and clamp by *upper* screw *only*.
4. Move the range arms till the arrow mark is opposite the angle, (T O B) on the arc, and clamp by the *lower* screw of the double clamp. The angle (T O B) may be measured by means of the director.
5. Turn the instrument over, and on the range arm will be found the distance (B T) and on the semi-circle the angle, (T B O) which is called the "battery angle."

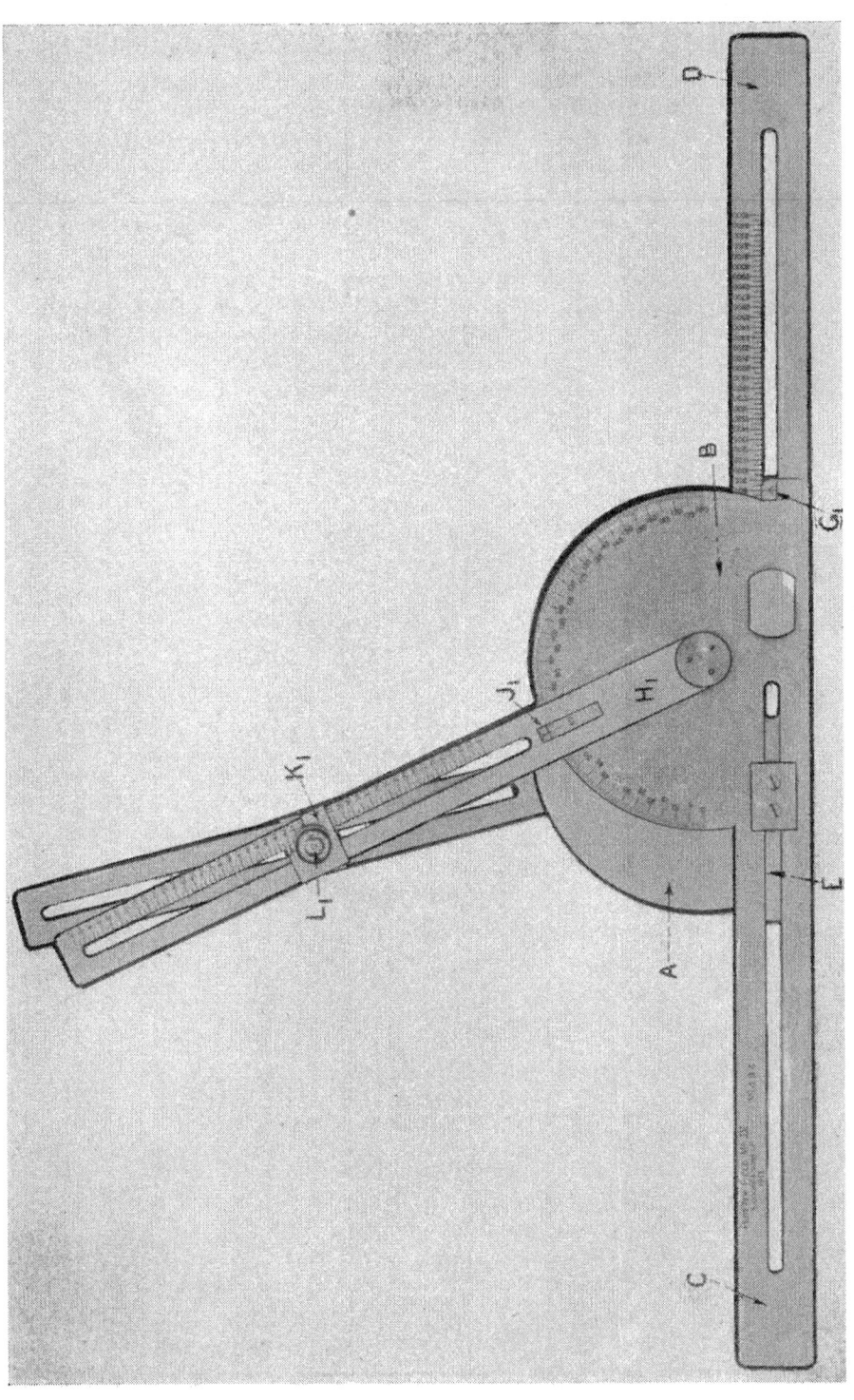

PLATE XXIX. [*To face page* 71.

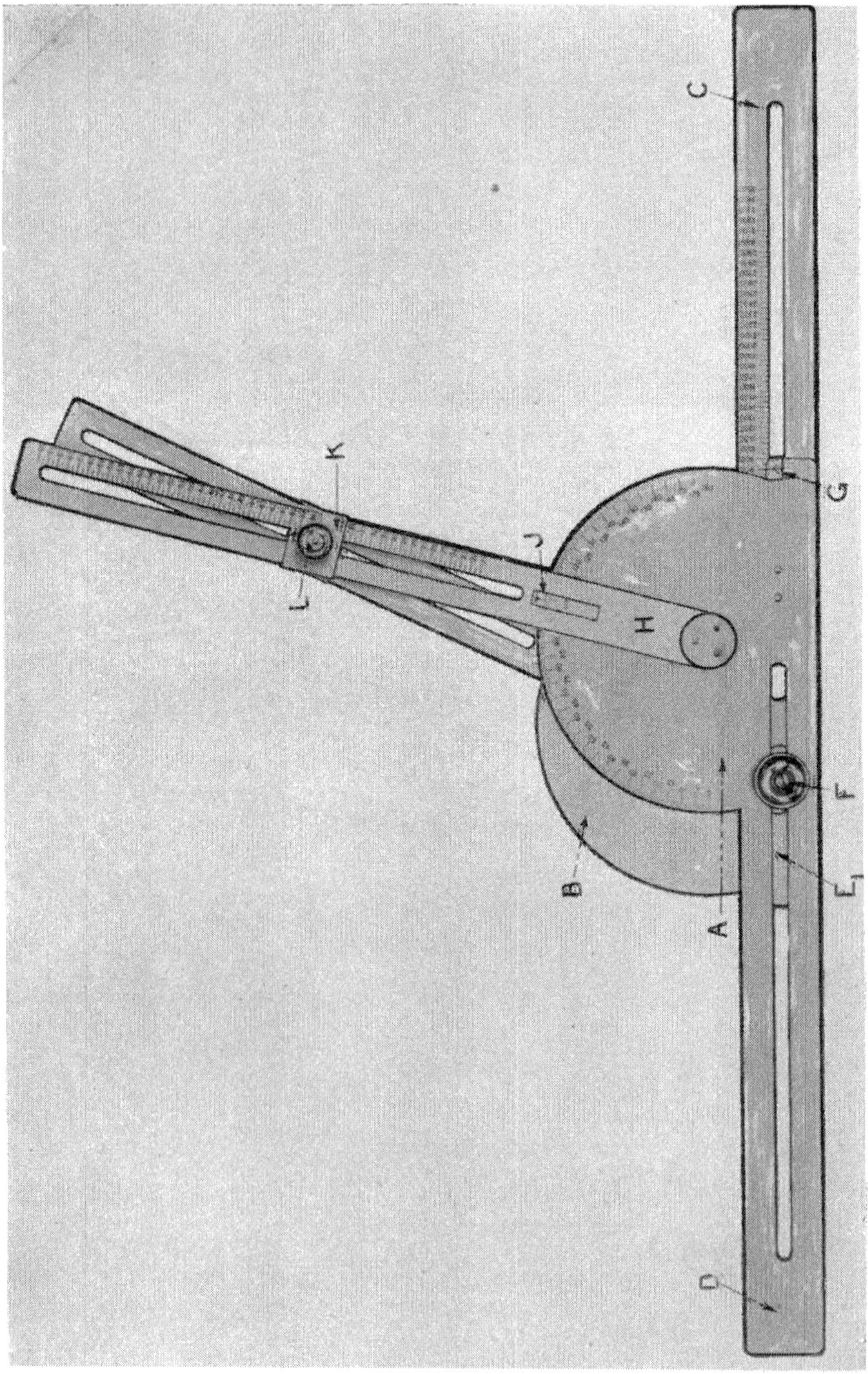

FIELD PLOTTER.

Thus, suppose that the base is 800 yards, the range from the right end of it to the target is 4,200 yards, and the included angle is 65°, and that the range from the left end of the base to the target and the included angle are to be found.

Proceed as follows :—

Loosen the base and two range clamps. Set the base to 800 yards (see Plate XXVIII.) and tighten up the clamp. Set the right range arm to 4,200 yards and tighten up the clamp. Revolve the right arm until it reads 65°, and tighten up the clamp at the back of the left range arm. Turn the plotter over (see Plate XXIX.) and the range from the left of the base to the target (on the left arm) will be found to be about 3,925 yards, and the included angle $104\frac{1}{2}°$.

For longer bases than 2,900 or longer ranges than 4,400 when using the Mark III Plotter, the graduations may be taken as double yards, the angles remaining the same.

The instrument is used in conjunction with a director, when the line of fire has to be picked up from a position at a considerable distance from the battery.

CHAPTER IV.

CLINOMETERS.

Clinometers may be divided into three classes, viz. :—

(1) Those of the Watkin Type.

(2) The Mark III Field Clinometer.

(3) The sight Clinometer.

THE WATKIN TYPE CLINOMETER.

The principal clinometers of this type in the service are :—

Clinometer, Watkin (or Field, Mark I). Used with machine guns.
Clinometer, Large. Mark I.
Clinometer, Inspectors. Mark I.
Clinometer, Inspectors. Mark II.
Clinometer, Field. Mark II.
Clinometer, B.L. 10 PR. Mark I.

Each Clinometer (Plate XXX.) consists of :—

A metal frame or body (A), having two truly surfaced surfaces at right angles to one another. The sides are connected together by a platform (B) on which is engraved the reader for the drum (C).

A main screw (Fig. 1) of hard steel which is rigidly attached to the body, and which has a double thread cut on it. A stop screw, with a large head is screwed into the top of the main screw to prevent the drum becoming detached.

A drum (Fig. 1) which consists of a sleeve, tube, nut and cap. The nut is of gunmetal and has a steel ring, with a dead hard bearing surface, let into it. It is fitted very accurately to the main screw, and to prevent any backlash, three or more holes are bored through it, into which are fitted backlash pieces. These pieces are forced against the main screw by flat German silver springs.

The tube is of brass or aluminium alloy, and is rigidly attached to the nut. Its exterior surface is accurately turned to receive the brass sleeve, on which a spiral graduated scale is engraved. It is accurately bored at the top to receive the cap which is held in position

To face page 72.]   PLATE XXX.

CLINOMETERS OF THE WATKIN TYPE.

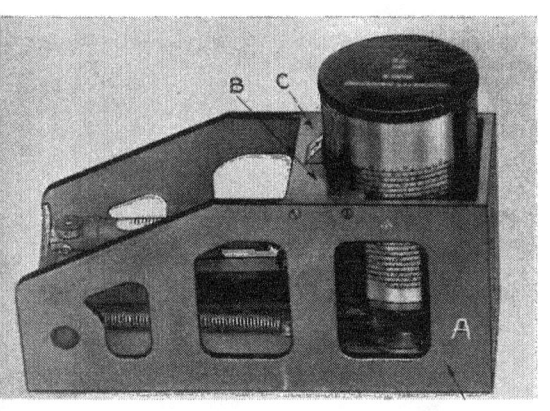

INSPECTORS, MARK II.

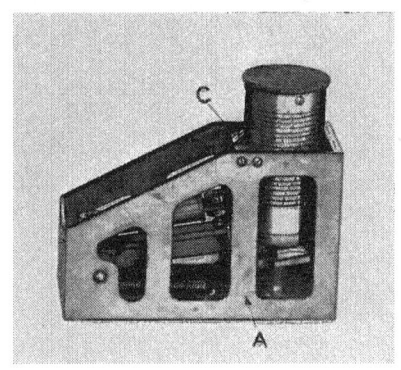

FIELD, MARK II.

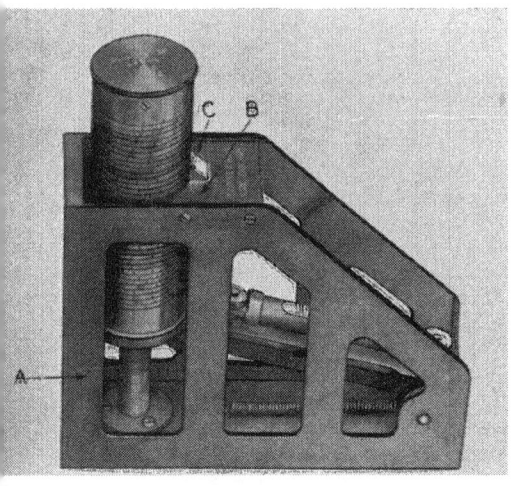

LARGE.

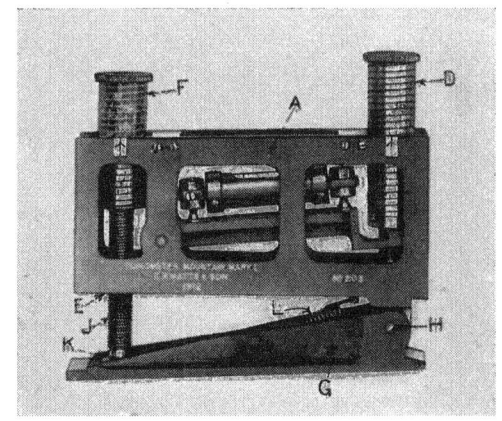

B.L. 10-P.R.

by three small screws. The graduations on the sleeve are filled with black for elevation and red for depression.

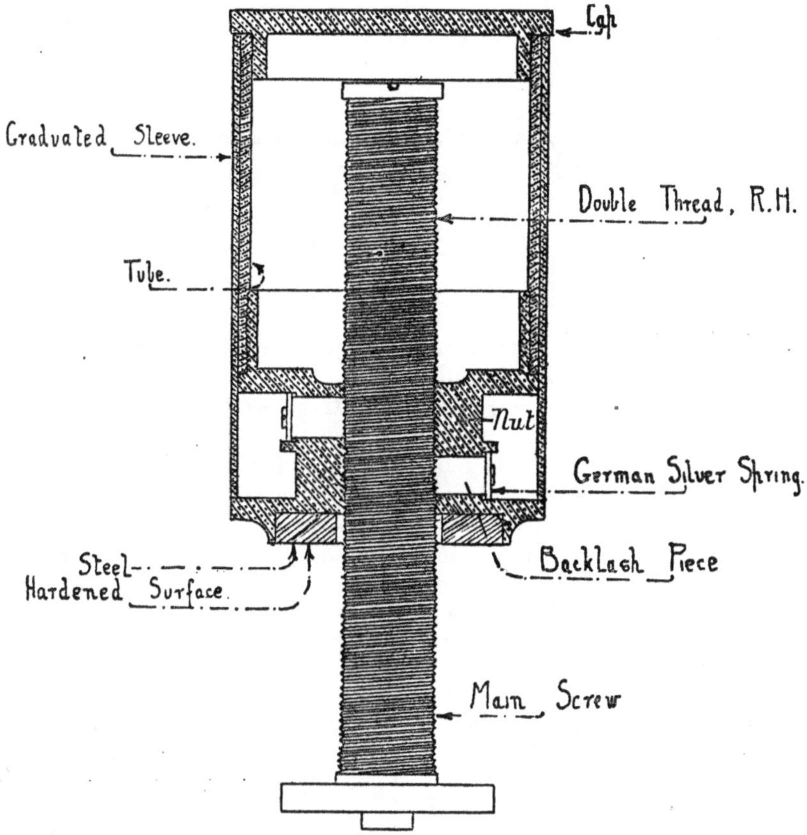

FIG. 1.
TYPICAL.

A bubble arm (Fig. 2) on which is mounted a cased spirit bubble. The case is clamped between nuts on vertical screws, which allow of the necessary zero adjustment. With Clinometers, which may be tilted to one side when being used for laying, it is important that the

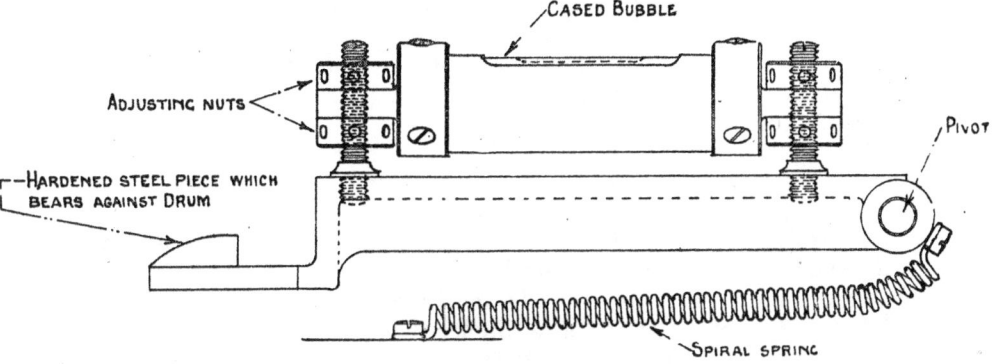

FIG. 2.

axis of the bubble should be parallel to the edge of the under surface of the body, or the clinometer will give inaccurate results. The hole at one end of the casing is therefore elongated, and adjusting screws provided for bringing it parallel. (Fig. 3.)

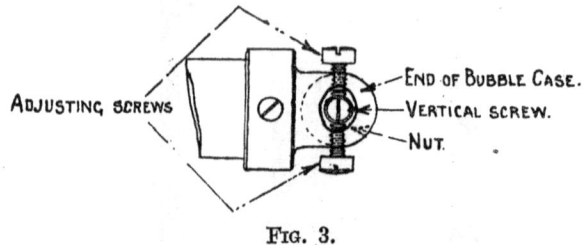

FIG. 3.

The bubble arm is pivoted at one end, and the upper surface of the other end has attached to it a piece of hard steel, which is carefully curved so as to allow of all the divisions on the drum being made practically equal to one another.

A spiral spring is attached by a screw to the bubble arm near the pivot, the other end being attached to the body in a similar manner, and prevents any backlash between the arm and the drum.

Clinometers when passed into the service, have very small errors, and those from which great accuracy is required have calibration tables issued with them. These tables show how many seconds error the clinometer has at various readings. After a time, however, the threads of the main screw and of the nut will wear, and the clinometer will not give such accurate readings. When this is the case, the clinometer should be checked with a standard one, or on a scale, and a fresh calibration table made for it.

After several years use it may be found that the backlash pieces are not doing their work correctly, fitting too tightly in their holes, due to oily dirt having accumulated there. The backlash pieces must never be removed except by an expert, and he must take the greatest care that they are replaced in the correct holes, and the right way up, or the threads will be ruined.

If the drum is ever taken off the main screw, the top of the screw and the nut should be marked so that the correct threads may be engaged when the nut is being replaced. If this is not done, the double threads, which may not be equally spaced, will be ruined and the accuracy of the clinometer upset.

The tests and adjustments for getting the bubble parallel to the base of the clinometer, and the method of use are dealt with on pages 77 and 177.

When setting a clinometer, the last turn of the drum should be clockwise (indicating a smaller angle), this ensures that there is no play between the drum and the bubble arm.

When laying with a clinometer it is important that the edge of the under surface of the body should be parallel to the side of the clinometer plane, or the laying may be incorrect. Suppose for example, that one wheel of a carriage is 10° higher than the other, and that the axis of the gun is horizontal. If the clinometer is set at zero, and placed on the clinometer plane parallel to its side, the bubble will be in the centre of its run ; but if it is placed across the clinometer plane, the bubble can only be brought to the centre of its run by setting the drum to 10°. In intermediate positions the clinometer will show elevation errors of between 0 and 10°.

As mentioned above, a similar error will result if the bubble is not mounted parallel to the edge of the under surface of the clinometer.

Clinometer, Large, Mark I.
(Plate XXX.)

The body (A) is made of gunmetal. The drum reads from $-40'$ to $+45°$. It is subdivided every 5'. To enable the clinometer to be set to read single minutes extra lines are marked to the right of the arrow on the platform (B), and these can be used as a vernier.

Thus (Fig. 4) if it is required to set the clinometer at, say 5° 1' or 5° 3' the 5° graduation would be brought opposite to the first line

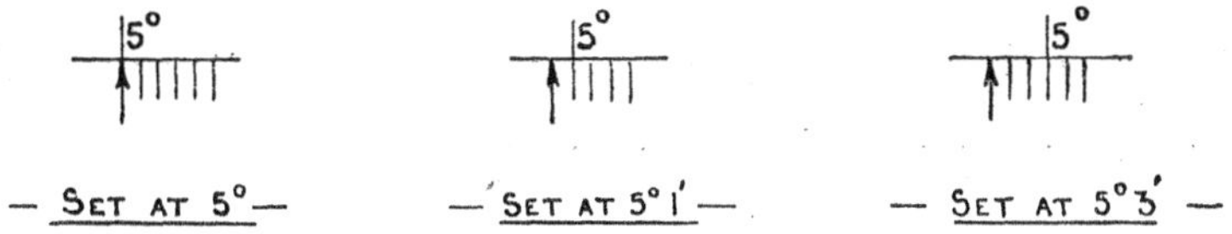

— Set at 5°—   — Set at 5° 1'—   — Set at 5° 3'—

Fig. 4.

to the right or the third line to the right of the arrow. As the 5' divisions are not exactly equal in length throughout the drum, the vernier should only be used for angles below 5°. In some cases, instead of the vernier being engraved, the 5' divisions are sub-divided and dotted every minute, these sub-divisions being read by the arrow.

There are three backlash pieces.

The bubble is a "Bubble, spirit, glass, D."

A leather case with a carrying strap and brass buckle is provided for carrying the clinometer.

The weight of the clinometer is about 6 lb. 3 oz., and of the case 2 lb. 4 oz.

Clinometer, Inspectors, Mark I.

This clinometer is very similar in appearance to the Mark II (Plate XXX).

The body is made of aluminium alloy, with a gunmetal plate riveted to the under surface. The drum cap and tube are also made of aluminium alloy, and other parts are brass, gunmetal or steel.

The bubble arm is carried on a pivot which is attached by screws to one side of the body.

The drum reads from $-30'$ to $+25°$. It is subdivided to read minutes (marked by lines) and half minutes (marked by dots). The scale is very open, due to the large diameter of the drum.

There are three backlash pieces.

The bubble is a "Bubble, spirit, glass, D." The casing is held at one end on a vertical spring and at the other end between two nuts.

A mahogany box with spring catch, two hooks and eyes, and a carrying strap is provided for carrying the clinometer.

The weight of the clinometer is about 5 lbs. 4 ozs. and of the box 2 lbs. 10 ozs.

Clinometer, Inspectors, Mark II.
(Plate XXX.)

This clinometer was introduced, as it was found that the base of the Mark I, which was made of aluminium alloy with a gunmetal plate riveted to it, was affected by changes of temperature. It also has a much longer nut, and six backlash pieces to steady the drum.

The body is a solid gunmetal casting. The pivot of the bubble arm passes through both sides.

The drum reads from $-30'$ to $+25°$. It is subdivided to read minutes (marked by lines) and half minutes (marked by dots).

The bubble is a "Bubble, spirit, glass, D," and the casing has adjusting screws for bringing it parallel to the edge of the base. Both ends of the casing are attached to the bubble arm by capstan nuts.

The same box is used for carrying either the Mark I or Mark II clinometer.

The weight of the clinometer is about 8 lbs. 12 ozs.

Clinometer, Field, Mark II.
(Plate XXX.)

The body is made of gunmetal.

The drum reads from $-30'$ to $+30°$ and is subdivided every $5'$.

There are three backlash pieces.

The bubble is a "Bubble, spirit, glass, C."

A leather case with brass buckle and a spring flap to pass over the waist belt is provided for carrying the clinometer.

The weight of the clinometer is about 3 lbs. 7 ozs. and of the case 1 lb. 5 ozs.

Clinometer, B.L. 10 P.R., Mark I.
(Plate XXX.)

This clinometer was designed for use with Mountain Artillery in India. It has two drums, one of which is set for the range in yards and the other for the angle of sight.

The body (A) is a framework on which are mounted the usual parts forming a clinometer.

The drum (D) is engraved in yards from 100 to 6,000, subdivided every 25 yards. (The graduations are for Shrapnel Shell with a charge of 16 ozs. 14 drs. Cordite, Size 5.) A zero is also marked on it for use when testing or adjusting the clinometer. The bubble is a "Bubble, spirit, glass, C" and its casing has an adjustment for getting its axis parallel to the side of the base plate (see page 73).

The front end of the body is bored and tapped at (E) to take the screw of the degree drum (F), upon which angles of sight are set. To prevent backlash the metal is cut through and the two halves are pressed against the screw by a flat German silver spring. The degree drum and its screw are rigidly fixed together.

The body is pivoted to the base plate (G) at (H) and the point of the degree scale screw (J) is kept in contact with a hardened steel disc (K) by means of a spiral spring (L). The degree drum is engraved from 0° to 10° elevation and 10° depression, each division representing 5 minutes. Elevation is indicated by black on brass and depression by white on black.

A teak box with brass carrying handle and two hooks and screws is provided for carrying the clinometer.

The weight of the clinometer is about 2 lbs. 6 ozs. and of the box 1 lb. 8 ozs. The external dimensions of the box are approximately $7\frac{1}{2}'' \times 6\frac{1}{2}'' \times 2''$.

When carrying out the zero test and adjustment the range drum must be set at "zero" and the degree scale at 0°.

Instructions for Setting, Testing, and Adjusting a Watkin Type Clinometer.

To lay a gun or howitzer at any angle up to 45°.—Unscrew the drum until the ↑ points to the elevation required, place the clinometer, thus :—

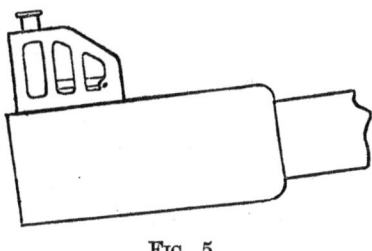

Fig. 5.

on the clinometer plane, and elevate the piece until the bubble of the spirit level is in the centre of its run.

For angles of depression.—Proceed as above, but reverse the direction of the instrument, placing it thus on the breech of the gun.

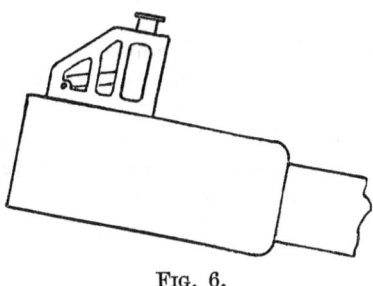

Fig. 6.

For angles of elevation greater than 45°.—Subtract the angle of elevation required from 90°, unscrew the drum to this reading; thus, for 60°, unscrew the drum to 30°, and place the instrument on the clinometer plane, thus :—

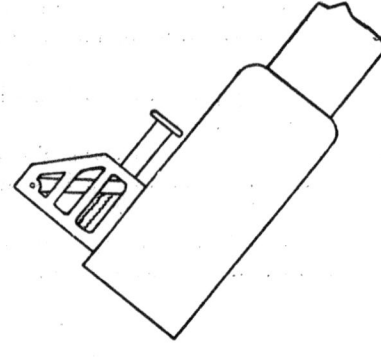

FIG. 7.

and elevate until the bubble is in the centre of its run.

(1) In order to preserve the clinometer in efficient working order, it is necessary to keep the working parts free from grit and dust as far as possible. As excess of oil is apt to cause the adhesion of grit, only sufficient is to be applied to make the screw work smoothly and to keep the steel parts from rusting.

(2) On no account should the instrument be taken to pieces, as it requires special tools to put it together again.

(3) Instruments are issued in correct adjustment, and with due care will remain correct for many years.

(4) To ascertain if the instrument is in adjustment :—

(a) Carefully clean the clinometer plane.
(b) Turn the drum to zero.
(c) Place the instrument on the clinometer plane, drum towards breech, and elevate or depress the gun till the bubble is in the centre of its run.
(d) Turn the clinometer end for end.
(e) Should the bubble not return to the centre, the instrument is out of adjustment.
(f) As the amount of error will generally be small, it is advisable to add or subtract the error, as the case may be, rather than correct the adjustment.
(g) To ascertain the error after complying with (d), drum towards muzzle, turn the drum until the bubble is again in the centre of its run; *one-half* the reading on the drum is the index error; what is practically a new zero point on the scale is thus determined.
(h) If the reading falls on the part graduated on black on the scale, *add the index error* when setting the clinometer for any required *elevation*; subtract the index error when taking a reading with the clinometer.

PLATE XXXI. [*To face page* 79.

CLINOMETER, FIELD, MARK III.

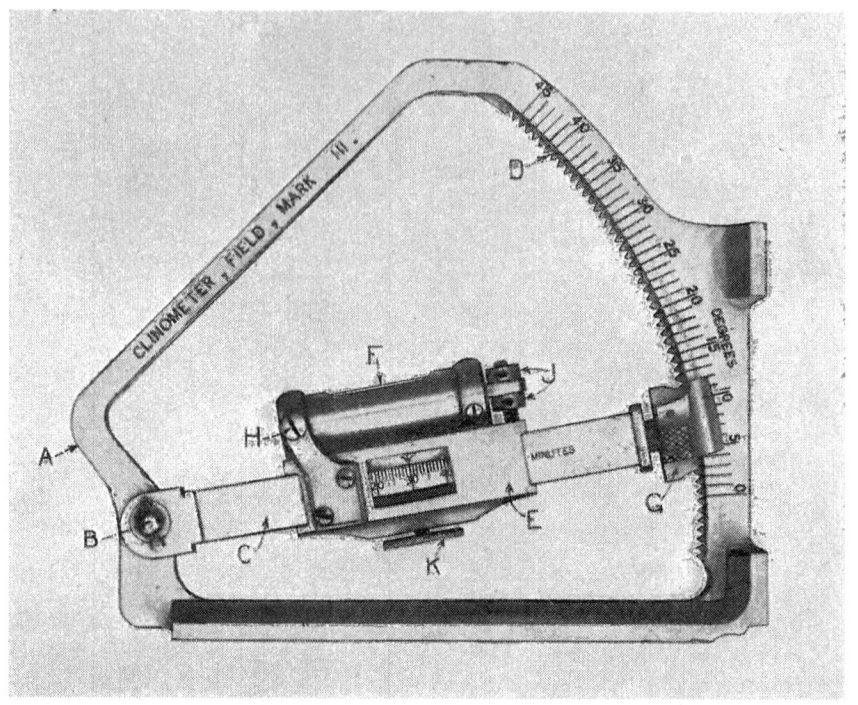

CLINOMETER, SIGHT.

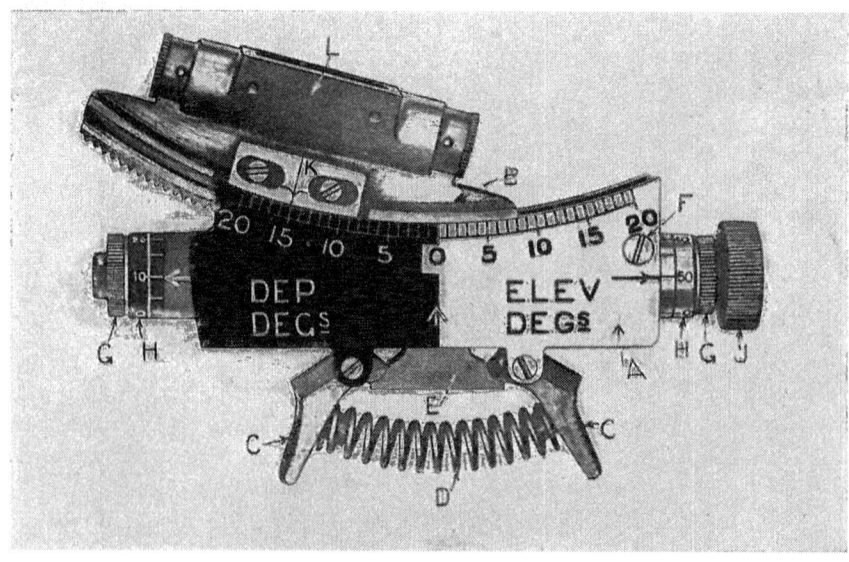

(i) If the reading falls on the portion graduated in red on the drum, *subtract the index error* for any required *elevation*; add it when taking a reading.

(5) If it is required to adjust the clinometer to have *no index* error, set the drum to the ascertained index error, and bring the bubble to the centre of its run by elevating or depressing the gun. Then, placing the drum at zero, manipulate the capstan-headed nuts (using a tempered steel wire just fitting the holes in the nuts) till the bubble is in the centre.

Reversing the instrument end for end should not alter the central position of the bubble; should it do so, proceed as before until there is no change.

In giving elevation by clinometer, great care should be taken that the clinometer plane is clean and free from paint, grit, &c., that the instrument is placed in the same position every round, that it is correctly set by the graduated scale and the elevation adjusted so that the air bubble may be in the same place each round, *always finishing off with depression*. The layer's eye should be in the same position relative to the clinometer for each round.

When *laying* with the clinometer, it is convenient to get one end of the bubble tangential to a line on the glass, being careful to always use the same line; but when ascertaining the index error, or adjusting a clinometer, the bubble must be brought to the true centre.

CLINOMETER, FIELD, MARK III.
(Plate XXXI.)

This clinometer is designed so that it can be very rapidly set. It consists of the following parts :—

A gunmetal body (A) with surfaces truly cut at right angles to one another. A hole for the pivot (B) of the arm (C) is bored through it, and teeth (D), each representing a degree, are cut on an arc on the opposite side.

In rear of the teeth graduations in single degrees from 0° to 44° are engraved on both sides. They are read by readers on the plunger (G).

A gunmetal arm (C) upon which can be slid a slider (E) having mounted upon it a cased " Bubble, spirit, glass, C " (F). The arm is curved, so that as the slider is moved to the right it is inclined at a greater angle to the base of the instrument. A complete movement of the slider will tilt the bubble through 1°. The actual angle through which it is tilted is indicated on both sides by readers on the slider in conjunction with scales on the arm. The scales are subdivided to show single minutes. A flat spring inside the slider keeps it bearing evenly on the arm. At one end of the arm is a plunger (G) having nine teeth cut on it which engage the teeth on the body. The plunger is forced outwards by a steel spiral spring.

One end of the bubble casing is pivoted to the slider on two screws (H) and the other end can be adjusted for zero by two capstan nuts (J).

The slider can be clamped in any position by a milled headed screw (K).

All parts except the steel pivot pin (B) are nickel plated.

The clinometer is carried in a leather case (No. 2) with brass buckle and short carrying strap.

The weight of the clinometer is about 1 lb. 13 ozs. and of the case 12 ozs.

To set the clinometer.—Press in the plunger (G) and move the arm (C) until the reader on the plunger (G) is opposite the required graduation on the degree scale. Release the plunger. Unclamp the screw (K) and move the slider until the arrow on it is opposite the required graduation on the minute scale. Clamp the screw (K).

The zero test and adjustment are the same as for the Watkin type clinometers (see page 78).

CLINOMETER, SIGHT, MARK I.
(Plate XXXI.)

The "Clinometer, Sight," is used in conjunction with the rocking bar sight of the 13 and 18-pr. Q.F. and 2·75 inch B.L. guns, when laying by quadrant elevation. It can be set to read the angle of sight, the range being set on the drum of the rocking bar sight.

It consists of the following parts :—

The Cradle (A) which is a manganese bronze casting. The upper surface is cut to form the arc of a circle in which the arc (B) can slide. Its under surface is shaped to fit on to a projection from the rocking bar sight, and is held to it firmly by two clips (C) which are forced outwards by a steel spiral spring (D). The clips are prevented from separating too far, and so allowing the spiral spring to become detached, by a "Stop, clip, retaining" (E).

A scale of degrees from 0° to 20° elevation and 20° depression is engraved on one face and is read by an arrow on the arc. The graduations for elevation are filled with black, and those for depression with white on a black ground.

The worm spindle (Fig. 8) is fitted in two bearings, the rear one of which is pivoted to the cradle at (F) (Plate XXXI). This allows of the worm being put out of gear with the arc by pressing the front end of the worm spindle downwards. A flat steel spring, one end of which is riveted to the cradle, and the other end of which presses the worm spindle upwards, tends to keep the worm spindle and arc in gear, and to prevent backlash between them.

Pinned on to each end of the spindle with a coned pin is a "bush, micrometer collar" which is screw-threaded externally to take a milled nut (G) (Plate XXXI) by which the micrometer collar (H) can be clamped to it. Between the nut and the micrometer collar is a washer having two feathers to prevent it turning. The micrometer

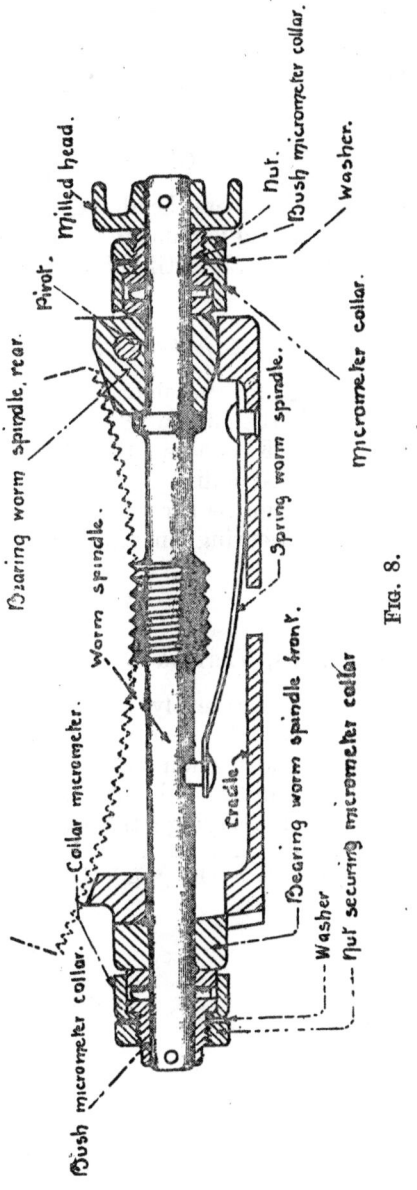

Fig. 8.

collars are divided every 5' and are coloured the same as the degree scale. One turn of the worm spindle represents 1°.

To the rear end of the worm spindle a milled head (J) is firmly attached.

The arc (B) is shaped to slide evenly in the cradle (A). On its under surface are cut teeth, into which the worm gears. Attached to it by two screws is an adjustable reader (K) for the degree scale. Its upper surface is shaped to take a " Bubble, spirit, glass, A " (L).*

The arc is prevented from becoming detached from the cradle by a stop screw passing through the rear of the cradle and coming in contact with stops at either end of the arc.

The weight of the sight clinometer is about 1 lb. 4 ozs.

To Set the Clinometer.

Press down the front micrometer head and slide the arc to one side until the correct degree reading is indicated. Release the micrometer head. Turn the milled head (J) until the correct minute reading is indicated.

To Test and Adjust the Clinometer.

This is done when aligning the sights, details of which may be found in the handbooks for the 13 and 18-pr. Q.F. guns.

The degree scale reader (K) can be adjusted by slackening the two screws passing through it, and sliding it to one side.

The micrometer collars can be turned independently of the worm spindle when the " nuts, securing micrometer collar " are loosened with a spanner.

Apparatus, Testing Clinometer.

This apparatus has been recently introduced for use at Coast Defence Stations. It is used for ascertaining the errors of a clinometer due to wear, &c. Calibration Tables, showing the errors at different readings, are made out and the necessary corrections applied when testing automatic sights, laying guns, &c.

---

* " A " bubbles will be replaced by " L " bubbles when they become unserviceable.

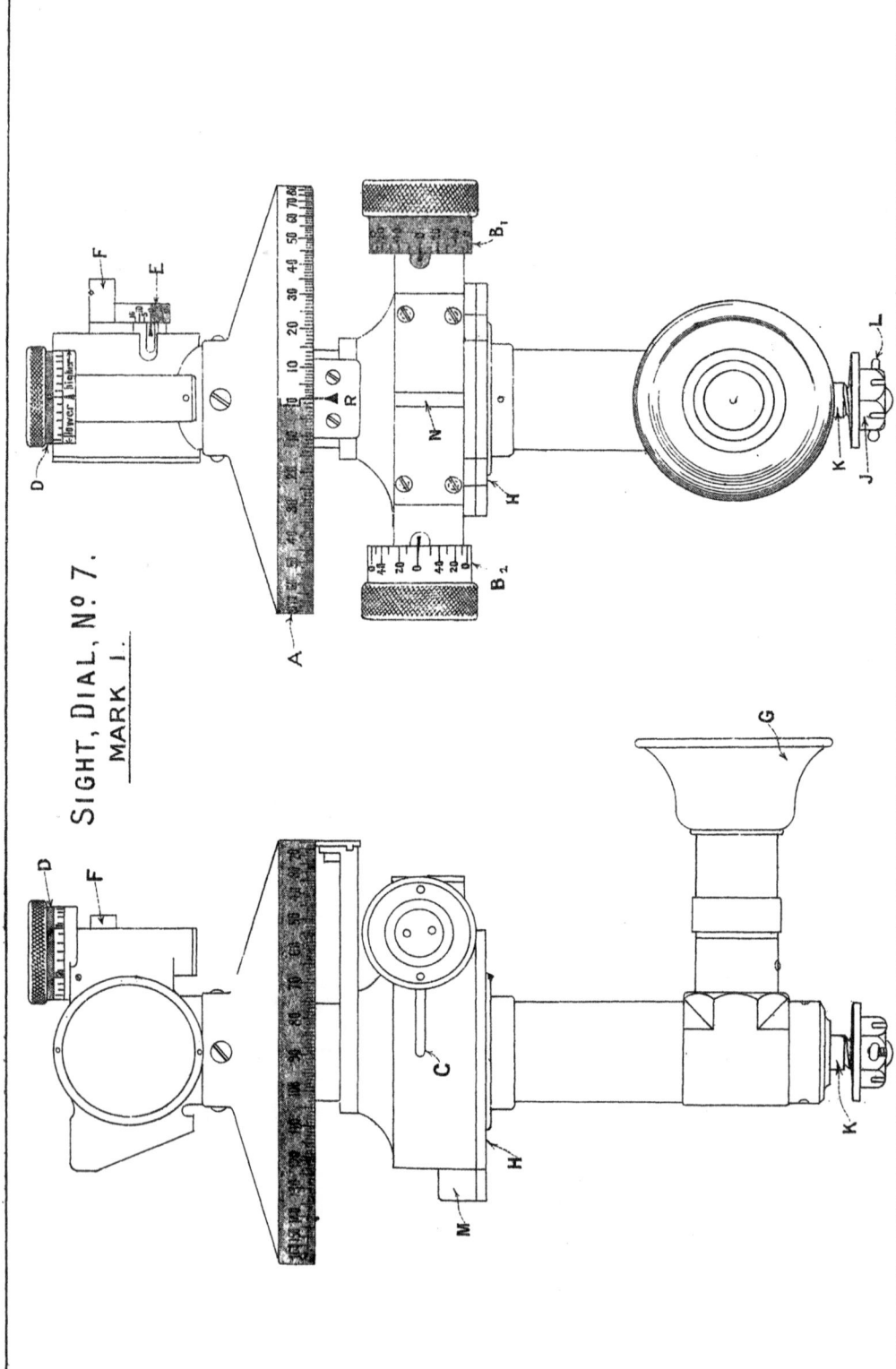

CHAPTER V.

SIGHT, DIAL, No. 7.

The principal advantages of the No. 7 dial sight over early patterns of dial sights are—

(1) The gun layer, whilst seated behind the shield can set his sight so that he can see through it in any direction. Although his head is protected by the shield, he can see over it, and also over his head. The position of his eye is always the same.

(2) Telescopic power is made use of.

(3) It can be used for either direct or indirect laying.

GENERAL ARRANGEMENTS.
(Plate XXXII.)

The telescopic arrangements are of an erecting type and give a magnification of four diameters and a field of view of 10°. Being of rather an intricate design the optical principles involved are fully described on pages 84 to 92. Two cross lines (Fig. 1) with gaps in their centres are engraved on a glass diaphragm which

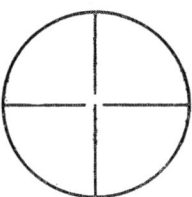

FIG. 1.

is fixed in front of the eyepiece. The point where they would intersect, if continuous, is laid on the target or aiming point. In sights of early manufacture the centre of the gap is used for laying on the target, &c., but in those of later manufacture, the lower half of the vertical line has been lengthened until it is in line with the horizontal line. The top of the lower half of the vertical line is therefore used for laying on the target or aiming point.

The top portion of the sight can be revolved horizontally through a complete circle, so that an object in any direction can be seen through it. The angle between this line of sight and the axis of the gun is indicated on a degree scale (A, Plate XXXII) and minute drums (B_1 B_2). The degree scale is marked from 0° to 180° "Right," on one side and from 0° to 180° "Left" on the other. "Right" graduations are white on a black background, and "Left" black on brass. The minute drums are similarly marked and used with the corresponding degree scales. The reader of the degree scale (R) can be adjusted by slackening the two screws and sliding it to one side.

Each complete revolution of the minute drums moves the top portion of the sight through 5°.

If it is required to set the sight rapidly, the upper portion of the sight can be thrown out of gear with the lower portion by pressing up the spring lever (C), the top portion can then be revolved until it is set approximately to the required reading. The lever (C) is then released and the sight is accurately set by turning the minute drum until the exact angle required is indicated.

To ensure the top and lower portions being correctly in gear, the minute drum should be revolved through half a circle after releasing the lever (C) before setting the angle ordered.

In case the point to be laid on is not in the same horizontal plane as the sight, an arrangement is provided by means of which the line of sight through the top prism may be elevated or depressed. This is effected by turning a minute drum (D), which is subdivided every 10 minutes, the degrees of elevation or depression being indicated on the scale (E). Graduations for elevation are black on brass, and for depression white on black. When the sight is used for direct laying the scale and drum must be set at zero.

An open sight (F) is provided for rough laying.

A detachable dermatine eyeguard (G) is provided, its object being to keep extraneous light out of the layer's eye, and to prevent him receiving any shock when the gun is fired.

A coned seating (H) rests on the carrier, and the sight is held down to it by means of the nut (J). When used with Carriers Nos. 1 and 3, a catch from the carrier engages with this nut; and when with Carrier No. 2 the stem (K) is passed through the carrier, a small disc spring placed round it so as to rest in the recess under the carrier, and the nut screwed home. The top surface of the nut is coned. The nut should be screwed up until there is no shake between the sight and the carrier, and the split pin (L) is then inserted. With the No. 2 carrier care should be taken to see that the sight is not nutted down so tightly as to prevent deflection being put on without undue force.

The sight is prevented from revolving in the Nos. 1 and 3 carriers by means of the projection (M). It is forced to revolve in the No. 2 carrier, when deflection is being put on, by means of the projection (N) and four screws which engage in the deflection scale of the carrier.

The carriers are so designed that, in the case of the Nos. 1 and 3, their cones and the coned seating of the sights are in contact: but in the case of the No. 2 they just do not touch, the rubbing surface being the flat portion at the top of the cone.

Considerations of Optical Arrangements.

The first principle of the optical arrangements is that a right angle prism (A B C, Fig. 2) is mounted at the top of a tube in such a way that it can be rotated in a horizontal plane, and that rays of light from an object (shown by a dotted line) will be reflected by it down the tube into a fixed prism (X Y Z) and by the latter to the layer's eye.

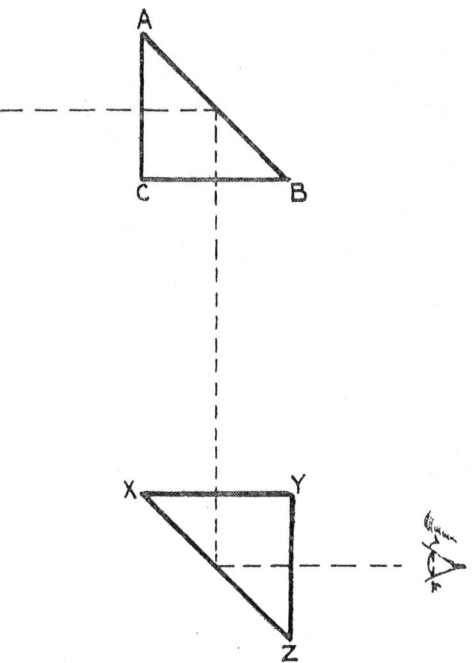

Fig. 2.

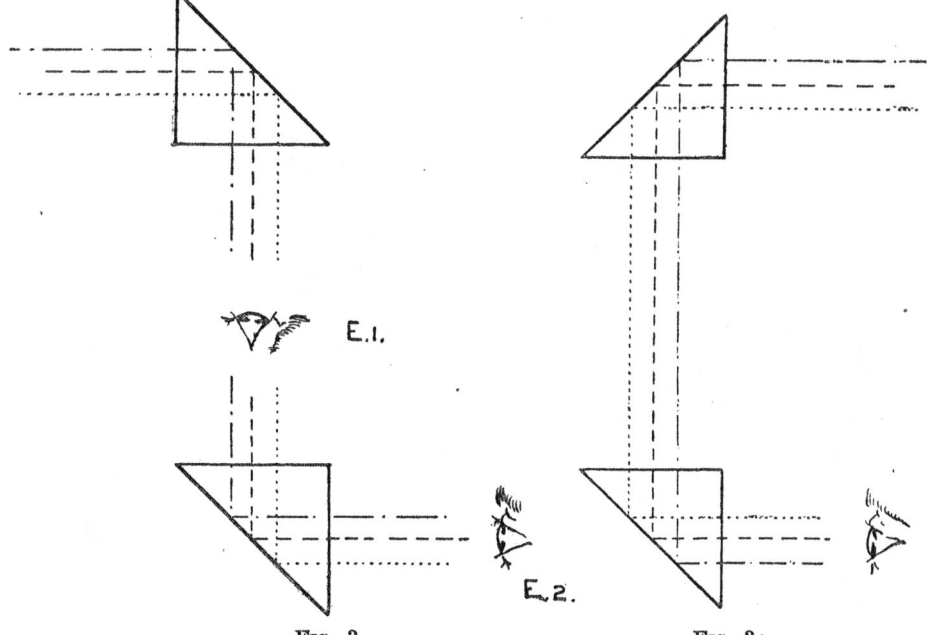

Fig. 3.   Fig. 3a.

The prisms act in the same way as mirrors, and the surfaces (A B, X Z) may be considered as mirrors. Now, as is well known, any object seen in a mirror will appear to be reversed in one direction. Writing held in front of a mirror for example, will be seen written backwards, but not upside down, or if the mirror is placed before the writing in a plane at right angles to it the writing will be seen upside down but correct as regards right and left (see Fig. 10).

The result of this fact is that, if two ordinary right-angled prisms were used, when they were in the positions shown in Fig. 3, the image of an object would appear to be correct both as regards "up and down" and "right and left."

The first prism has the effect of making the object appear upside down when the eye is applied beneath it at (E 1), the second has a similar effect on this upside down image and makes it appear correct both as regards "up and down" and "right and left" when the eye is applied at (E 2). Dotted lines show the paths of rays from an object.

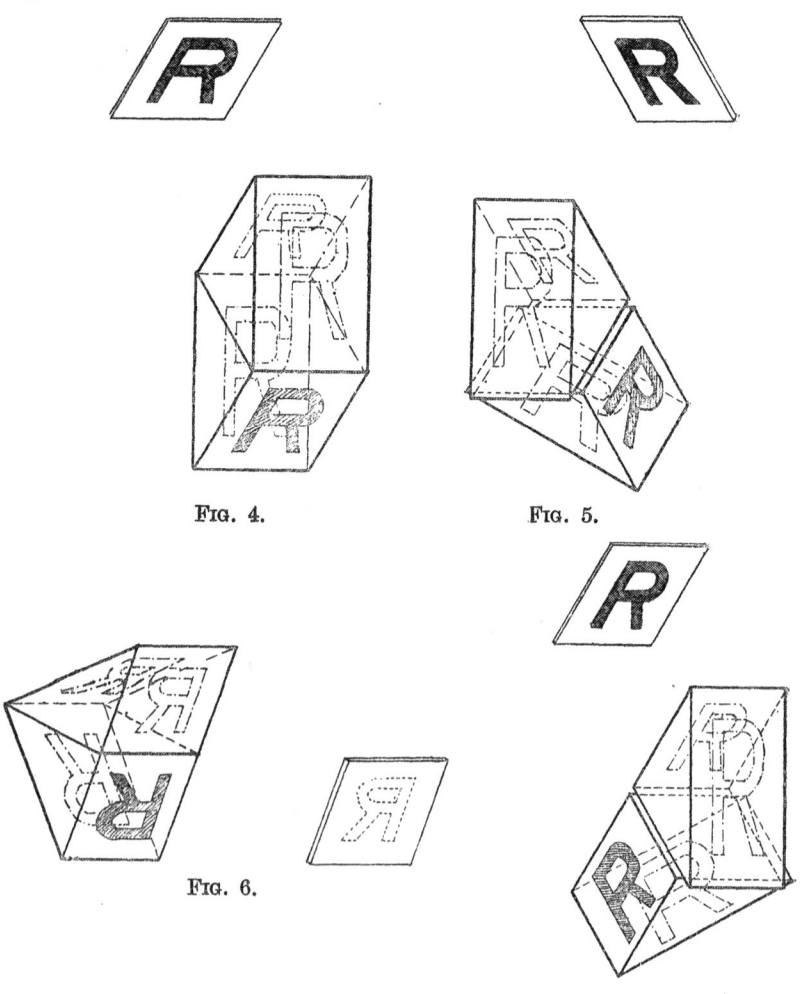

FIG. 4.   FIG. 5.

FIG. 6.

FIG. 7.

On the other hand if the prisms are placed in the positions shown in Fig. 3A the object will be seen upside down, and reversed as regards "right and left."

To make this more clear, and to show the effect of the top prism being revolved in a horizontal plane through angles of 90°, the prisms are shown in Figs. 4, 5, 6, 7 in contact with one another. The places where rays of light projected from the letter (R) placed in front of the top prism pass through the surfaces of the prisms or are reflected by them are shown in thin lines.

From these figures it will be noted that, when the prisms are placed as in Fig. 4 the object is seen correct as regards both "up and down" and "right and left," and that as the top prism is revolved clockwise in a horizontal plane, the image of the object seen in the lower prism appears to revolve clockwise through a corresponding angle, but in a vertical plane (Figs. 5, 6, 7).

In the actual sight an arrangement is introduced which insures the layer always seeing the object correct both as regards "up and down" and "right and left." This consists of a prism (Fig. 8), which is made to revolve on a vertical axis at half the speed of the top prism.

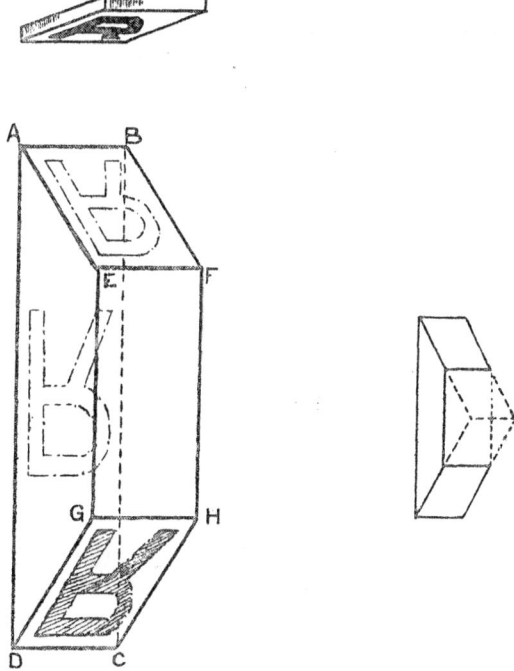

Fig. 8.

This prism is an ordinary right angle one, with the right angle portion cut off, as it is not required. The portion (A B C D) is the flat reflecting surface. (A B F E, C D G H) are flat surfaces inclined at 45° to (A B C D). If the letter R is printed on a piece of paper and held face downwards at right angles to the axis of the prism, the rays of light from it travelling vertically downwards will meet the surface (A B F E) (as shown in thin lines), be refracted by the glass on to (A B C D), and reflected by it through the surface (C D G H). Meeting the air here they will pass vertically downwards.

The reflecting surfaces will have caused the R to appear upside down when the eye is placed vertically below the prism.

The effect of holding the prism vertically below the letter R and revolving the former is that the R appears to revolve twice as quickly as the prism is turned. If the prism is revolved through 45° the R will appear to have turned through 90° and so on, as shown in Fig. 9.

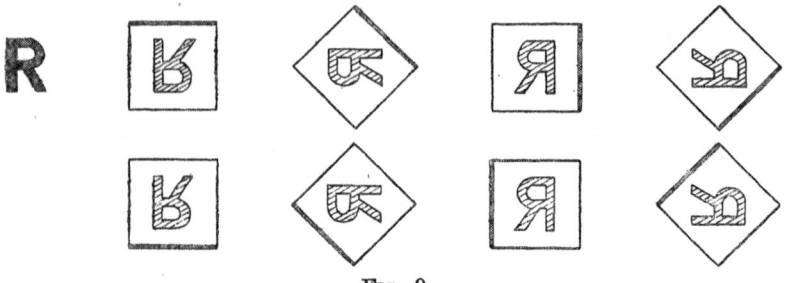

FIG. 9.

(The thick line represents the reflecting surface of the prism.) This is due to the well known fact that if a mirror is revolved through a certain angle the reflection of a fixed object appears to move through double that angle. This is shown in Fig. 10.

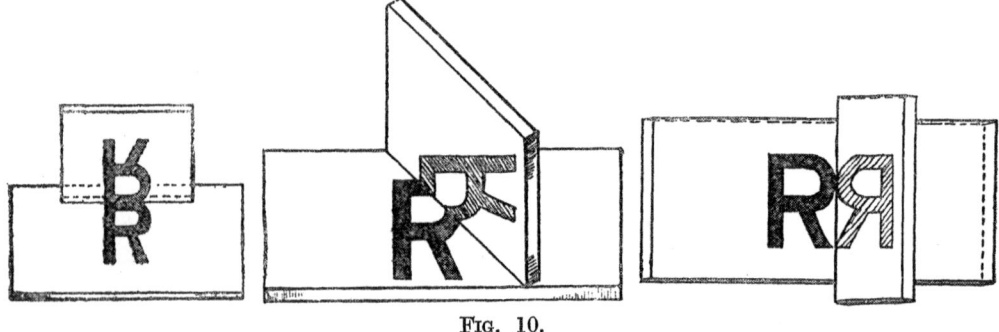

FIG. 10.

It will be noted in Fig. 9 that the R appears in the same position, when the reflecting surface is in a certain position, as it does when the prism has been moved through another 180°.

It is immaterial in what part of the sight this erecting prism is placed, but in the actual sight it is mounted between the upper and lower prisms.

We have up to the present, considered two sets of prisms, viz. :—

(1) The upper and lower right angle prisms, which when the upper one is revolved horizontally causes the object to appear to revolve at the same speed, but in a vertical plane.

(2) The erecting prism, which, when it is revolved, causes the object to appear to revolve at twice that speed.

If, therefore, we arrange the prisms so that when the upper prism is revolved at a certain rate the erecting prism is revolved at half that rate, the object will not appear to move as regards "up and down" or "right and left."

Fig. 11.

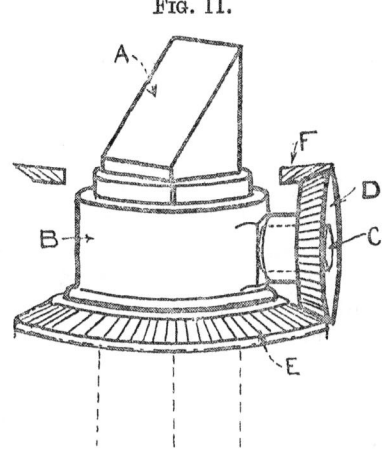

A.—Erecting Prism
B.—Prism Mount
C.—Axis of Pinion
D.—Pinion
} These all revolve together in a horizontal plane.

E.—Lower Bevel Wheel, which is connected to body and does not move.
F.—Upper Bevel Wheel, which revolves with the upper prism.

This is arranged in the sight as follows :—

The erecting prism (A, Fig. 11) is fixed in a mount (B), from which projects the pivot (C) of a pinion (D). This pinion engages with the bevel wheels (E, F), the first of which is fixed to the body of the sight and the other one to the "bracket worm wheel" to which is fixed the upper prism. The upper prism and the upper bevel wheel always revolve together.

The erecting prism (A) and its mount (B) with the axis (C) of the prism (D) will, however, only revolve at half this rate.

The relative movements of the parts are similar to those of a gun carriage being moved along the ground by means of a drag rope running off the top of the wheel tyre (Fig. 12). As is well known

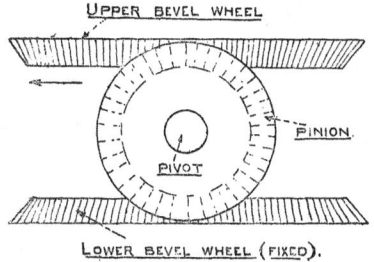 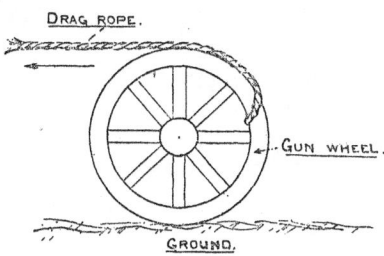

Fig. 12.

the carriage will advance only half the distance through which the rope is pulled. The rope will represent the upper bevel wheel, the wheel will represent the small bevel pinion, and the ground will represent the lower bevel wheel.

Up to the present we have seen that the prisms can be arranged as under:—

(a) Upper and lower prisms combined to make the object appear correct, or reversed as regards *both* "up and down" and "right and left."

(b) Erecting prism to make the object appear reversed as regards *either* "up and down," or "right and left."

To magnify the object it is necessary to insert an object glass, which will reverse the image as regards *both* "up and down" and "right and left." It is therefore necessary to arrange the three prisms so that the image will be reversed as regards *both* "up and down" and "right and left," and this reversed image can then be corrected by the object glass.

It is impossible to effect this with the three prisms described above, which have only three reflecting surfaces, and it is necessary to introduce one more reflecting surface which will reverse the image as regards either "up and down" or "right and left." This is effected by making the lower prism with two reflecting surfaces inclined at 90° to one another, instead of only one reflecting surface (Fig. 2). Such a prism is known as a roof prism.

Such a roof prism is shown in Fig. 13. (A B C) is a horizontal and (B C D) a vertical surface. The reflecting surfaces (A B D,

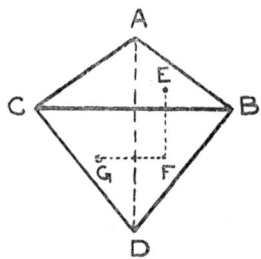

FRONT VIEW.

FIG. 13

A C D) are at right angles to one another and at 45° to the surfaces (A B C, B C D).

A ray of light passing vertically downwards would enter the upper surface of the prism at (E), be reflected at (F) horizontally by the surfaces (A B D) to (G) on the surface (A C D), and by that surface horizontally through the rear face (B C D).

Similarly a ray of light entering the left half of the upper surface (A C B) would be reflected by the left reflecting surface (A C D) to the right reflecting surface (A B D) and horizontally through the rear face (B C D).

The actual prism in the sight is of rather more complicated shape, other surfaces being formed on it by which it is held in position. Roof prisms have to be exceedingly accurately made or a double image would result.

The actual arrangement of prisms and lenses is shown in Fig. 14.

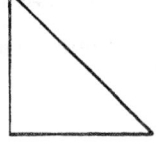

Upper Prism inverts "up and down."

Erecting or Centre Prism inverts "up and down," and counteracts effect of Upper Prism.

Object Glass inverts "up and down" and "right and left."

Lower Prism inverts both "up and down" and "right and left," and counteracts effect of Object Glass.

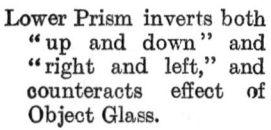

Diaphragm with cross lines.

Eyepiece lenses do not invert in any way.

FIG. 14.

The telescopic arrangements give a magnification of four diameters and a field of view of 10°. The eyepiece is fixed, and cannot be focussed, but, owing to the low power, both the view and cross lines will be in correct focus for all except those with very abnormal eyesight. The advantage of having the eyepiece fixed is that it can be made watertight like the remainder of the sight.

Details of the Mark I Sight.

To enable the sight to be laid on an aimimg point above or below the normal, the upper prism (A, Fig. 15) can be elevated or depressed by means of a milled head (B).

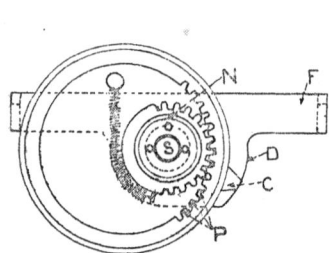

Arrangement by which the crosshead with open sights is made to move twice as quickly as the Upper Prism.

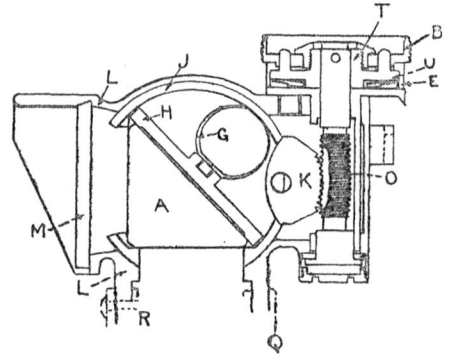

Sectional Elevation through centre.

Fig. 15.

Each turn of the milled head elevates or depresses the line of sight through 5°. The degrees are indicated by a reader (C) on the "Case upper prism holder" in conjunction with a degree scale, marked every 5°, engraved on the cross head (D); and the odd degrees and minutes by a reader on the "Case," and a "drum, graduated, micrometer head" (E), which is subdivided every 10'. Elevation is indicated by black on brass and depression by white on black.

The open sights on the cross head (F), used for picking up the target or aiming point, are arranged to move at twice the speed of the upper prism with its reflecting surface.

The upper prism (A), the reflecting surface of which is silvered, rests in the upper prism mount (J) upon a brass packing piece, being pressed on to it by means of a spring (G) acting on a plate (H). Side movement is prevented by means of a cap which screws into the side of the prism holder.

The holder, upper prism (J), has a recess cut in it, into which the "toothed segment (K)" is accurately fitted and kept in position by means of a pin. One side of the prism holder is recessed and has annular teeth (P) cut on it. Its outer surface fits accurately into the case upper prism holder (L), which forms a bearing for it.

The case, upper prism holder (L), screws on to the top of the worm wheel (Q), and is prevented from turning independently of it by means of screws (R). A glass window (M) prevents rain entering the sight, and the left side is closed with a cap. A hole is bored through the right side, through which passes the pivot (S) of the cross head. On this pivot is mounted and pinned the "pinion, cross head" (N), the teeth of which engage with the annular teeth on the prism holder.

SIGHT, DIAL, No. 7.

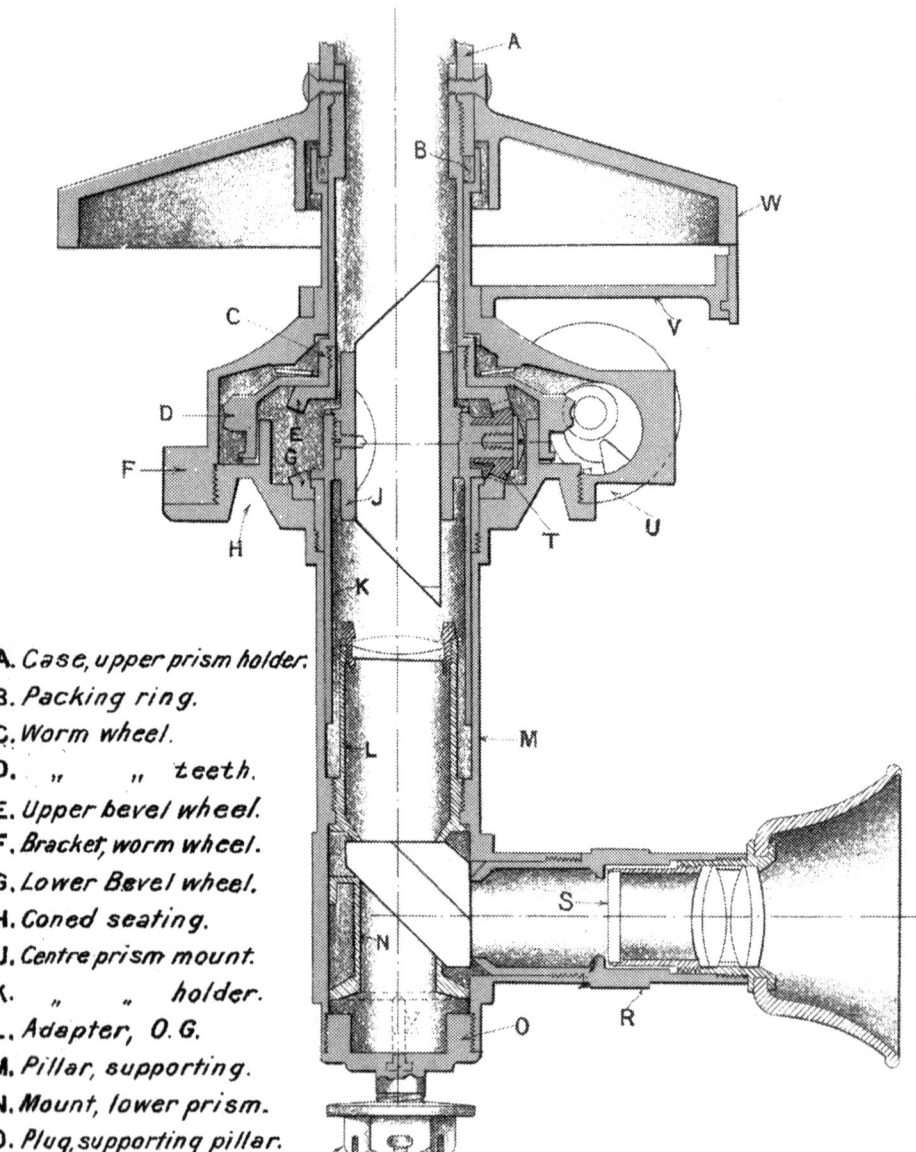

A. Case, upper prism holder.
B. Packing ring.
C. Worm wheel.
D. "   "   teeth.
E. Upper bevel wheel.
F. Bracket, worm wheel.
G. Lower Bevel wheel.
H. Coned seating.
J. Centre prism mount.
K. "   "   holder.
L. Adapter, O.G.
M. Pillar, supporting.
N. Mount, lower prism.
O. Plug, supporting pillar.
P. Nut, plug, S.P.
R. Case, eyepiece.
S. Diaphragm, with cross lines.
T. Bevel pinion.
U. Ring, milled, micrometer head.
V. Bracket, reader dial plate.
W. Degree scale plate.

As the teeth of the latter are struck to twice the radius of those of the former, any movement of the cross head will be twice that of the prism. The cross head has open sights cut on it.

The prism holder is elevated by means of a worm (O) in the "case" which gears with the toothed segment (K). Fixed to the top of the worm are a milled head (B) clamping cap (T), clamping collar (U) and graduated micrometer drum (E) which can be adjusted. They are similar to those on the traversing arrangements described later on.

Plate **XXXIII** shows a section of the sight, but the upper prism holder case, &c., are omitted, as they are shown in Fig. 15.

The parts which are fixed are shown in red, those which move with the upper prism holder in blue, and those which move with the centre prism in green.

The degree scale plate (W) is made of gunmetal, and is fixed to the top of the worm wheel and upper prism holder case by means of four screws. It is graduated every degree from 0°–180° " Right " and " Left." The former graduations are white on black and the latter black on brass.

The worm wheel (C) is of steel. Its upper portion is threaded to take the upper prism holder case. Teeth (D) are cut round its largest circumference, each tooth representing 5°. It is fitted internally with a bevel wheel (E) which actuates the gear, which revolves the centre prism.

The centre prism holder (K) is of steel. Its upper portion is threaded to take the centre prism mount (J). Pivoted on a projection is the bevel pinion (T), which gears simultaneously with the bevel wheels in the worm wheel and in the pillar supporting.

The centre prism mount (J) is of brass and is threaded to screw into the top of the centre prism holder. The centre prism is firmly held in it, and is so adjusted that if the mount and prism are revolved through 180° the cross wires in front of the eyepiece will remain laid on the same point as before.

The pillar supporting (M) is of steel. It is accurately bored to form a bearing for the centre prism holder, and the lower bevel wheel (G) is firmly attached to it. Near the top it is threaded to screw into the worm wheel bracket. Beneath this is formed the cone seating (H) which fits over the cone on the top of the carrier. Its lower end is threaded to receive the " plug, supporting pillar " (O) and above this is formed a seating for the " mount, lower prism, in two halves " (N). About half way up it is threaded to receive the " Adapter object glass " (L).

A projection near the lower end is threaded to receive the " case, eyepiece " (R).

A small plate is fitted near the coned seating which *during manufacture* can be removed and a tommy inserted to revolve the lower bevel wheel until vertical objects are seen through the sight to be perfectly vertical. Four screws are then inserted to fix the bevel wheel permanently. This adjustment must never be made after the sights are issued to the Service.

Adjustments for verticality can only be made by engaging the correct teeth of the bevel pinion with those of the two bevel wheels.

The plug, supporting pillar (O) is threaded to take a castellated nut (P), which can be prevented from turning by means of a split pin. This nut is adjusted so that the catches of the Nos. 1 and 3 carriers pressing on its upper surface, which is slightly coned, prevent the sight from lifting. In the case of the No. 2 carrier, the small disc spring of the carrier presses against the upper surface of the nut.

The mount, lower prism holder (N), is shaped to support the lower prism, which is prevented from rising by coming in contact with the " Adapter, object glass " (L), and from moving to one side by coming in contact with the front of the " Case, eyepiece " (R).

The adjustment of the lower prism is somewhat difficult, and depends upon the adjustment of the two sets of screws (X) one of which is shown in dotted lines. Each set consists of an upper screw which presses the prism holder and the prism upwards until they are firmly secured, but not strained, and a lower screw which prevents grit from entering the screw hole.* If the upper screws are not properly adjusted, the prism will either be loose or strained, and consequently give bad definition, or it may easily be fractured.

The adapter, object glass (L), holds the object glass and its cell and is screwed well home in the pillar supporting. The object glass is burnished in its cell.

The case, eyepiece (R), screws into the " pillar, supporting " and one end is threaded to take the eyepiece. A glass window on one side is provided to allow light from a lamp to reach the diaphragm (S) in the eyepiece cell, if the sight is used at night.

The eyepiece cell contains two achromatic lenses, separated by a distance tube, and a glass diaphragm, with cross lines engraved on it, in an extension. The rear end is recessed to take the dermatine eyeguard.

The bracket, worm wheel (F) (see also Fig. 16), is of steel and is threaded to screw on to the top of the " pillar, supporting." Its upper portion forms a bearing for the top of the worm wheel.

Two projections are formed on it, the front one (B) fits in a recess in the Nos. 1 and 3 carriers and prevents the sight turning ; the rear one (C) fits into a groove in the deflection scale of the No. 2 carrier and with the assistance of four screws ensures the sight revolving when deflection is being put on.

One side of the bracket is bored through to take the traversing gear (Fig. 16) the principal parts of which are :—

The " bearing, worm spindle " (D), which is bored eccentrically to take the " Spindle, worm " (W). One end of it is threaded to take the " collar, actuating." When the lever (D 1) on the latter is pressed upwards, the bearing revolves and owing to the worm spindle being mounted eccentrically in it, it is withdrawn from the worm wheel (W W). A spiral spring (E), the ends of which fit into the worm wheel bracket

---

* In sights of recent manufacture the lower screw is made longer and is screwed home until it comes in contact with the upper screw, thus locking it in position.

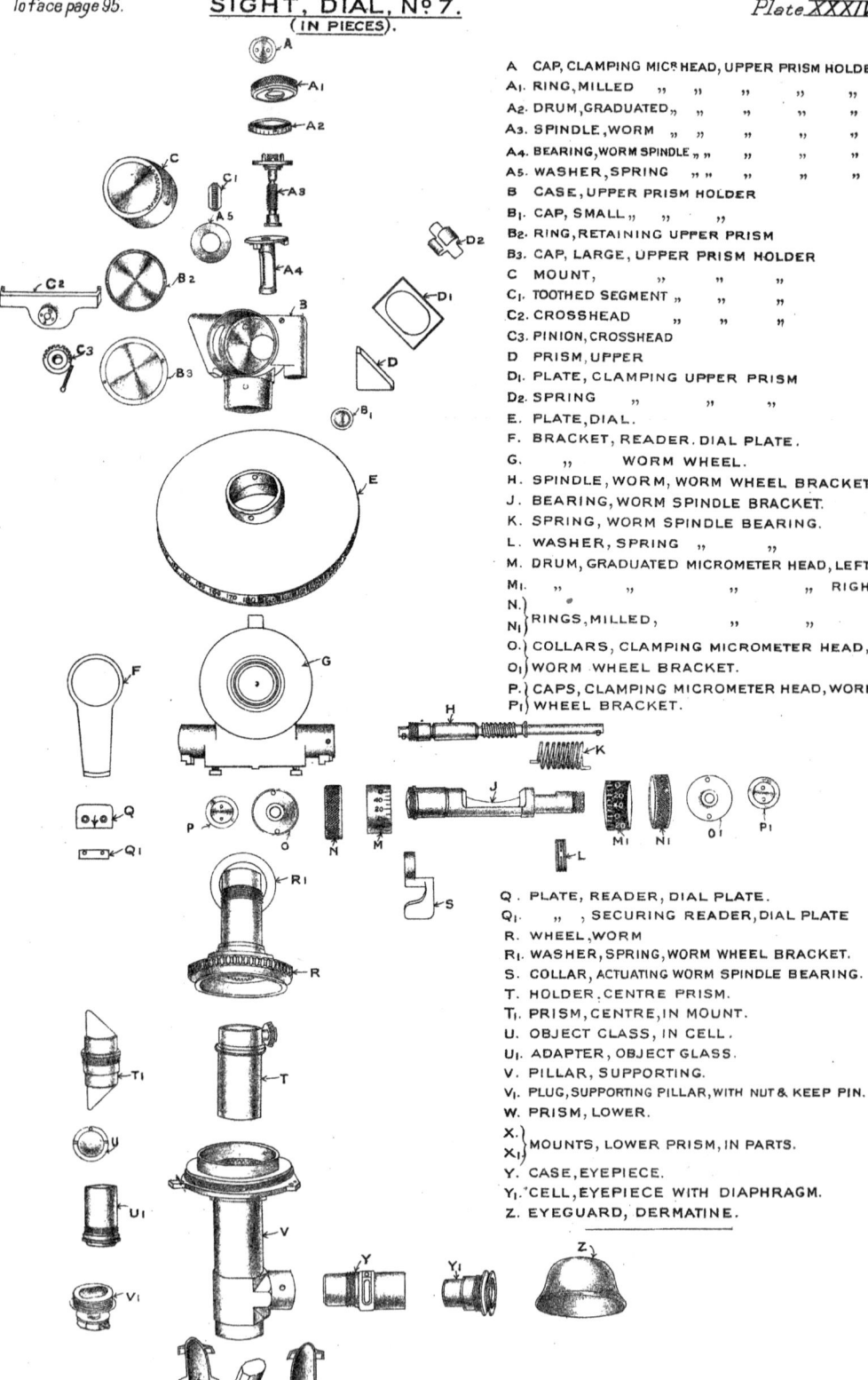

To face page 95.   **SIGHT, DIAL, No. 7.**   Plate XXXIV.
(IN PIECES).

A. CAP, CLAMPING MICR HEAD, UPPER PRISM HOLDER.
A1. RING, MILLED   ,,   ,,   ,,   ,,   ,,
A2. DRUM, GRADUATED ,, ,,   ,,   ,,   ,,
A3. SPINDLE, WORM   ,,   ,,   ,,   ,,   ,,
A4. BEARING, WORM SPINDLE ,,   ,,   ,,   ,,
A5. WASHER, SPRING   ,,   ,,   ,,   ,,   ,,
B. CASE, UPPER PRISM HOLDER
B1. CAP, SMALL ,,   ,,   ,,
B2. RING, RETAINING UPPER PRISM
B3. CAP, LARGE, UPPER PRISM HOLDER
C. MOUNT,   ,,   ,,   ,,
C1. TOOTHED SEGMENT ,, ,,   ,,
C2. CROSSHEAD   ,,   ,,   ,,
C3. PINION, CROSSHEAD
D. PRISM, UPPER
D1. PLATE, CLAMPING UPPER PRISM
D2. SPRING   ,,   ,,   ,,
E. PLATE, DIAL.
F. BRACKET, READER. DIAL PLATE.
G. ,,   WORM WHEEL.
H. SPINDLE, WORM, WORM WHEEL BRACKET
J. BEARING, WORM SPINDLE BRACKET.
K. SPRING, WORM SPINDLE BEARING.
L. WASHER, SPRING ,,   ,,
M. DRUM, GRADUATED MICROMETER HEAD, LEFT.
M1.   ,,   ,,   ,,   ,,   RIGHT.
N. }
N1.} RINGS, MILLED,   ,,   ,,
O.) COLLARS, CLAMPING MICROMETER HEAD,
O1.) WORM WHEEL BRACKET.
P.) CAPS, CLAMPING MICROMETER HEAD, WORM.
P1.) WHEEL BRACKET.
Q. PLATE, READER, DIAL PLATE.
Q1.   ,,   , SECURING READER, DIAL PLATE
R. WHEEL, WORM
R1. WASHER, SPRING, WORM WHEEL BRACKET.
S. COLLAR, ACTUATING WORM SPINDLE BEARING.
T. HOLDER, CENTRE PRISM.
T1. PRISM, CENTRE, IN MOUNT.
U. OBJECT GLASS, IN CELL.
U1. ADAPTER, OBJECT GLASS.
V. PILLAR, SUPPORTING.
V1. PLUG, SUPPORTING PILLAR, WITH NUT & KEEP PIN.
W. PRISM, LOWER.
X. }
X1.} MOUNTS, LOWER PRISM, IN PARTS.
Y. CASE, EYEPIECE.
Y1. CELL, EYEPIECE WITH DIAPHRAGM.
Z. EYEGUARD, DERMATINE.

and the bearing, causes the worm to re-engage with the worm wheel when the lever is released.

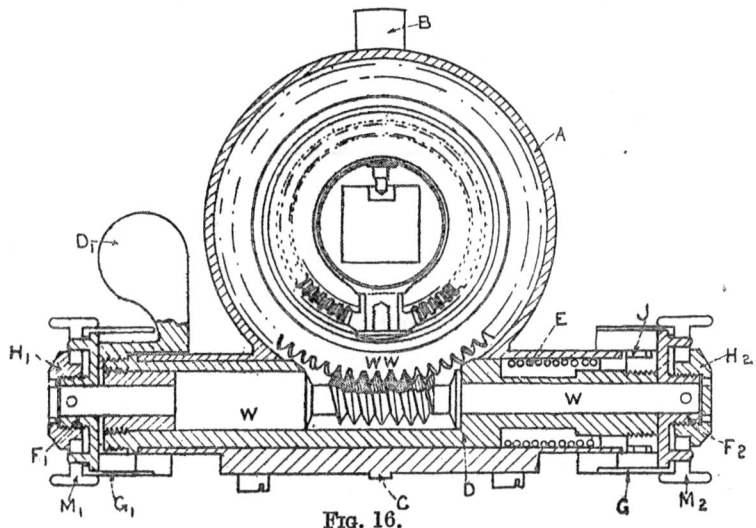

Fig. 16.

Pinned to each end of the wormspindle is a "collar, clamping" (F_1 F_2), two pins on which fit into two holes in the milled ring (M_1 M_2). The micrometer drums (G G_1) are clamped between the collars and rings by means of the "caps, clamping" (H_1 H_2). This arrangement allows of the micrometer drums being moved independently of the milled rings when the sights are being aligned.

A spring washer (J) prevents any side play between the "bearing, worm spindle" and the "bracket, worm wheel."

A stop prevents the lever on the actuating collar being lifted far enough to foul the dial plate.

A packing ring (B, Plate XXXIII) is placed between the top of the worm wheel bracket and the worm wheel to prevent moisture entering the sight.

Several washers, screws, stops, &c., have not been mentioned in the above description.

Special tools are required for taking of the sight apart.
Plate XXXIV shows the dial sight taken apart.
The weight of the sight is about 5 lbs. 11 ozs.

Mark II.

The Mark II sight differs from the Mark I described above in the following particulars :—
1. The vertical scale graduations on the upper prism holder crosshead, and the micrometer head, excepting the zero and index marks, are omitted.
2. Certain internal parts are made rust proof.
3. The milled rings of the traversing gear are longer.

CASE No. 7 DIAL SIGHT. No. 1.

A stout leather case is provided for carrying the No. 7 dial sight, when it is not permanently attached to a carrier. The case can be strapped in a vertical position to the shield of the 4·5-inch Q.F. howitzer or in the B.L. 60-pr. carriage limber, two brass sockets at the sides taking most of the weight.

The case is fitted internally with blocks of cork covered with leather, shaped to the sight.

The lid of the case folds downwards, two straps prevent it lowering too far.

When inserting or removing the sight, it must on no account be lifted by the dial plate.

The weight of the case is about 5 lbs. 10 ozs.

The case can be used for either the Mark I or Mark II sight; but if the sight has the long pattern milled heads on the traversing gear, the corresponding packing piece in the case must be removed.

INSTRUCTIONS FOR USE OF No. 7 DIAL SIGHT AND No. 2 CARRIER.

The sight should be placed in the socket at any convenient height to suit the position of the aiming point, and as soon as the gun is laid, the sight is run down and an auxiliary aiming point picked up if the original aiming point cannot be used.

All scales should be set at zero to commence with.

On receipt of the order to lay .. .. degrees off an aiming point or the director, the quick release thumb-piece should be raised, the dial plate (A, Fig. 17) turned in the required direction by moving the cowl (B) with the right hand, until the reading is within about 4° of the correct setting. Then, if whole degrees only are involved, set the dial plate (A) to the exact reading by means of the drum (D) or (E). Should the required reading, however, involve both degrees and minutes, the dial plate (A) should be set as above to the number of degrees, and the lower graduated drum (J) or (K) to the number of minutes.

Angles to the right are shown on the scales "white figures on black ground." "WHITE IS RIGHT."

Angles to the left are shown "black figures on yellow ground."

When laying on the aiming point or director the traversing lever should be used to move the gun, small final adjustments may be made by using the traversing gear.

The crosshead or finder (F) on the side of the cowl will be used to get the gun roughly on to the aiming point, and when an aiming point to the left of the gun is chosen the No. 2 of the detachment will assist his layer by using the finder.

The upper prism in the cowl can be elevated or depressed by means of the micrometer head (G) to assist the layer to get on to his aiming point.

[N.B.—It must be remembered that if the sight is used for direct laying the vertical scale of the cowl must be at zero, otherwise a false angle of sight will be automatically put on.]

SWITCHING. " ....*degrees more right.*"

The drum on the right (D) of the dial sight will be manipulated by the right hand always away from the body. The dial plate will thus move to the right, or counter-clockwise.

" ....*degrees more left.*"

The drum on the left (E) of the dial sight will be manipulated by the left hand always towards the body. The dial plate will then move to the left, or clockwise.

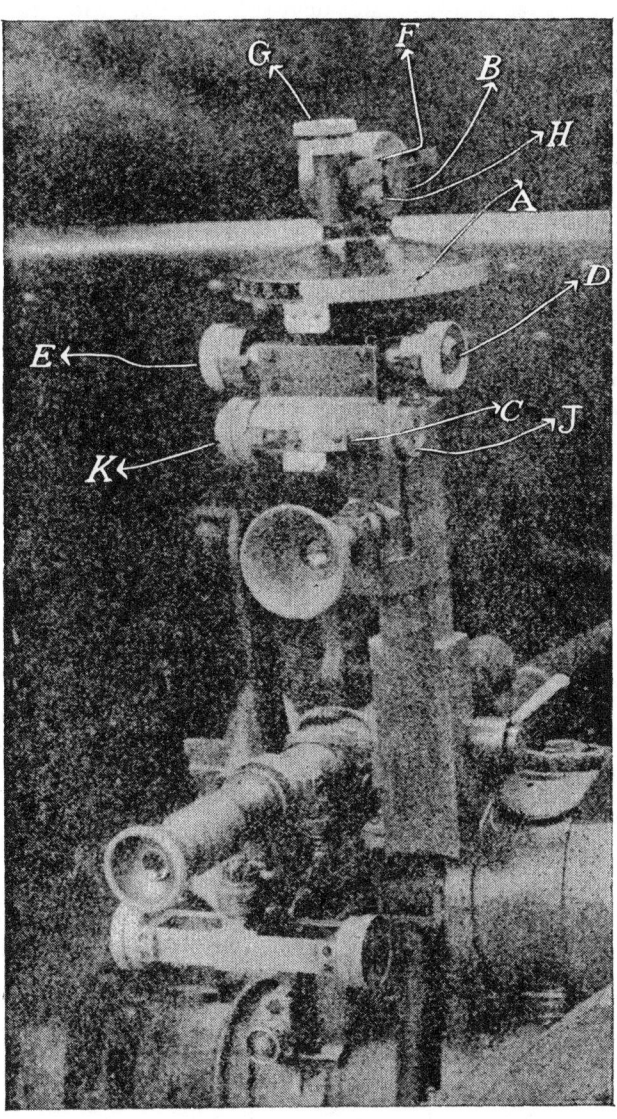

FIG. 17.

(B 10585)

"....*minutes more right or left*" will be put on in a similar manner by using the graduated drum (J) or (K) of the carrier.

If the switch necessitates the trail being lifted, the layer, *after* putting the required amount on his scale, will order the trail to be raised, will put his traverse back to zero, and will relay on his aiming point.

If a gun is ordered to give "parallel lines" to the other guns, the layer should set his lower deflection leaf (C) to zero and measure the angle from the aiming point selected by his section commander, by using the dial plate (A). If the arrow is not opposite an exact degree he will set it to the next degree lower, *i.e.*, if it is showing say 57° 20′ Right, he will set the dial plate (A) to 57° Right and will complete the measurement on the lower deflection leaf (C), using the graduated drum (J) or (K).

The guns receiving the order "Parallel lines to No....." must remember to put their deflection scales (C) to zero before putting on the reading ordered.

Auxiliary aiming point.

If after the gun is laid, the original aiming point for any reason becomes obscured, the layer will pick up an auxiliary aiming point by lifting the thumb-piece and moving the dial plate (A) round till he picks up with the eyepiece any point he wishes to use for an auxiliary aiming point, and if the arrow is not opposite an exact degree he will act as laid down above.

When a layer is running off his traverse he should simply direct the trail to be raised, put his traverse back to zero, and relay on the aiming point without touching the scales on the sight.

WRENCH, ADJUSTING No. 7 DIAL SIGHT AND CARRIERS.

This wrench is made of forged steel and has four arms for adjusting the No. 7 dial sight and its carriers when the sights are being aligned with the gun.

CHAPTER VI.

THE TELEMETER, ARTILLERY.

The telemeter is an instrument which enables the range of a distant point to be found by taking two observations of that point from the ends of a base.

The base used may vary from 50 to 150 yards, according to the pattern of telemeter employed.* The length of the base is measured by means of the telemeter itself.

The telemeter can, if necessary, be used by one man alone, but as a rule a rangetaking party consists of two men—the rangetaker and his assistant.

It is the most accurate field rangefinder in the Service, but its usefulness is limited by the fact that it cannot be used for taking the range of moving targets and that it is somewhat slow in use.

The telemeters in the Service are known as the "Telemeter, Artillery," and there are four Marks, I, II, III and IV.

The following table shows the equipment required for each Mark of telemeter :—

Mks. I and II.	Mk. III.	Mk. IV.
1 Telemeter Artillery, Mks. I or II.	1 Telemeter, Artillery, Mk. III.	1 Telemeter, Artillery, Mk. IV with leather case and adjusting key.
1 Leather Case, with waistbelt.	1 Leather Case, with waistbelt.	1 Cord Mk. IV, Telemeter Mk. I.
1 Cord, metallic, 19 ft., Mk. III, or 27 ft., Mk. I.	1 Cord, metallic, 29 ft., Mk. I.	1 Tape Mark IV, Telemeter Mk. I.
1 Tape, steel, 20 ft., Mk. II.	1 Tape, steel, 29 ft. Mk. I.	2 Stands Mk. IV, Telemeter Mk. I.
1 Pocket, cord, Mk. II.		2 Buckets, picket, tripod, Mk. I.
1 Pocket, tape, Mk. II.		
1 set of 3 Pickets, Tripod†, either (a) Mk. I or (b), Mk. I* or II, and, with (a)— 2 Buckets, picket, small. 2 Straps, picket. With (b)— 2 Buckets, picket, tripod, Mk. I.	As for Mks. I and II.	

* NOTE.—By working in "half-yards" or "double-yards" it is possible to use bases between 25 and 300 yards, as explained on p. 115.

† NOTE.—The Pickets Tripod are called A, B, or C pickets, to distinguish them—see p. 102.

The Marks I, II and III Telemeters are generally similar to one another, but the Mark IV differs considerably from the earlier Marks.

A full description of the Mark IV Telemeter will be found on page 103. The following description applies to the Marks I, II and III. (See Plates XXXV and XXXVI.)

The telemeter consists of the following parts :—

The frame, with cover and two telescope sockets, protecting ring for range drum (B), compensating screw (K), with guard (Y), and three pivots, one (P) for the horizon mirror frame and compensating arm, one (Q) for the base bar, and one (H) for the steel index arm.

The range drum (T) and drum screw (S).

The compensating arm (I) and spring ($b\ b$), with frame for the horizon mirror (X) and right angle pointer (M).

The graduated base bar (W D) with spring ($a\ a$) and slider (E).

The steel index arm (F G) with spring ($c\ c$), and two index mirrors (L and N).

The telescope.

The Frame.

The frame is of gunmetal in the Mark I and of aluminium alloy in the Marks II and III, and has a leather backing screwed to it. Two recesses are formed in the leather backing to fit over the head of the tripod picket.

The cover is attached to the frame by screws, and carries the two telescope sockets and shutters. The shutters, which have a small hole in the centre, can be slid in over the telescope sockets so that the instrument can be used without the telescope, if necessary.

The protecting ring has an arrow engraved on it which serves as an index for reading the range scale.

The compensating screw is on the right side of the frame. It is used for setting the horizon mirror, and is protected by the compensating screw guard.

The Range Drum.

The range drum is a brass cylinder having a spiral range scale engraved on it. It is fitted with two stops, one of which comes into action when the range drum is at "infinity," and the other prevents the drum from becoming detached.

The drum screw has a double thread.

Backlash between the drum screw and its socket is taken up by means of a plunger and spring. The range scales are graduated as follows :—

Marks I and II from 500 to 6,000 yards.
Mark III from 500 to 10,000 yards.

The Compensating Arm, &c.

The compensating arm is carried on a pivot on the frame and the end of the arm rests on the point of the compensating screw, against which it is held by a spiral spring ($b\ b$).

To face page 100.Plate XXXV.

The Telemeter Artillery Perspective View. (Cover removed).

T.T.—The Range Drum.
B.—The protecting ring for range drum.
S.—The drum screw.
I.—Compensating arm.
K.—The Compensating Screw.
Y.—The screw Guard, (revolving).

W.D.—The base bar.
E.—The Slider.
F.G.—The steel index arm.
X.X.—The horizon mirror.
L.N.—The index mirrors.
P.—The compensating arm pivot.

a. a.—Base bar spring.
b. b.—Compensating arm springs.
c. c.—Index arm spring.

Scale about ⅔ full size.

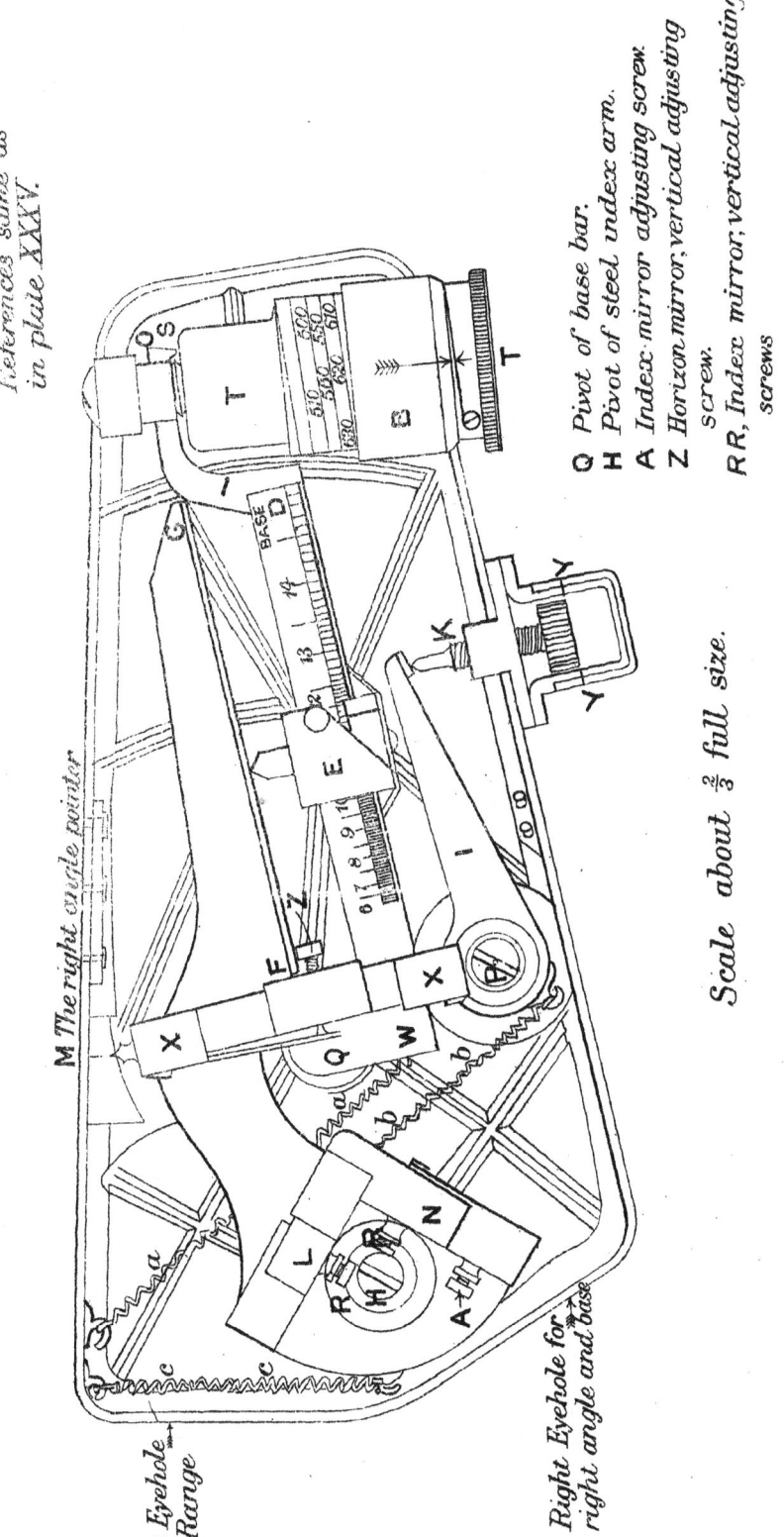

Attached to the compensating arm is a frame which carries the horizon mirror, and at the end of this frame is the right angle pointer. A line is engraved on a plate on the left side of the frame under this pointer. When the pointer is vertically over the line the horizon mirror is in such a position that the reflected lines of sight are at right angles to the direct line of sight (the drum being set at infinity).

The horizon mirror is a rectangular sheet of glass, the lower half of which is silvered, the upper half plain.

THE BASE BAR, &c.

The graduated base bar is pivoted to the frame at one end; the other end carries a hardened steel bearing piece which rests on the shoulder of the drum screw and is kept pressed against it by the base bar spring ($a\ a$). A scale of bases is engraved upon it, divided to read single yards, and graduated as follows:—

Marks I and II from 60 to 145 yards.
Mark III from 90 to 150 yards.

The slider is a steel saddle which fits on the base bar and can be moved along it. It is held down on the base bar by a spring. It carries a hardened steel projection which bears against the steel index arm.

THE INDEX ARM, &c.

The index arm is of steel, and is pivoted at one end to the frame. The other end rests on the point of the slider and is kept pressed against it by the index arm spring ($c\ c$).

Above it, near the pivot, are mounted the two index mirrors, which are completely silvered and are at right angles to one another. They can be adjusted vertically by the adjusting screws (R R), and one of them can be adjusted horizontally by the adjusting screw (A).

THE TELESCOPE.

The telescope is of the Galilean pattern, and has a field of view of about 2° and magnifies four times.

It is focussed by screwing the eyepiece in and out. For use, it fits into the telescope sockets, the shutters being pushed to one side. When not in use it is carried in the pocket on the side of the telemeter case.

THE LEATHER CASE, &c.

A leather case is provided for carrying the telemeter. It has a shoulder strap and waist belt. A small pocket on the outside of the case carries the telescope.

THE METALLIC CORD.

The following are the metallic cords in use:—

Cord, metallic, 19 feet, Mark II ⎫
,, 19 feet, Mark III ⎬ for Telemeters Marks I and II.
,, 27 feet, Mark I ⎭
,, 29 feet, Mark I. Telemeter Mark III.

The cords are of silk, covered with copper wire, except the 19 feet Mark II, which is covered with brass wire.

One end is fixed to a wooden shuttle, on which the cord is wound, the other end is furnished with an S hook which enables the cord to be attached to the button of the (A) picket.

The cords are used for marking the sub-base as explained on page 111. The cord is passed through a hole in the shuttle and a knot is tied in the cord at the following distances from the outer bend of the S hook :—

19 and 27-foot cords, 6 yards.
29-foot cords, 9 yards.

The spare cord is then wound on the shuttle and made fast.

Should the cord be broken care must be taken to join it up and retie the knot so that the above measurements are not altered.

The length of the cord should be checked by comparing it with the steel tape.

THE STEEL TAPE.

The following are the steel tapes in use :—

Tape, steel, 20 feet, Mark II.
Tape, steel, 29 feet, Mark I.

The tapes are plain ribands of steel, with a loop at one end for fixing to the button of the (A) picket, or carrier of the stand, the other end being made fast to the interior of a case into which the whole tape can be wound.

There is a small piece of brass soldered on to the tape at the following distances from the loop :—

20-foot tape, 6 yards.
29-foot tape, 9 yards.

In a few tapes the brass piece is replaced by a hole bored through the tape.

THE POCKETS, CORD AND TAPE.

The Mark II pockets for the cord and tape are of leather, with a loop on the back through which the waist belt passes. They are closed by a buckle and strap. That for the cord is square ; the other is rounded off.

These pockets are for use with Marks I, II and III Telemeters only.

THE TRIPOD PICKETS.

The " picket, tripod, Mark II " is of ash, and consists of the head and three legs. The legs are attached to the head by a thick leather hinge ; they are jointed in the middle to enable them to be folded up and provided with a sliding brass sleeve which is slipped over the joint and keeps it rigid when the tripod is in use.

The legs are fitted with steel points.

A set of " pickets, tripod " consists of three pickets, the (A), (B) and (C).

To face page 103. Plate XXXVII.

Telemeter Artillery. Mark IV.

A.A. Telescope Sockets.
C. Range Drum Reader.
D. Range Drum.
E. Drum Screw.
F. Compensating Screw.
G. Compens'g Arm with Horizon Mirror.
H. Percentage of Error Reader.
J. Hor: Mirror Frame Spring.
K. Compensating Screw Guard.
L. Graduated Base Bar.
M. Spring for ,, ,,
N. Slider.
P. Index Arm.
Q. Index Mirrors.
R. Index Mirror Frame Spring.
S. Percentage of Error Scale.
T. Hole to insert Adjusting Key.
V. Screw adjusting Horizon Mirror.
X } Screw adjusting Index Mirrors.
X'}

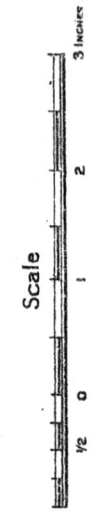

Plan.
Covers Removed.

Scale

PLATE XXXVIII. [*To face page* 103.

Telemeter, Artillery, Mark IV.

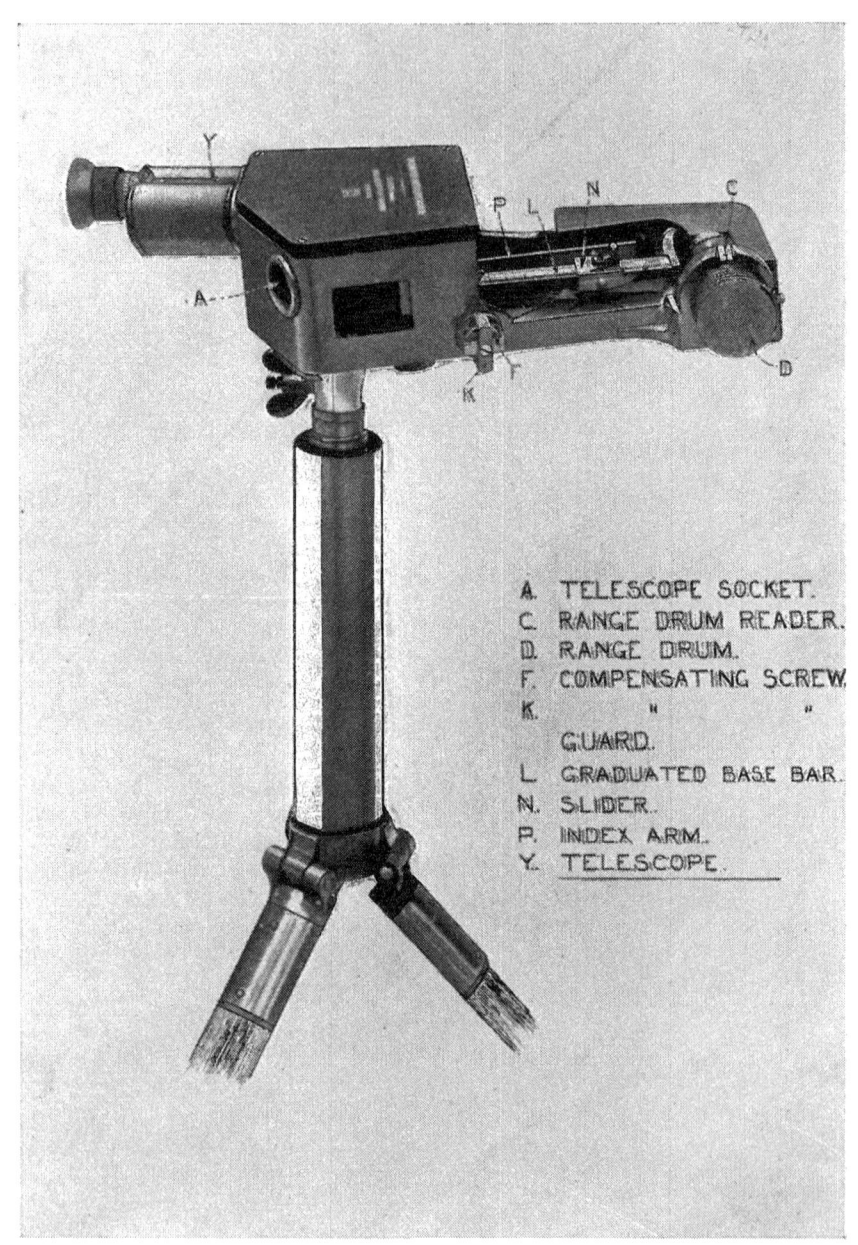

A. TELESCOPE SOCKET.
C. RANGE DRUM READER.
D. RANGE DRUM.
F. COMPENSATING SCREW.
K. "   "   GUARD.
L. GRADUATED BASE BAR.
N. SLIDER.
P. INDEX ARM.
Y. TELESCOPE.

The (A) picket is fitted with a movable cross head, and with a brass button to take the S hook of the metallic cord.

The (B) and (C) pickets, which are exactly alike, except as regards their flags, are interchangeable, and have plain heads.

Each of the three pickets carries a linen flag (attached to it by means of straps).

The (A) and (C) picket flags have a black vertical line and a black horizontal line painted on them; the (B) picket flag has a black vertical line only.

The picket, tripod Mark I* is similar to the Mark II.

The picket tripod Mark I is similar to the Mark II, except that the legs are not jointed.

The "straps, picket" are attached to the (A) and (B) pickets, when the picket is carried on horseback.

The pickets tripod Marks I, I* and II are for use with telemeters Marks I, II and III only.

The Bucket, Picket, Small.

This is a small leather bucket, about 9 inches high, used for carrying the picket tripod Mark I.

For use it is attached to the stirrup-iron by means of a strap; the feet of the picket tripod rest in the bucket, the head of the picket being held by the "strap picket," which is passed round the range-taker's arm.

The bucket is reversible, and may be attached to either the near or the off side stirrup.

The Bucket Picket Tripod, Mark I.

This bucket is of leather, about $3\frac{1}{2}$ inches in diameter, and is used for carrying the pickets tripod Marks I* and II. It is provided with a suspending strap which is passed round the hind arch of the saddle, and with a short arm of leather stiffened with steel. The surcingle is passed through a loop on this arm.

The bucket is reversible, and may be carried either on the near on the off side of the horse.

TELEMETER ARTILLERY, MARK IV.

The Telemeter.

(Plates XXXVII and XXXVIII.)

The principal parts of the telemeter are as follows :—

The frame with covers, two telescope sockets (A, A, Plate XXXVII), two spring clips to take the stand, and the range drum reader (C).

The range drum (D), and drum screw (E).

The compensating screw (F), compensating arm with horizon mirror (G), " Percentage of error " reader (H), and spring (J).

The compensating screw guard (K).

The graduated base bar (L), spring (M), and slider (N).

The steel index arm (P), with two index mirrors (Q Q) and spring (R).

The percentage of error scale (S).

The telescope (Y, Plate XXXVIII).

The adjusting key.

The Frame, &c.

The frame is an aluminium casting. Aluminium covers to protect the mirrors and range drum screw are secured to it by means of screws. Two brass telescope sockets (A A) are fitted in the rear face. Featherways are cut in them into which the feather on the telescope fits, thus ensuring that the telescope is always inserted in the same position. The range drum reader is engraved on an annular projection (C).

A small hole (T) between the telescope sockets allows of the adjusting key being inserted to engage the adjusting screw (X 1).

Brass pieces are screwed to the base and form two spring clips into which the top of the stand can be fitted. There is a spring arrangement to take up play.

There are two small recesses immediately beneath the points where the lines of sight to the target and to the other end of the base line intersect. These recesses fit over a small spring plunger at the top of the stand.

The Range Drum, &c.

The range drum (D) consists of a hollow brass cylinder with ranges from 500 to 20,000 yards engraved on it. It is fitted with two stops, one of which comes into action when the range drum is at infinity, and the other prevents the drum becoming detached. The drum screw arrangement is on the differential principle, so arranged that the spiral on the drum is of a greater pitch than the thread on the drum screw (E). This allows of the value of the graduations being indicated by large figures. Backlash between the drum screw and its socket is taken up by a spring plunger.

The Compensating Screw, &c.

The compensating screw (F) passes through a spring bearing in the flange on the right of the body. Its point acts upon one end of the compensating arm (G), which is a bent lever pivoted to the frame. The other end of the arm forms a frame for the horizon mirror, and at the end of this is fixed the percentage of error reader (H).

The lower half of the horizon mirror is silvered, and the upper half transparent. It can be vertically adjusted by means of the screw (V). A spiral spring (J) prevents any play in the above arrangements.

The Compensating Screw Guard.

The compensating screw guard (K) is fitted outside the compensating screw. It can be revolved through a quarter of a circle, and either allows access to the compensating screw, or prevents it being accidentally moved.

The Graduated Base Bar, &c.

The graduated base bar (L) is pivoted to the frame at one end, and the other end, which is of hardened steel, is pressed against the point of the drum screw (E) by a spiral spring (M). The bar is graduated from 50 to 125 yards, each division being 1 yard.

The slider (N) is made of steel, a flat spring beneath it keeping it pressed down on the base bar. A hardened steel projection bears against the flat surface of the index arm (P).

A line is cut on the slider by means of which the graduations on the base bar are read.

The Steel Index Arm, &c.

One end of the index arm (P) is pivoted to the frame, and the other end is pressed against the slider (N) by means of a spiral spring (R). Above it near the pivot are mounted two index mirrors (Q Q), which are completely silvered, and set at right angles to one another. Two adjusting screws (X) allow of the mirrors being adjusted vertically, and another one (X 1) allows of the right mirror being adjusted horizontally.

The Percentage of Error Scale.

The percentage of error scale (S) is fixed to the frame and indicates what percentage of the range recorded on the range drum should be *deducted*, when the angle at the left of the base, between the base and the line to the target, is not a right angle.

The Telescope.

The telescope (Y, Plate XXXVIII) is of the prismatic type, and has a magnification of six diameters. It is focussed by revolving the eyepiece. A feather near the object glass fits into the featherways in the sockets and insures the telescope being always inserted in the same position.

The field of view is 5° 30′, and is coloured by means of a tinted diaphragm, with the exception of a small circle of 1° in the centre.

This arrangement facilitates picking up a target, but does not impair accuracy, as coincidences are always made in the uncoloured circle, which is of about the same size as the complete field of view in previous Marks of telemeters.

The Adjusting Key.

The adjusting key has a milled head at one end, and at the other a square hole, which fits over the adjusting screw (X 1, Plate XXXVII) in the right index mirror frame.

THE CASE.

The case is made of leather, and is carried by means of a shoulder strap and waist belt. It is fitted with pockets for the telescope, metallic cord, steel tape and adjusting key.

THE METALLIC CORD.

The metallic cord consists of a silk core wound round with copper wire. When issued it is 17 feet long. At one end is fitted a brass S hook for attaching it to the neck above the ball and socket on the stand. The other end passes through a wooden shuttle, one half of which is white, and the other black. A knot is tied in the cord so that when the cord is taut, the distance from the centre of the neck of the stand to the centre of the shuttle (or from the bearing surface of the S hook to the nearest edge of the shuttle, when held at right angles to the cord), is exactly 15 feet.

THE STEEL TAPE.

The tape is made of spring steel, and has a brass piece brazed on to it exactly 15 feet from the inside of the loop at the end. It can be wound into its leather case. It is used for checking and adjusting the length of the metallic cord.

THE STAND.
(Plate XXXIX.)

The stand consists of three jointed ash legs (A A A) which are pivoted beneath a metal tube (B), which has white and black lines painted on it. Above the tube is a ball and socket joint (C), which can be clamped by means of a butterfly nut (D). The ball is fitted with a small circular plate (E) which fits into the spring clips beneath the telemeter. It has a small spring plunger (F), which engages the recesses in the telemeter frame. A strap (G) is fitted to one leg, so that the legs can be bound together when not in use.

METHOD OF CARRYING THE EQUIPMENT.

A rangetaker's party consists of :—

1st rangetaker (No. 1).
2nd rangetaker (No. 2).
Horseholder.

The equipment is carried as follows :—

No. 1 carries the telemeter strapped over his shoulder so that it may rest behind the elbow, just clear of the hip. The instrument is kept from jolting by the waistbelt, which is passed through the loop of the leather case and buckled in front. His stand or tripod picket (B or C) is carried in the bucket on the saddle on the near side.

No. 2 carries his stand or tripod picket (A) in the bucket on the saddle on the off side.

[To face page 106.] PLATE XXXIX.

STAND, MARK IV, TELEMETER (MARK I).

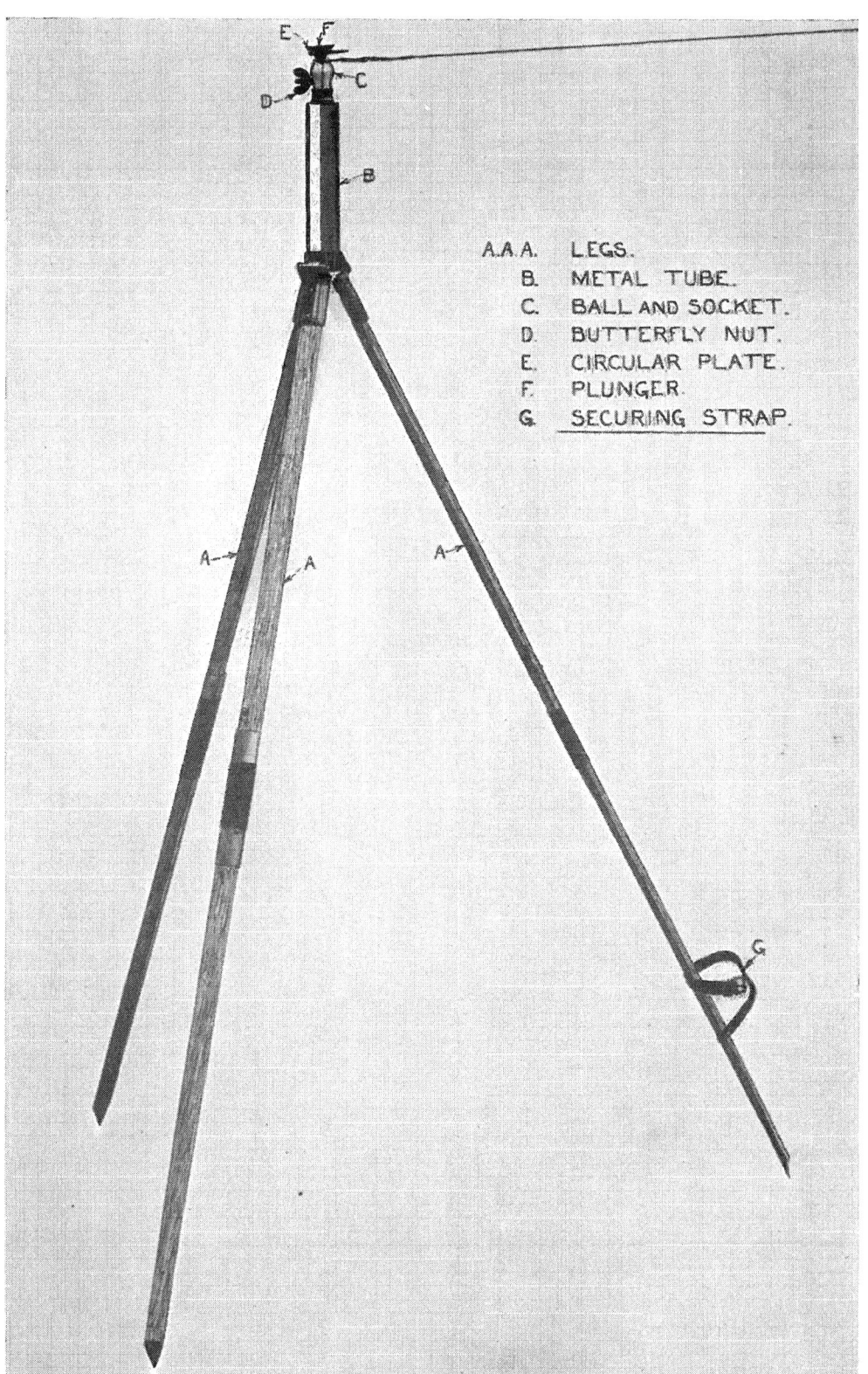

A.A.A. LEGS.
B. METAL TUBE.
C. BALL AND SOCKET.
D. BUTTERFLY NUT.
E. CIRCULAR PLATE.
F. PLUNGER.
G. SECURING STRAP.

The bucket is attached to the saddle in a similar manner to the cavalry rifle bucket, the suspending strap passing round the hind arch, the surcingle to be passed through the loop of the arm.

It is reversible and may be carried on either the near or the off side of the saddle. The spare picket tripod is carried on a limber.

USE OF THE INSTRUMENT.

The principal application of the telemeter in artillery operations is to solve practically, without calculation* or actual measurements, the following problem :—

To find the distance to any visible point, from the ground occupied by the range-finding party.

This is technically termed " taking a range."

The physical conditions necessary in order to take a range with the telemeter from any point P to any object O (Fig. 1), are that a position may be found to the right or left of P from which both O and P are visible, and at which a point Q may be marked such that either the angle O P Q or the angle O Q P shall be, approximately, a right angle.

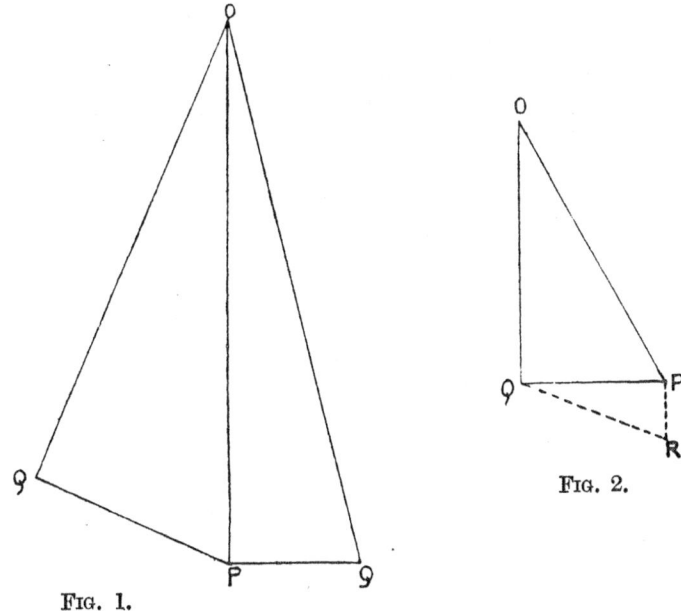

FIG. 1.   FIG. 2.

In practice the mode of proceeding is usually as follows :—

The object being O (Fig. 2), a picket is placed at P by No. 2 and the rangetaker (No. 1) by means of the instrument, finds a point Q such that angle P Q O is approximately a right angle, and places a second picket there.

---

* There are certain cases when, although the limits of the instrument are exceeded it is still possible to find the correct range. In those exceptional cases a simple calculation is required. (*See* p. 115.)

He then, standing at Q, measures with the instrument the base P Q by means of a sub-base P R, which is marked at right angles to P Q by No. 2, by means of the metallic cord.

After this, setting the base so found on the base bar of the instrument, he proceeds to P, and by an observation at that point reads off the range O Q on the drum.

Three things, therefore, have to be done by means of the instrument—

1. To fix the right angle (within certain limits).
2. To find the base.
3. To take the range.

It is best to consider 1 and 3 first.

Step 1.—To Fix the Right Angle approximately and set the Horizon Mirror.

The drum must be set to zero (↑) and the pointer on the horizon mirror frame to the zero mark on its scale, and the slider to the stop nearest the pivot of the base bar.

No. 2 plants his stand (or A picket) at the point from which the range is required.

No. 1 moves out to the left end of the base and looking through the right telescope socket moves backwards or forwards until he sees the reflection of the A picket roughly in coincidence with the target. He then plants his stand or picket, places the instrument on it, fits the telescope into the right socket and by means of the compensating screw makes an exact coincidence of the A picket and target, and turns up the compensating screw guard.

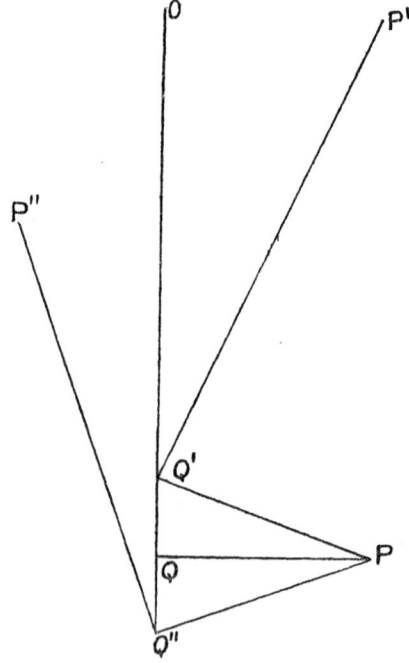

Fig. 3.

In Fig. 3, let P represent the A picket, and O the target. The range-taker has moved out to the left of P to some point Q′ or Q″. From this position, looking through the right eyehole, he will see the image of the picket at P reflected towards P′ or P″, at right angles to P Q′ or P Q″, and the target will be seen in the unsilvered portion of the horizon mirror either to the left or right of the image of the picket (which is seen in the silvered portion of the horizon mirror), as in Figs. 4 and 5.

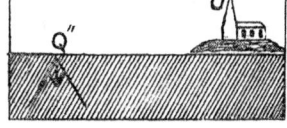

Fig. 4.   Fig. 5.

Then by moving backwards or forwards as may be necessary he will be able to find a point Q at which the object O and the reflected image of P coincide (Figs. 3 and 6), and this fixes the right angle, approximately.

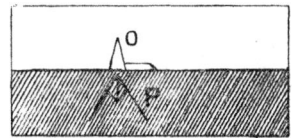

Fig. 6.

Having thus found the right angle point approximately, he plants his stand or picket and sets the horizon mirror accurately, as described above.

Step 3.—To take the Range.

Assuming that the right angle stand or picket has been planted as described above, and that the base has been measured and set on the base bar (by Step 2, which remains to be described), the next step is to take the range.

The range taker (No. 1) taking care not to alter the setting of the horizon mirror, moves to the right end of the base, puts the telescope into the left telescope socket, and sets the instrument on the A picket or stand. Looking towards the target through the telescope he will then see the image of the B picket (or stand) reflected in the direction P S, parallel to Q O (Fig. 7), *i.e.*, to the right of the target.

He then turns the range drum counter-clockwise, and this will make the image of the picket move to the left. He continues to turn the drum until the target and the image of the B picket are seen in exact coincidence; the range of the target will then read off on the drum.

What has been described as Steps 1 and 2 amounts to this:—

First an approximate right angle O Q P, (Fig. 8) has been made at Q, and the horizon mirror has been set so that, when looking

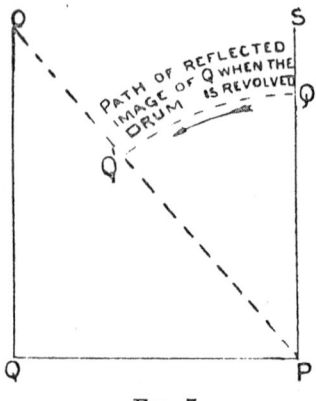

FIG. 7.

through the right telescope socket, the mirror reflects this angle O Q P. Then the other index mirror and the horizon mirror reflect the supplement of this angle, and therefore when the instrument is set on the stand at P and the left eyehole used, the image of Q is reflected in the direction P S, parallel to Q O.

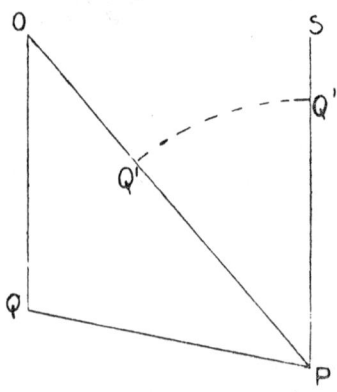

FIG. 8.

After this, the instrument remaining in its last position P, the reflected angle at that point is altered by revolving the drum so that Q' (the image of Q) is no longer reflected at the angle Q P S to Q' P, but at the smaller angle Q P O.

Now the longer the range is, the less does the angle Q P O differ from the angle Q P S, and therefore the fewer are the turns which it is necessary to give to the drum to make Q' move from S and coincide with O.

From the above it is easy to see how by engraving a scale on the drum, such scale can be made to record the actual range, that is, the particular value of O P in every instance.

So far, however, it may not appear how the reading on the drum is applicable to every range independent of the length of the base, for it is evident that if P Q *(Fig. 8) were shorter, the angle* O P Q *would be greater, and vice versâ, although the length of* Q O *remained unaltered. This difficulty is met by the use of the base bar, which enables the movement given to the index mirror by each turn of the drum to be increased or diminished according to the position of the slider. By this contrivance it is arranged that in proportion as the base is longer for any given range, the greater is the movement of the index mirror corresponding to any given number of turns of the drum, and therefore (Fig. 8) the greater the resulting deviation of the reflected image* Q' *from the direction* P S.

Thus, within certain limits, the necessary compensation is effected to enable the one scale on the drum to be made use of whatever the length of the base may be.

Step 2.—To find the Base.

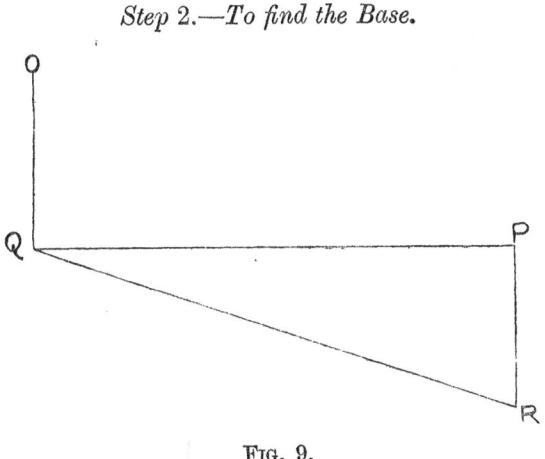

Fig. 9.

In Fig. 9 let P represent the range (or A) picket and Q the right angle (or B) picket, the target O lying in the direction Q O, The base to be found is P Q and the procedure is as follows :—

No. 2 unwinds the metallic cord, attaches the S hook to the stand or picket at P and extends the cord to its full length in the direction P R, at right angles to Q P, holding the shuttle in his right hand and raising or lowering it as required until it lies in the same plane as the top of the picket at P and the target O.

The right angle is obtained by the help of the movable crosshead on the A picket. No. 2 turns the crosshead until one of the notches is laid on the B picket ; then looking along the other notch he picks up an aiming point in the direction of the target. When he extends the sub-base he holds the shuttle so that it is in line with the aiming point, and the top of the A picket. The Stand Mark IV Telemeter is not provided with a crosshead, and No. 2 therefore has to judge the right angle.

He holds it steady until No. 1 has completed his observation.

No. 1 places himself at Q with his instrument resting on the stand. He sets the drum to zero and the slider on the base bar to the ength of the sub-base (*i.e.*, the length of the metallic cord), which has been extended by No. 2. As described in Step 1, he sets the horizon mirror, by means of the compensating screw, so that the reflected image of P is seen in exact coincidence with the target O. Then, without moving the compensating screw, he turns the drum until he sees the reflected image of the shuttle, held up by No. 2, in exact coincidence with the target O. The drum then records the distance P Q. What has been done in this step is to measure the angle P Q R.

In the triangle Q P R (Fig. 9) the side P R is fixed and the angle Q P R is a right angle : therefore the shorter the side P Q the greater is the angle P Q R, and *vice versâ*.

With the drum at zero the mirrors were set so that P was reflected in coincidence with O ; then the drum was turned, thereby moving the index mirror until R was reflected in coincidence with O. The amount of movement of the index mirror is therefore a measure of the angle P Q R, and this movement as registered by the scale on the drum, is a measure of the side P Q.

READING THE SCALES.

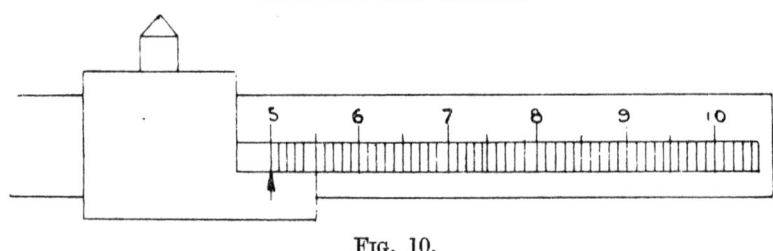

FIG. 10.

Fig. 10 shows how the scale on the base bar is engraved and figured.

For setting a *sub-base* on the base bar the numbered divisions represent yards ; in the above diagram the slider is set for a sub-base of 5 yards (as used for the telemeter, Mark IV).

If a sub-base of 9 yards is used the slider must be moved so that the arrow on the slider is opposite the division marked 9.

For setting a *base* on the base bar, the numbered divisions represent tens of yards, and the sub-divisions single yards.

Thus Fig. 10 shows the slider set for a base of 50 yards ; Fig. 11 shows the slider set for a base of $85\frac{1}{2}$ yards.

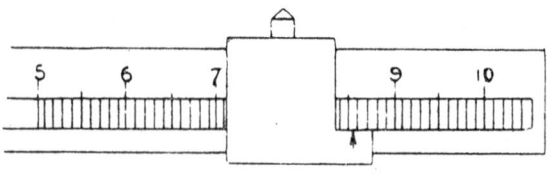

FIG. 11.

The scale on the range drum is a scale of yards. The numbers from 500 to 990 give the actual range in yards, while those from 10 to the end of the scale express hundreds of yards. Thus the arrow pointing to 850 would indicate a range of 850 yards; the arrow pointing to 23 or 77 indicates a range of 2,300 or 7,700 yards.

When measuring the base, the reading on the drum must be divided by 10 to get the true base length; thus if the arrow points to 855 on the drum the base is $85\frac{1}{2}$ yards; if the arrow points to 972 the base is 97·2 yards.

Preliminary or Position Drills.

This part of the subject can only be acquired by practice under a competent instructor, who will show how each operation is performed by going through the various movements himself.

For reference, however, the various positions are here described.

Planting Pickets.

The A picket is planted with the flag to the left. The B picket is planted with the flag to the right. The leg should be opened out sufficiently to ensure that the picket is firmly planted, and that the head of the picket is vertical. The A stand for the Mark IV telemeter should be planted with one leg to the rear to prevent it from being pulled over by the metallic cord when the sub-base is extended.

To lay out a Sub-base.

No. 2 turns the crosshead of the A picket on to the right-angle picket, and then looks over that line of the cross which is at right angles to the base, and takes up a line for the *sub-base*. He then—

1. Hooks the S of the cord to the button of the range-picket, or head of the Mark IV stand.
2. Extends the cord in the correct line, paying it out carefully, and taking care not to disturb the picket.
3. Holds the shuttle upright at the level of the top of the picket and object under observation, keeping, however, the line taken up. (To do this he must sometimes raise the hand considerably, sometimes lower it.) The shuttle should be turned with the edge towards the No. 1.
4. On a signal from No. 1, No. 2 drops the shuttle, steps up to the picket, unhooks the cord, and winds up.

Service Drill.

The range-finding party consists of No. 1, the range taker, and No. 2, the assistant, both of whom should be qualified range takers.

The method of carrying the equipment is laid down on p. 106.

Duties of No. 1.

No. 1 directs No. 2 where to plant the A picket or stand, and will satisfy himself that it is correctly planted and that the object is visible from the head of the picket when planted. He hands the metallic cord to No. 2, and moves out with the B picket or stand to the far end of the base. He should always use as long a base as the conformation of the ground will admit of, for the longer the base the more accurately will the range be found.

He sets the drum to zero, and the slider on the base bar to the division representing the length of the sub-base (see p. 112) and the pointer on the horizon mirror to the zero on its scale. Then, looking through the right eyehole he will move backwards or forwards till he sees the target and the reflected image of the A picket roughly in coincidence; he is then near the right angle point, and will plant his stand or picket firmly and put the telescope in the right socket. He then rests the instrument on the head of the picket and with the compensating screw sets the horizon mirror so that the target and A picket are seen in *exact* coincidence. He then turns up the guard over the compensating screw, which must not be touched again until the range has been found. Having set the horizon mirror he signals to No. 2 to extend the sub-base, and (still using the telescope in the right socket) turns the drum until the shuttle and the target are seen in exact coincidence, and reads off the base, which he at once sets on the base bar.* He then crosses over to the A picket, puts the telescope into the left telescope socket, rests the instrument on the picket and turns the drum until the target and the B picket are seen in coincidence, and reads off the range on the drum. He then signals to No. 2 to bring in the B picket.

Coincidence must always be made as nearly as possble in the centre of the field of view.

No. 1 should always plant the B picket as near the right angle point as the conformation of the ground admits of, because any deviation from this point will result in the range being found too long. There may be occasions however when, on account of the nature of the ground, or in order to take advantage of cover, it may be advisable to plant the B picket some distance from the right angle point. Under these circumstances the range given by the instrument will be too long, and No. 1 should inform the B.C. of this fact. The Mark IV telemeter is provided with a scale under the pointer on the horizon mirror which shows what percentage must be subtracted from the range found in order to get the true range.

Thus, suppose the pointer on the horizon mirror is over the figure 2 on the scale marked " Subtract %," and the range read on the drum is 8,600 yards, the true range is 2 per cent. less, *i.e.*, 8,428 yards.

Duties of No. 2.

No. 2 plants the A picket as directed by No. 1, and lays out the sub-base as described above.

As soon as No. 1 has measured the base No. 2 crosses over to the B picket, and on getting a signal from No. 1, he brings it in.

No. 2 must be careful when extending the sub-base not to move the A picket. Should he inadvertently do so, he must signal to No. 1, who will then check the setting of the horizon mirror, and if necessary correct it.

---

* If the telemeter is out of adjustment for parallelism (see Test 4, p. 124), it is as well to check, and if necessary correct the setting of the horizon mirror after setting the base on the base bar.

Working in Half Yards or Double Yards.

Cases may arise when it is convenient or even necessary to use a base either longer or shorter than any of those marked on the base-bar of the telemeter.

In these cases a simple calculation is required.

The principle which governs all cases of calculation is that the scales on the base bar and cylinder do not necessarily refer to yards, but will answer for any linear unit it is found convenient to work in, as for example, metres.

It is usual to work in half yards and double yards.

Half yards for bases shorter than those marked on the base bar.

Double yards for bases longer than those marked on the base bar.

Working in Half Yards.

For this a sub-base of, say, 6 *yards* is treated as 12 half yards, and is accordingly set as *twelve* on the base bar.

The working is otherwise exactly as usual, but the range finally obtained is read in half yards, and must, therefore, be halved for the distance in yards.

Example—

Sub-base of 6 yards is set 12 on the base bar.
Base reads 70, and is set on the base bar.
Range reads 1,900 (half yards).

$$\frac{1,900}{2} = 950 \text{ yards.}$$

Working in Double Yards.

Either a single or a double sub-base may be used.

(*a*) When a single sub-base of, say, 6 yards is used it is set 6, the base is read as usual in yards and divided by 2 to get it in double yards.

This base (in double yards) is then set on the base bar. The range finally is read in double yards, and must, therefore, be doubled for the distance in yards.

Example—

Sub-base, 6.

 Base reads ..   ..   160 yards.
  Divide by 2   ..   80 double yards.

Slider set to 8.

 Range reads 2,300 (double yards).

  $2,300 \times 2 = 4,600 =$ distance required in yards.

The above case (a) is the only one in which a calculation is required before setting the base.

(*b*) When a double sub-base of, say, 12 yards is used.

In this case the sub-base is treated as 6 double yards, and set accordingly at 6 on the base bar.

The rest of the working is as usual. The range finally obtained is read in double yards, and must be multiplied by 2 for the distance in yards.

Example—

Sub-base 12 yards is set 6 on the base bar.
Base reads 90 and is set on the base bar.
Range reads 2,100 (double yards).

$2{,}100 \times 2 = 4{,}200$ yards.

Variations in the Drill for Casualties.

The variations which are recognised in the drill are those necessary to meet the following casualties :—

Diminished Numbers with Complete Equipment.

No. 1 or 2 working alone.

When either No. works alone he has to lay out the sub-base for himself as follows :—

Having planted the A picket he lines himself with it and the object at cord's length, and then, if the range is estimated to be under 3,000 yards, takes a side pace in the direction of the C picket, and then plants the B picket. The side pace so taken must be in length according to the estimated range, as follows, for a sub-base of 6 yards :—

Estimated range 1,000 yards .. pace of 18 inches.
    ,,   ,,   2,000 ,, .. half pace of 9 inches.

Full Numbers with Equipment Incomplete.

(a) *One picket wanting.*—The spare picket should be used.

(b) *Two pickets wanting.*—The remaining picket is used in this case as an A picket; the base is measured in the usual way and set on the base bar, and No. 1 marks the right angle point with a sword or other substitute for a picket. If there is nothing handy which can be used for this purpose, No. 1 when setting the horizon mirror will mark the spot where he stands by digging his heel into the ground, or with a stone, and when he goes over to the A picket to read the range No. 2 will stand on exactly the same spot and act as a picket.

(c) *The cord lost.*—Lay out the sub-base with the tape.

(d) *Cord and tape lost.*—Where the ground admits of it, the base is found by pacing; if this cannot be done a sub-base of convenient length is put out by pacing, and this sub-base is set on the base bar.

Whenever it is necessary to measure a base or sub-base by pacing, both Nos. 1 and 2 should pace the distance twice or three times and the mean should be taken.

DIMINISHED NUMBERS WITH EQUIPMENT INCOMPLETE.

The following is the only case for which special directions can be given :—

No. 1 working alone with only Two Pickets.

No. 1 plants one picket as an A picket (A Fig. 12); then having fixed the right angle C and planted the other picket as a C picket, he obtains the base A C thus :—Stretching the cord from the C

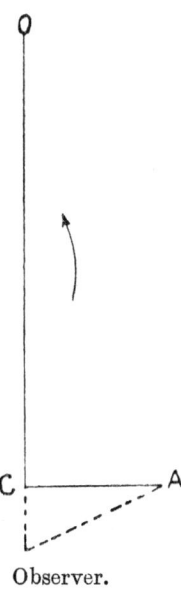

Observer.

FIG. 12.

picket in line with the object O he stands so that his eye may be just the distance of the cord from the C picket, and in this position he reflects A picket upon the object by turning the drum (slider set to the length of the cord used). This will give the base A C.

DOUBLE SUB-BASE.

To lay out a double sub-base, the three pickets are used and No. 1 superintends.

First, a sub-base is laid out with the cord in the usual way from the A picket, and the C picket is placed to mark the end of it.

Then a second length of the cord is laid out from the C picket in exact line with the A and C pickets, and the B picket is planted to mark the end of it.

The C picket is then taken away.

N.B.—No. 1, working alone, can not lay out a double sub-base unless he has three pickets.

Theory of the Telemeter.

The Mirrors.

Let E be the eye looking through the unsilvered part of the horizon mirror F at the object O. Let A be the picket, the reflection of which falls first on the index mirror N at the angle β, and from it passes off at the angle β', and falls upon the horizon mirror (silvered portion) at the angle η, and from it again to the eye at the angle η'. Let θ be the angle at which the mirrors are to each other, and a the angle between the object and the picket.

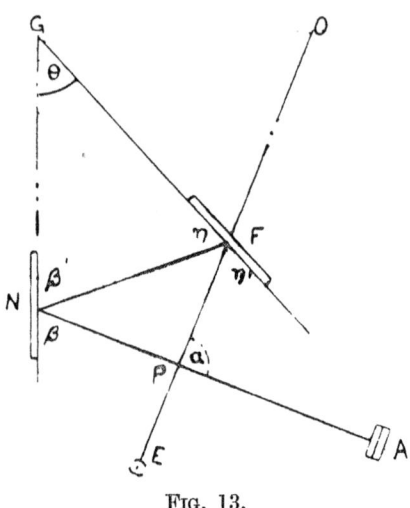

Fig. 13.

By the optical law—

Angle of incidence = angle of reflection.
$$\beta = \beta'.$$
$$\eta = \eta'.$$

Now by Euclid the exterior angle = the sum of the two interior opposite angles.

Therefore—
$$\eta' + PFN = \theta + \beta' = \theta + \beta.$$
$$\beta + FNP = \theta + \eta = \theta + \eta'.$$

Adding—
$$\beta + \eta' + PFN + FNP = 2\theta + \beta + \eta'.$$

That is—
$$PFN + FNP = 2\theta.$$

But—
the angle $a = PFN + FNP.$

Therefore—
$$a = 2\theta.$$

If then—
$$\theta = 45°, \ a = 90°.$$

In the telemeter the parts are so arranged that—

(1) When the right-angle pointer is set at zero the horizon mirror is inclined at 45° to both the index mirrors, and therefore the angle between the direct and reflected lines of sight is a right angle, both when using the right telescope socket and when using the left telescope socket.

(2) The point of intersection of the direct and reflected lines of sight (point P in Fig. 13) is vertically above the centre of the top of the stand or tripod picket.

Thus, if the telemeter is placed with the right spring clip on the stand, and the telescope in the right socket, the reflected line of sight is reflected at right angles to the direct line of sight and to the right of it. If the left spring clip and left telescope socket are used the reflected line of sight is reflected at right angles to the direct line of sight, and to the left of it (the range drum and right angle pointer being, of course, at zero).

The Range-finding Triangle, and the Compensating Action of the Double Index Mirrors.

The conditions required for solving the range-finding triangle A O C, Fig. 14, are that we should know the base A C and the angle A O C, the angle A C O being always a right angle. But inasmuch as we are unable to get at the point O to measure the angle, we must find a line A D at right angles to A C, and measure the angle D A O, which is equal to the angle A O C. This is done in taking the range with the instrument.

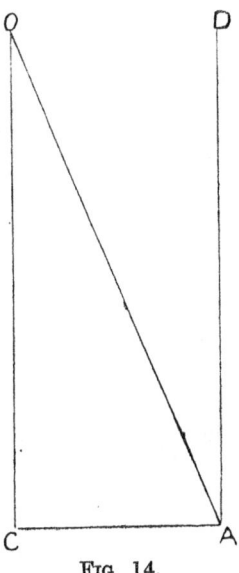

Fig. 14.

First consider the instrument as used when the right-angle pointer is set at zero. In this case both index mirrors are at 45° to the horizon mirror.

Then if O be the object (Fig. 14) and A C the base, an exact right angle O C A is made by the use of the right eyehole, and (the drum being at zero) an exact right angle C A D is made by the use of the left socket, where D is the reflected image of the picket C.

Here the range A O, which is approximately equal to C O is recorded by the instrument as A C, Cot A O C, and is therefore found correctly.

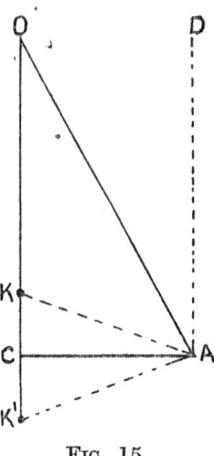

Fig. 15.

Next, suppose that for convenience the observer has left the exact right-angle position and advanced to K or retired to K^1, Fig. 15, and has completed coincidence of A and O by use of the compensating screw. The two index mirrors are now no longer each at 45° to the horizon mirror, but the increase in the angle on the one side is exactly balanced by the decrease of the angle on the other, so that A O C remains unaltered. If, therefore, the true right-angle base A C were set on the base bar, the range recorded by the instrument would be as before—A C, Cot A O C. But instead of A C, the base set is A K or A K^1, hence the range recorded is A K Cot A O C or A K^1 Cot A O C, and the error introduced depends upon the difference between A K or A K^1 and A C.

Example.—Let A C = 100 yards, Cot A O C = 10, then the true range, as recorded by telemeter, with pointer at zero, = A C Cot A O C = 100 × 10 = 1,000 yards; but if the C picket has been displaced to K or K^1 and the compensating screw made use of, then the range recorded will be AK Cot A O C or A K^1 Cot A O C.

Let C K = C K' = 10 yards, then A K = $(\sqrt{\overline{AC}^2 + \overline{CK}^2})$ or 100·5 yards and the range recorded will be 1,005 yards, showing an error of ½ per cent.

N.B.—It will be noticed that the error caused by a deviation from the true right angle is always *plus*.

Measuring the Base.

In measuring the base A C (Fig. 16) a small range-finding triangle A C B, similar to the triangle O C A in the preceding figures, is worked out. As we are, however, in this instance at the station C we can obtain the angle A C B, which A B subtends, by first making a coincidence between A and O, with the compensating screw, and then turning the drum until B and O are in coincidence.

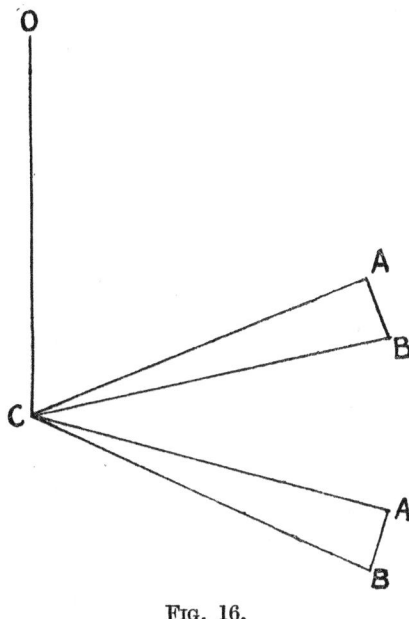

Fig. 16.

This is done as follows :—

The telemeter is placed on the stand at C (drum at zero, telescope in the right socket). Let O be the distant object and A the picket or stand marking the other end of the base and B the shuttle held up by No. 2. The horizon mirror is set by means of the compensating screw in such a position that the picket at A is seen in coincidence with the object O. The drum is then turned, thus altering the angle between the index mirror and the horizon mirror, and consequently the direction of the reflected line of sight, until the shuttle B is seen in coincidence with the object at O. The amount of movement of the drum is a measure of the angle A C B, and if the slider be set to the division on the base bar which marks the length of the sub-base (A B), the length of the base A C will be read off on the drum.

(See page 112 as to setting bases and sub-bases on the base bar, and reading ranges and bases.)

It should be noted that the points A B C and O must all be in one plane, otherwise the angle A C B will not be correctly measured. If the point B is either above or below the plane passing through O A and C the angle A C B will be measured too small, an error which will cause the base read to be greater than A C. This error will always produce a plus error in the range found.

Object of the Slider.

Suppose O an object, distant 1,000 yards, A C a base of 120 yards, and D C a base of 60 yards. The angle A O C will be double the angle D O C, and generally, if A C $= n$ D C, the angle A O C $= n$ times the angle D O C.

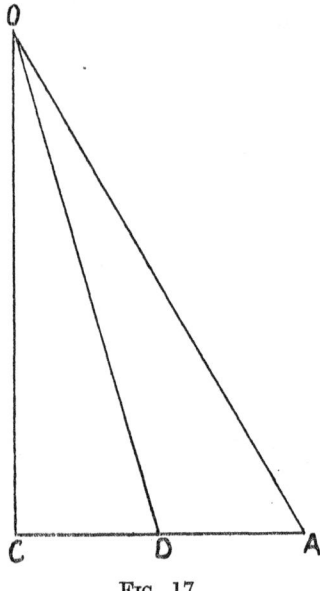

Fig. 17.

As there is only one given position of the drum and screw for any given range, some arrangement had to be devised by which the inclination of the mirrors might be altered, irrespective of the screw, so as to cause them to assume a greater inclination for a large base than for a small one.

This is arrived at by means of the arm W D (Plates XXXV and XXXVI), with the slider E bearing against the arm F G. As these two arms pivot at N and W, it is evident that the further the slider is away from W the greater will be the movement of the arm F G (and consequently of the mirror fixed to it), for any definite movement of the screw Y.

Testing and Adjusting the Telemeter.

The following tests have been written for the Mark IV telemeter, but are also applicable to the Marks I, II, and III, the words " picket tripod " being substituted for " stand " where necessary.

The tests and adjustments are only to be carried out by a qualified officer or artificer.*

---

* The adjustment of the Marks I, II and III telemeters is more difficult than that of the Mark IV and should, as a rule, only be undertaken by the A.O.D. No adjusting key is issued with the Marks I, II or III telemeters.

The third test is by far the most important.

If the second test shows an error of 4° or 5° the range recorded is not likely to be more than 1 per cent. wrong ; but if the third test shows the adjustment of the instrument to be only one minute out, the following errors may be expected :—

Range.	Base.	Error.
5,000 yards.	50 yards.	150 yards.
5,000 yards.	100 yards.	75 yards.
10,000 yards.	120 yards.	225 yards.

(1) *The Mirrors should be in Correct vertical Adjustment.*

Test.—Fix the telemeter to a stand and plant it firmly on the ground. Select two perfectly vertical objects, *e.g.*, factory chimneys, edges of houses, &c., the lines of sight to which intersect at approximately right angles. If none are available hang up two plumb bobs. By means of the compensating screw (and, if necessary, also the range drum) make coincidence between the two objects, looking through the telescope fixed in the right socket. The objects should be in coincidence for their entire lengths, and not appear to be crossed.

Repeat the above test with the telescope in the left socket.

Adjustment is effected by elevating or depressing the reflected lines of sight by turning the adjusting screws (X, X, V, Plate XXXVII). A tommy to fit the heads of the adjusting screws can be made out of a nail. The last movement of the screws should be clockwise. To get at the screws the cover must be removed, the four screws securing it to the frame being withdrawn. Care must be taken to keep the direct and reflected lines of sight in the same plane. If the objects, upon which the adjustment is being carried out, appear to separate, they must be brought into coincidence again by means of the compensating screw.

(2) *When the reader of the " percentage of error " scale is at 0, the direct and reflected lines of sight from the left hand telescope socket must be at right angles to one another.*

Test.—Before this test can be carried out, it is necessary to lay out a perfectly straight line and place a mark on a line at right angles to it as follows :—

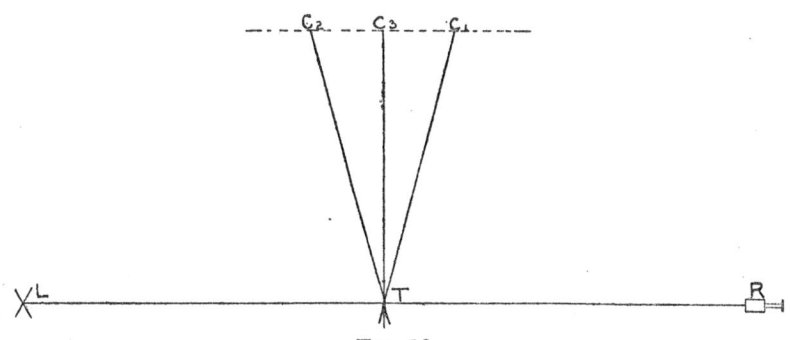

Fig. 18.

Plant a tripod firmly at T (Fig. 18). Select a distant point L as far off as possible. Take a telescope mounted on its stand at least 200 or 300 yards from T, and plant it at R, so that when T and L are seen through it, they are exactly in line with one another. It must be arranged that the points R, T, L, are all in a straight *line*; and L and T must be in the focus of the telescope at the same time.

Set the range to infinity and the slider to 125 yards, fix the telescope in the left socket, and the left spring clip of the telemeter to the tripod T. Observe L by reflection and make a point C_1 (T C_1 being approximately at right angles to L T R) coincide with it by means of the compensating screw.

Remove the telemeter from the stand and refix it by means of the right spring clip. Insert the telescope in the right socket. Observe R (centre of object glass) by reflection, and see if C_1 is in coincidence with it. If it is, L T C_1 and R T C_1 are right angles. If it is not, mark a point C_2, which is seen in coincidence with R. Place a mark C_3 midway between C_1 and C_2, L T C_3 and R T C_3 should then be right angles. Repeat the operation to make certain that L and C_3 (and R and C_3) make *exact* coincidences. If possible C_1, C_2 and C_3 should be chalk marks on the side of the building at least 300 yards away; but if no building is available pickets may be used as marks. If in the above L and C_3, seen through the telescope in the left socket, are in exact coincidence, the reader of the "percentage of error" scale should read 0.

Adjustment.—Bend or file the reader until it is opposite 0. This adjustment should very rarely be necessary.

(3) *The angles made by the direct and reflected lines of sight from the left and right sockets must together be equal to two right angles.*

Test.—Place the left spring clip of the telemeter on the stand at T and the telescope in the left socket. Set range drum at infinity and slider at 125 yards. By means of the compensating screw make L coincide with a point C_1, C_2 or C_3 (Fig. 18) approximately at right angles to L R T. Place the right spring clip of the telemeter on the stand and the telescope in the right socket. R should then be seen in coincidence with the same point C_1, C_2 or C_3.

Adjustment.—Insert the long key in the hole between the telescope sockets until it engages the head of the adjusting screw of the right index mirror (X^1, Plate XXXVII). Turn it until the two points coincide, the last movement being clockwise. Check.

(4) *The base bar and steel arm must be parallel throughout their entire lengths.*

Test.—Set drum to infinity, and by means of the compensating screw make an exact coincidence between two well defined objects approximately at right angles to one another. Moving the slider along the bar should not upset the coincidence. The telescope may be in either socket.

Adjustment.—This can only be carried out by an expert. If the test is not correct see footnote on p. 114.

(5) *The metallic cord must be exactly five yards long.*

Test.—Measure it by means of the steel tape. For the points from which the measurements should be made see p. 106.

Adjustment.—Retie the knot near the shuttle in the correct position.

CHAPTER VII.

ONE-MAN RANGE-FINDERS.*

As the name implies, a one-man range-finder is one in which a single observation alone is required for determining the range of an object, and in this respect it differs essentially from a range-finder of the double observer type, such as the service Mekometer or Telemeter, in which two observations from the ends of the base are necessary.

In both types of instruments the range is obtained virtually by the measurement of the parallax of the object, that is, of the angle subtended at the object by the base of the instrument.

This base, in the case of one-man range-finders, is very short, and other things being equal, the accuracy obtainable is directly proportional to the base length, and also to the magnifying power of the telescope employed.

The chief advantages of the one-man type of range-finder as compared with the Mekometer and Telemeter are :—

(1) Only one observer is required.

(2) Its rapidity and handiness in use.

(3) Ranges of moving objects can be taken continuously.

(4) The facility with which it can be tested and adjusted in the field.

And the chief disadvantages :—

(1) Increased size and weight.

(2) Delicacy.

(3) Liability to be affected by mirage.

All service one-man range-finders are, at present, built on the "coincidence" system, in which the field of view is divided into two parts by a fine dividing line, and the range of the object is determined by bringing the image of the object on one side of the dividing line into exact coincidence with the corresponding image on the other side of the dividing line.

The range-finder consists, in fact, of two telescopes mounted in a common frame, and having a common eyepiece in the middle of the frame, the objectives being situated near the ends of the frame, and suitable reflectors being provided to reflect the rays of light from the two ends into the eyepiece.

The range-finder itself forms the base of a triangle, having at its vertex the object, the range of which is determined by measuring the parallax.

---

* For Test for Range Takers see Appendix B, p. 182.

Fig. 1 is a typical diagram of the telescope arrangements of the range-finder.

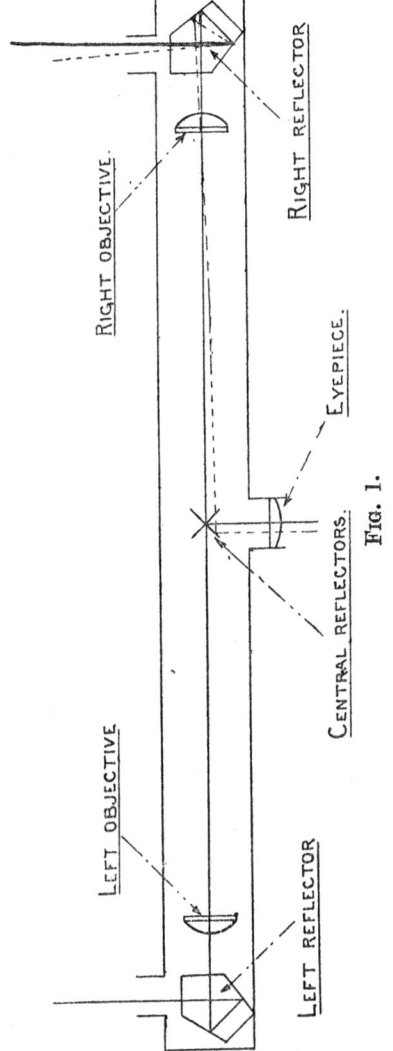

Fig. 1.

Two beams of light from the distant object are received by the reflectors at the ends of the base and are transmitted through two objectives towards the centre of the range-finder, where another pair of reflectors reflect the beams outwards through the eyepiece. Each objective forms an image of the distant object in the focal plane of the eyepiece, and the observer therefore sees in the field of view two images of the object, separated by the dividing line. The image seen in the upper part of the field of view is formed by (say) the left-hand telescope portion of the instrument, and that in the lower part by the right-hand telescope.

In coincidence range-finders various arrangements of the field of view have been adopted. For field range-finders the most common are :—

(1) The erect image system.
(2) The inverted image system.
(3) The inset image system.

(1) The erect image system.—

In this system the field of view is divided in half by a horizontal dividing line, the two halves of the field of view forming one continuous picture, and natural objects are seen erect. To measure the range, the instrument is directed in such a way that the dividing line cuts across the object at right angles, and the working head of the instrument is then turned until the part of the image above the dividing line coincides with the part below it, *i.e.*, until the edges of the object appear continuous and without any break at the dividing line. The range is then read off on the range scale. (See Figs. 2 and 3.)

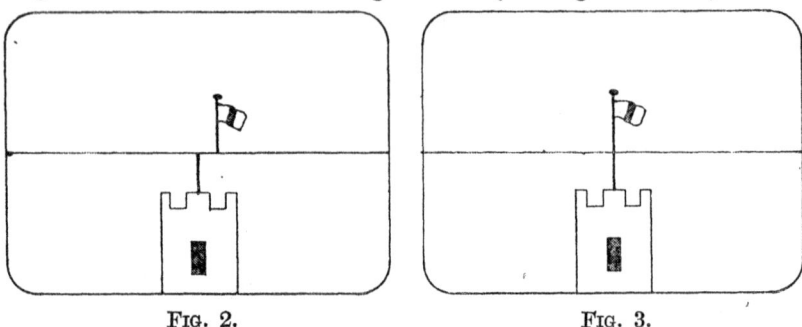

FIG. 2.   FIG. 3.

(2) The inverted image system.—

In this system the field of view is divided in half by the dividing line, but the upper half of the field is inverted.

To measure the range the instrument is directed in such a way that the dividing line is at right angles to the vertical edges of the object, and the tops of the two images of the object are just touching the dividing line; the working head of the instrument is then turned until one image is vertically above the other, *i.e.*, until the edges of the object coincide on the dividing line, and the range is read off on the range scale. (See Figs. 4 and 5.)

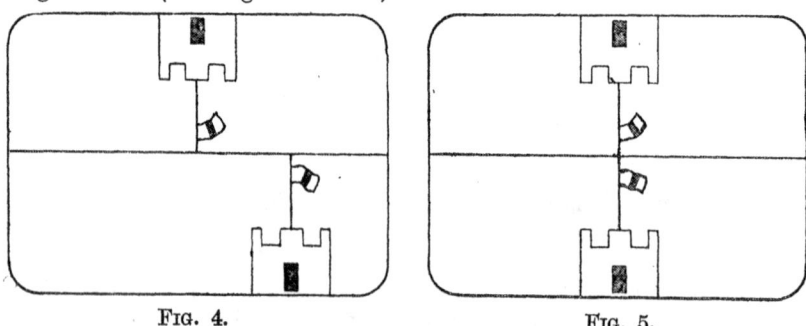

FIG. 4.   FIG. 5.

This system makes it easier to get accurate coincidence on objects of small size or irregular outline, such as bushes, stones, tufts of grass, &c. On the other hand it makes it rather more difficult to pick up the object in the first place, and to keep it under observation in windy weather, when it is difficult to hold the range-finder quite steady.

In order to get over the first of these disadvantages the inset image system has been adopted.

(3) The inset image system.—

In this system the image from one end of the instrument is confined within a small rectangle inserted in the middle of the field of view from the other end. (See Figs. 6 and 7.)

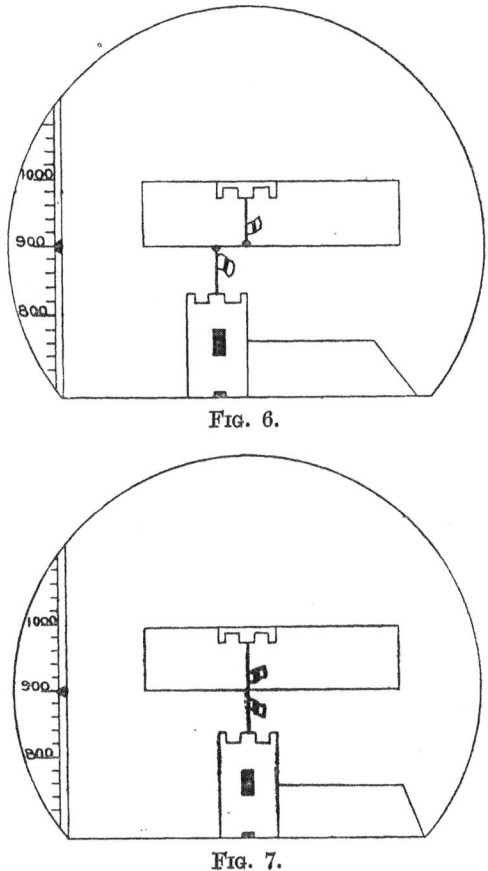

Fig. 6.

Fig. 7.

The lower edge of the rectangle forms the dividing line.

The inset image may be either erect or inverted.

This system combines some of the advantages both of the erect and inverted image systems, in that it gives a large field of view and so facilitates picking up the object whose range is required, and makes it possible to keep under observation a certain amount of ground beyond the object.

Reverting to Fig. 1.—

Suppose a distant object is viewed by rays indicated by the continuous lines, and that the two images are seen in correct coincidence or alignment (as in Figs. 3, 5 and 7). If, now, the object approaches the left end of the instrument, the beam of light received by the reflector at the right end will have a new direction, such as is shown by the dotted line, and the two images will no longer appear in correct coincidence, but will occupy such relative positions as are shown in Figs. 2 and 6.

(B 10585) I

The interval between the two images might serve as a measure of the distance of the object, since the nearer the object comes, the greater will the interval be; but the measurement of this interval would be too difficult to make accurately and would take too long. Optical or mechanical devices are therefore provided for altering the course of one of the beams of light within the instrument, so as to bring the two images into correct coincidence, and a scale is provided to show the range of the object, this range scale being moved by the gear which brings the two images into coincidence.

Two of the optical devices referred to will be explained :—

    (1) The travelling deflecting prism, as used in the Barr & Stroud range-finder.

    (2) The double rotating prisms, as used in the Zeiss range-finder.

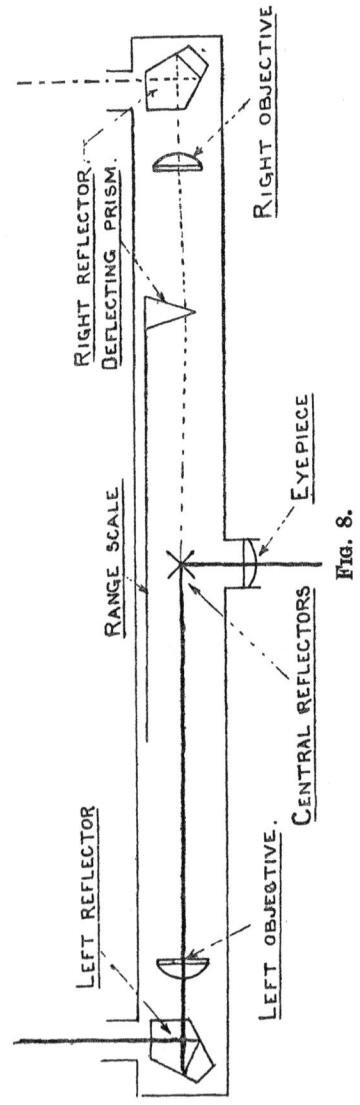

Fig. 8.

(1) Fig. 8 shows the general arrangement of the Barr & Stroud range-finder.

The end reflectors are pentagonal prisms, which have the property, within certain limits, of bending a ray of light through a constant angle. Any ray of light falling on the pentagonal prism through the end window is twice reflected inside the prism and comes out at right angles to its original direction. (See Appendix A.)

The deflecting prism, and range scale attached to it, are mounted between guides (not shown in the diagram) and can be moved along the range-finder by means of a milled head on the outside of the body of the range-finder.

When the range-finder is turned so that the object is seen in the centre of the inverted field, the rays of light from the distant object enter the left window as shown by the continuous line, are reflected at right angles by the left reflector, pass through the left objective and are reflected outwards through the eyepiece by the central reflector.

The rays from the same object enter the right window as shown by the dotted line, are reflected at right angles by the right reflector, pass through the right objective and the deflecting prism, which bends them as shown in the figure, and are reflected outwards through the eyepiece by the central reflector.

When the deflecting prism is in such a position that the rays of light from the right-hand reflector strike the central reflectors at the same point as the rays from the left-hand reflector, the two images are seen in coincidence (*i.e.*, one vertically above the other) and the range scale indicates the correct range of the object.

The action of the deflecting prism will be readily understood by referring to Figs. 9, 9A, 10, 10A, 11 and 11A.

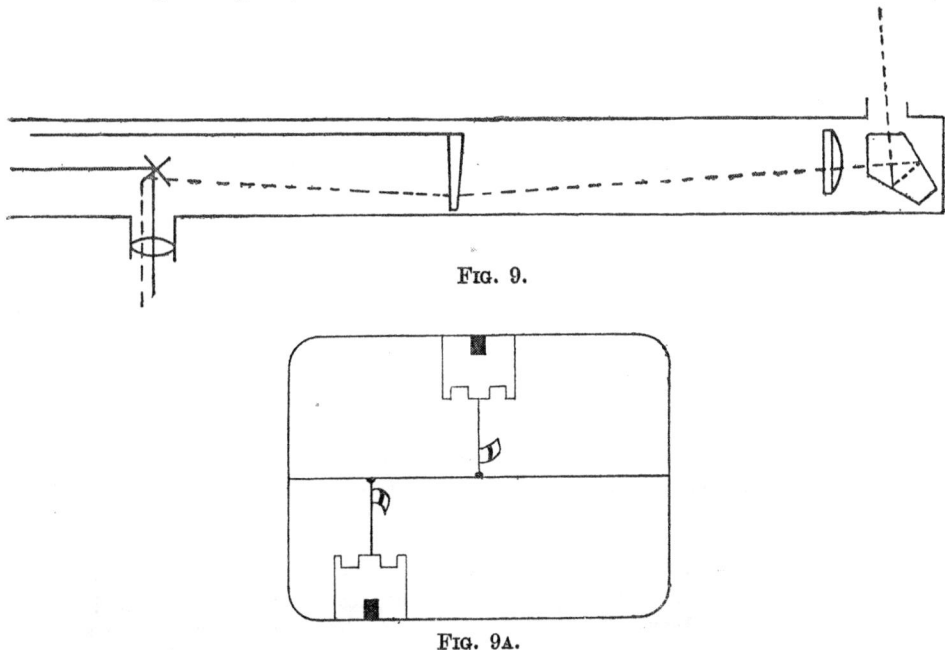

FIG. 9.

FIG. 9A.

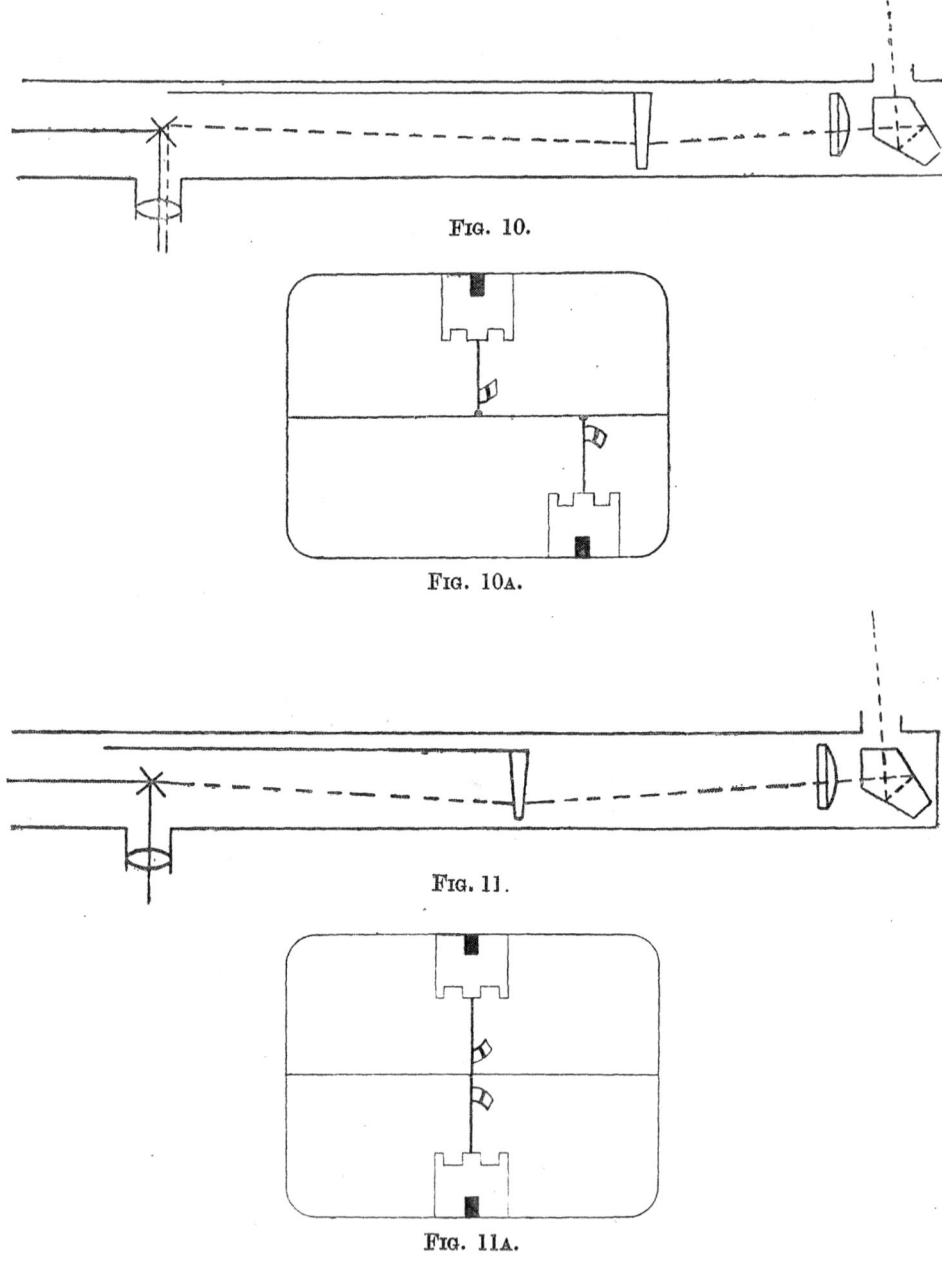

Fig. 10.

Fig. 10a.

Fig. 11.

Fig. 11a.

In Fig. 9 the deflecting prism is too much to the left, and the erect image is seen to the left of the inverted image (Fig. 9a) and the range shown on the range scale is too long.

NOTE.—Figs. 8 to 11 are typical diagrams only. In the range-finder the actual course of the rays of light is more complicated, and it would not be possible to show them clearly in a diagram of this kind. The diagrams, however, explain the action of the deflecting prism.

In Fig. 10 the deflecting prism is too much to the right, and the erect image is seen to the right of the inverted image (Fig. 10A) and the range shown on the range scale is too short.

In Fig. 11 the deflecting prism is in the correct position, and the two images are seen in coincidence (Fig. 11A) and the range scale shows the correct range.

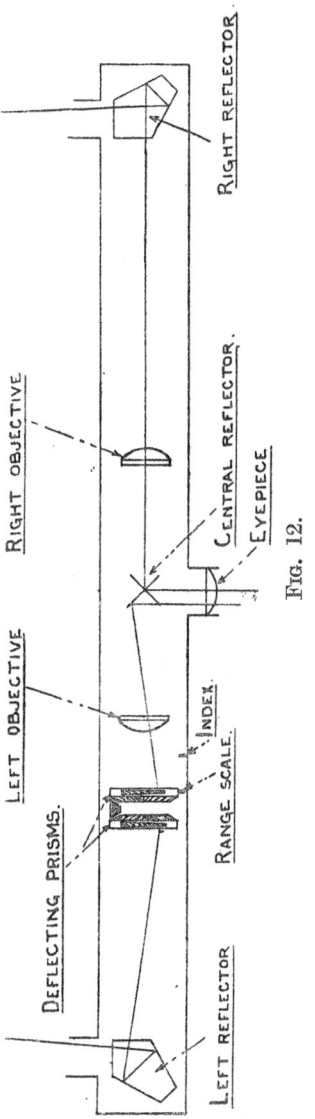

Fig. 12.

Fig. 12 shows the general arrangement of the Zeiss range-finder.

The end reflectors are pentagonal prisms, as in the Barr & Stroud instrument, and the instrument has two objectives, central reflectors and an eyepiece, generally similar to those of the Barr & Stroud instrument, but differing in details of design and arrangement. The deflecting prisms and range scale are, however, of an entirely different design, as shown in Fig. 13.

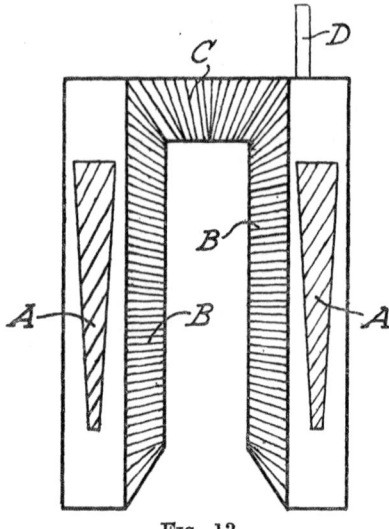

Fig. 13.

Two wedge-shaped prisms (A, A) are mounted in brass mounts which have bevel teeth (B, B) cut on their circumference, and the two prism mounts are geared together by means of a bevel pinion (C). The bevel pinion is connected to the working head of the instrument. When the working head is revolved by the observer, the bevel pinion is turned round, and causes the wedge-shaped prisms to revolve in opposite directions.

The range scale (D) is attached to one of the deflecting prism mounts, and the index is fixed to the body of the range-finder. The deflecting action of the wedge-shaped prisms is shown in Figs. 14 and 14A.

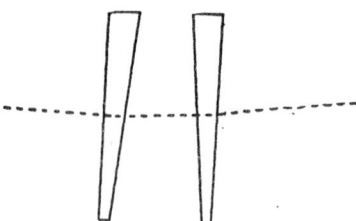

Fig. 14.

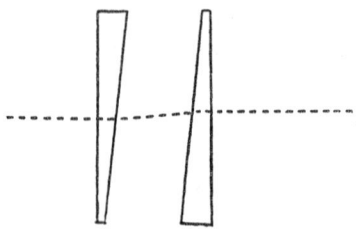

Fig. 14A.

When the two prisms are placed so that their thick ends are opposite one another, a ray of light falling on them will be twice deflected in the same direction, as shown in Fig. 14. In this position the deflecting prisms cause their maximum deflecting effect. When the thick end of one prism is opposite the thin end of the other prism (Fig. 14A) the ray of light is twice deflected, but in opposite directions, and consequently passes out in a direction parallel to its original course. In this position the deflecting prisms cause their minimum deflecting effect.

In intermediate positions the deflection of the ray of light is intermediate between the extremes.

It will be seen from Fig. 13 that a quarter of a revolution of the prism mounts will suffice to change from the maximum to the minimum deflection, and a further quarter revolution produces the maximum deflection in the opposite direction, and as the range scale is attached to one of the prism mounts and the index is fixed to the body of the instrument, it follows that the total length of the range scale must be not greater than half of the circumference of the prism mount. This involves such a small scale, with the graduations so close together, that it would be difficult to read them accurately with the naked eye. A telescope is therefore provided inside the instrument, arranged in such a way that the scale can be seen through the eyepiece at the same time as the object whose range is being taken.*

Fig. 15 shows the appearance of the field of view, the range scale and index being seen at the left edge.

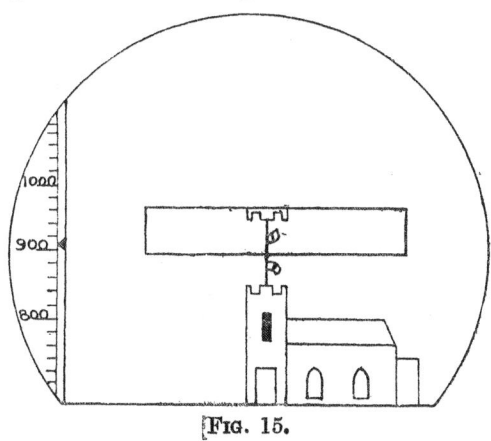

FIG. 15.

RANGE TAKING.

With the coincidence type of range-finder the range is measured by moving the working head until a correct coincidence is obtained. In instruments of the erect image type, by " making coincidence "

---

* In later patterns of Zeiss Range-finders (1912), the range scale is not directly attached to one of the prism mounts, but is placed on a separate revolving mount geared to the prism mount in such a way that the scale moves through (approximately) a complete revolution while the prism moves through a half revolution. In this way a longer or more open scale is obtained.

is meant bringing the two halves of the image together until they form a complete and continuous image, without any lateral displacement of the part above the dividing line from that below it.

Fig. 2 shows the appearance of a flagstaff when the two halves of the image are not in coincidence, and the range scale is not indicating the correct range.

Fig. 3 shows the appearance of the flagstaff when coincidence has been obtained, and the range scale is reading the correct range. The very smallest lateral displacement of the two halves of the image may mean a considerable error of range, and it is therefore essential to hold the instrument perfectly steady and to make coincidence with the greatest care, and to be satisfied with nothing but the best possible coincidence.

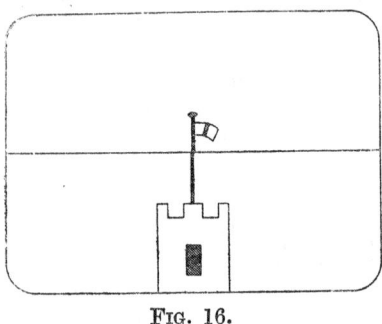

Fig. 16.

Fig. 16 shows a bad coincidence, the upper part of the flagstaff is perceptibly to the right of the lower part.

In instruments of the inverted image type "making coincidence" means bringing the two images into alignment in such a way that when the dividing line cuts the edge of the image at right angles there is no lateral displacement between the corresponding edges of the two images above and below the dividing line.

Fig. 4 shows the appearance of a flagstaff before coincidence has been obtained.

Fig. 5 shows a correct coincidence.

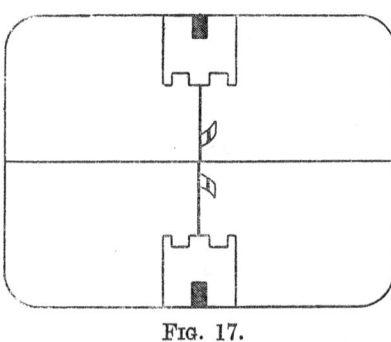

Fig. 17.

Fig. 17 shows a bad coincidence, the upper image being perceptibly to the right of the lower image.

The easiest objects to make coincidence upon are flagstaffs, telegraph poles, chimneys, &c., and these should be selected for taking ranges to during preliminary instruction and when testing the instruments as laid down on page 140.

Coincidence can be made on almost any objects which can be clearly seen, such as bushes, trees, tufts of grass, stones, men, &c.

The points to which particular attention should be paid are :—

(1) Focus the eyepiece correctly.

(2) Always use a stand or other support for the instrument; it is important that the range-finder should be perfectly steady when coincidence is being made.

(3) Always make coincidence in the centre of the field of view, and with the dividing line at right angles to the part of the object which is being observed.

(4) Take three observations, and give the mean range. If one observation differs much from the other two, discard it, and take another.

If the object which is being observed is not vertical, the range-finder must be tilted to one side or the other until the dividing line is at right angles to the edge which is being observed.

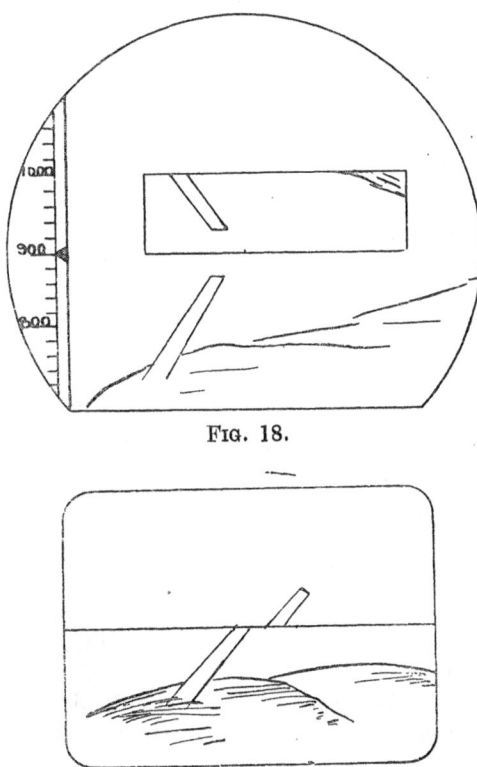

Fig. 18.

Fig. 18a.

Figs. 18 and 18a show the appearance of a sloping post in the field of view when the instrument is held horizontal.

Before attempting to get coincidence on such an object, the range-finder must be tilted until the dividing line appears as in Figs. 19 and 19A.

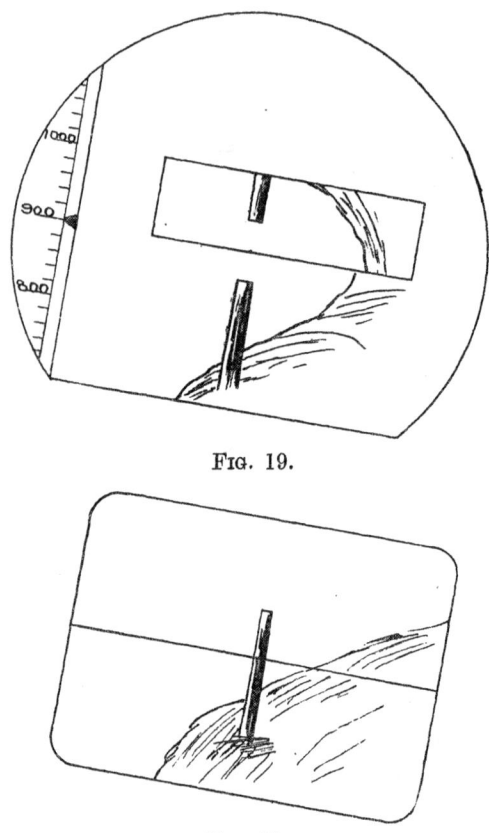

Fig. 19.

Fig. 19A.

The reason for this is that if the "halving" adjustment is not correct, a coincidence made with the dividing line at an angle to the post would not give the correct range; but if the instrument is tilted so as to bring the dividing line at right angles to the post, a small error in the halving adjustment will not seriously affect the range recorded. This point is more fully explained on page 141. When taking the range of a horizontal object, a sky line, or shelter trench, the instrument should be held vertically.

Under favourable conditions of light and weather accurate coincidence can be made by simply bringing the two images into alignment, as already explained; but on hot days, when the heated air can be seen "trembling," so to speak, it is very difficult to make accurate coincidence, as the images appear to be continually shaking and moving from side to side.

Under these conditions coincidence must be made very deliberately, the images being brought into coincidence and then watched for some moments. If the upper image moves first to one side and then to the other side of the lower and moves by about the same amount to either side, the coincidence is correct; but if the upper image moves only to one side, or moves more to one side than the other, the coincidence is not correct, and the working head must be moved.

The following method of working, known as the "above and below" method, is a very good one for observing a stationary object, and should be used when time permits.

Having brought the two images into the centre of the field and into coincidence, move the working head until the upper image is not in exact coincidence but just perceptibly to the right of the lower image, and note the reading of the scale. Then move the working head until the upper image is the same amount to the left of the lower image, and again note the reading of the scale. The mean, or average, of these two readings will be the true range of the object.

After a little practice it will be found possible and desirable to move the working head backwards and forwards between the two positions which give equal displacement to the right and left, and then to bring it midway between these two positions. The scale will then show the correct range of the object, and the necessity for noting the two readings and taking their mean is thus avoided.

The great accuracy obtainable by this method may be explained as follows.

Suppose that the range of the object is exactly 1,000 yards. At that range a movement of the scale of 6 yards does not produce a want of alignment which can be readily detected. Consequently when trying to get exact coincidence the observer may get readings varying from 994 to 1,006 yards. A movement of the scale of 10 yards will, however, produce a want of alignment which can be distinctly seen. If, then, the observer sets the scale to 990, he will see the images perceptibly out of alignment in one direction, and if he sets the scale to, say, 1,014, he will see them out of alignment in the other direction by about the same amount. The average of these two readings gives the range as 1,002 yards. Now, if he sets the scale first to 990 and then to 1,020, the second setting would put the images twice as much out of alignment as the first, and this difference would be very distinctly visible. Even then, however, the mean range would be 1,005, and as the observer can easily see the difference between a want of alignment which is just perceptible, and one that is double that amount, he would correct the second setting, and consequently is able, by this method, to get very accurate results.

Range Taking on Moving Targets.

The range of a moving object can be taken by bringing the two images into coincidence in the normal way and the coincidence can be checked by using the astigmatiser; but if the object is moving at all rapidly the "above and below" method cannot be used.

The range may also be obtained by taking the range of some point on the road or ground in front of the object and watching until the object comes up to that point. This method would usually be adopted when it is intended to open fire on the moving object, as it gives time for setting the sights, &c.

The Use of the Astigmatiser.

Some instruments are provided with astigmatisers which can be brought into use when required, but which are not normally in use. The astigmatisers are primarily intended for use when taking the ranges of lights or objects glinting in the sun, or illuminated by searchlights, but they are also useful for observing and checking coincidences obtained on ill-defined objects, such as stones or bushes.

When such objects are astigmatised they appear in the field of view as vertical streaks of light, or as a collection of dark and light vertical streaks, the corresponding portions of which, above and below the dividing line, can easily be recognised and brought into coincidence.

In instruments of the Barr & Stroud pattern, the astigmatisers are brought into use by pushing forward a small lever which is attached to the left handle of the instrument.

The object whose range is to be taken should be found and brought into the centre of the field, and a rough coincidence made with the astigmatiser not in use. The astigmatiser lever is then pushed forward and the coincidence completed.

The eyepiece of some of the earlier pattern range finders must be re-focussed when using the astigmatisers. The astigmatisers should not be used unless the light on the object is good, or the object itself is luminous.

The present patterns of Zeiss Range-finders are not provided with astigmatisers.

Hints to Range Takers.

(1) Always focus the eyepiece carefully.

(2) Always use the stand or some support for the instrument, if possible.

(3) Always make coincidence in the centre of the field of view, and with the dividing line at right angles to the object observed.

(4) Check the coincidence by using the astigmatiser.

(5) Always take three observations, and give the mean range; if one of these observations differs much from the other two, discard it and take another observation.

(6) Correct any halving error as soon as possible.

(7) It is often a help to close the left eye for a moment when making coincidence.

(8) Use the dermatine rayshades when the light is bright, when looking towards the sun, or when it is raining.

(9) Never leave the adjusting heads exposed.

(10) Keep under cover as much as possible.

(11) Handle the instrument with care.

Adjustments.

In the preceding pages it has been assumed, when the two images of an object are brought into coincidence in the field of view, that:—

(a) The "halving" is correct;

(b) The range indicated by the scale represents the true distance of the object;

but the instrument may get out of adjustment in either or both of these respects, and two adjustments are therefore provided, viz. :—

  (1) The halving adjustment.
  (2) The coincidence adjustment.

(1) THE HALVING ADJUSTMENT.

In instruments of the "erect image" type the halving is correct when the image of an object seen in the range-finder is complete and continuous and the dividing line cuts across it. The halving is incorrect if any part of the image is seen both above and below the dividing line, or if any part of the image is missing and not seen either above or below the dividing line. In the former case a part of the image is duplicated; in the latter a part of the image is deficient. (See Figs. 20, 21 and 22.)

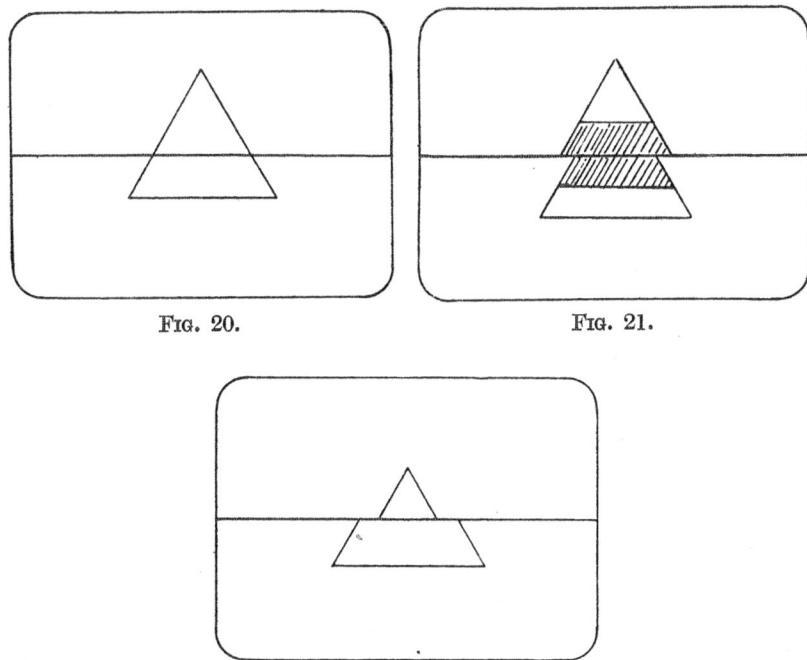

FIG. 20.   FIG. 21.

FIG. 22.

In Fig. 20 the halving is correct, and a complete image of the triangle is seen, with the dividing line cutting across it.

In Fig. 21 a part of the image is seen both above and below the dividing line, the part which is "duplicated" being shown shaded.

In Fig. 22 a part of the image is "deficient."

In instruments of the "inverted image" system the halving is correct when the two images of any object are the same distance above and below the dividing line respectively, so that if the range-finder is gradually depressed so as to make the two images approach the dividing line, they will touch it simultaneously.

The halving is incorrect if one image is touching the dividing line and the other is either above or below it. (See Figs. 23, 24 and 25.)

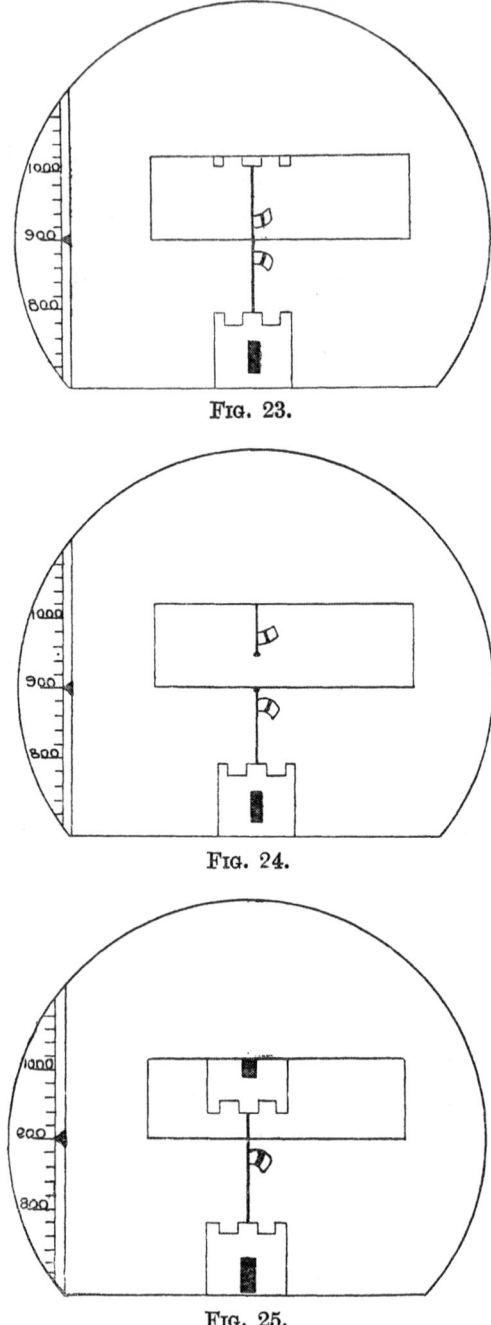

Fig. 23.

Fig. 24.

Fig. 25.

In Fig. 23 the halving is correct, and the top of the flagstaff in both images is just touching the dividing line.

In Figs. 24 and 25 the halving is incorrect.

In either system the halving errors are the result of a movement of the images in a vertical direction, *i.e.*, at right angles to the dividing line.

TO ADJUST THE HALVING.

Mount the range-finder on its stand or on a steady support, and direct it on some well-defined object. It is best to choose an object some distance away (say 2,000 yards or over) provided it can be clearly seen. Make an accurate coincidence, uncover the halving adjusting head and turn it as may be necessary until the halving is correct. Then cover the adjusting head.

For instruments of the inverted image type any object whose top is clearly defined may be used for the halving adjustment, but for instruments of the erect image type it is necessary to choose some object having sloping sides, such as the gable end of a house, a church spire or a bell tent, or some oval or circular object, such as the full moon, &c. If no suitable natural object is available, two aiming posts stuck in the ground and leaning towards one another so as to form an equilateral triangle can be used. They should be some 500 yards from the instrument.

(2) THE COINCIDENCE ADJUSTMENT.

When the coincidence adjustment is correct the range scale should show the correct range of any object on which an accurate coincidence has been made.

If it does not do so, then the coincidence adjustment is incorrect and must be put right.

The range-finder is so constructed that the coincidence adjustment, once set, is not likely to go wrong in the course of ordinary service. It is nevertheless advisable to test the setting before using the range-finder. Any alteration of the coincidence adjustment should only be undertaken very deliberately and carefully, and as far as possible when the conditions of weather and light are favourable.

The instrument may be tested and adjusted by either of the three following methods :—

(1) Adjustment on a known range.
(2) Adjustment on an infinitely distant object, such as the moon or a star.
(3) Adjustment on an artificial infinity, such as the adjusting lath.

Before testing or adjusting the coincidence adjustment the halving must be accurately adjusted.

(1) ADJUSTMENT ON A KNOWN RANGE.

If the range of a suitable object, such as a flagstaff or tower, at a range of at least 3,000 yards* is *accurately* known, proceed as follows.

---

* The more distant the object, the more accurately can the adjustment be made.

Test.—Set the instrument up on its stand, and take a series of 10 observations on the distant object, writing down the range obtained each time. Work out the mean of these 10 readings.

If the mean is within ·75 per cent. per thousand yards of the true range the adjustment is correct.

For example: suppose the true range of the object observed is 4,760 yards. This is roughly 4·8 thousands. The error allowed therefore is $4·8 \times ·75$ per cent. of the range, or $4·8 \times ·75 \times 48$ yards, *i.e.*, 172 yards—say 170 yards.

If, therefore, the mean of the 10 readings is between 4,590 and 4,930, the adjustment is correct.

If it is not, set the correct range on the range scale, examine the coincidence, and note to which side the upper image is displaced from the lower.

Uncover the coincidence adjustment head, and turn it until the coincidence is correct.

Check by taking a second series of 10 readings on the object, and work out the mean as before. If the mean range is not within the percentage given above, the adjustment must be repeated.

When correct, cover up the adjusting head. When the instrument reads correctly on any one range, it will read correctly at all other ranges which are shorter.

(2) Adjustment on an Infinitely Distant Point.

An infinity point, marked with a star, is engraved on the range scale. When coincidence is made on an infinitely distant object, such as the moon or a star, this mark should come opposite the reader.

On either side of the infinity mark there are equally spaced graduations which are used when taking readings on an infinitely distant object.

The adjustment is tested by taking a series of observations on the object and noting the reading of the scale each time; the divisions beyond the infinity mark being reckoned as + and those below it as —.

If the mean of the observations is 0, the adjustment is correct; but if the mean is more than $\pm$ ·3 the adjustment should be corrected.

The following is an example of the method. Supposing observations are taken of the edge of the moon, and the readings are:—

$$+ 2·0$$
$$+ 2·5$$
$$+ 3·2$$
$$+ 2·8$$
$$+ 2·2$$
$$+ 3·2$$
$$+ 2·8$$
$$+ 2·5$$
$$+ 3·0$$
$$+ 3·2$$

Total + 27·4

Mean + 2·74

This shows that the scale is reading too high.

Set the infinity mark opposite the reader and examine the coincidence; the error of alignment will be clearly visible. Correct it by means of the coincidence adjusting head.

Then take a fresh series of observations; suppose they are as follows :—

$$\begin{aligned}
&+ 1\cdot 0 \\
&+ 0\cdot 8 \\
&- 0\cdot 2 \\
&- 0\cdot 5 \\
&0\cdot 0 \\
&+ 0\cdot 2 \\
&+ 0\cdot 5 \\
&- 0\cdot 2 \\
&+ 0\cdot 2 \\
&+ 0\cdot 5 \\
\hline
&\text{Total } + 2\cdot 3 \\
\hline
&\text{Mean } + 0\cdot 23
\end{aligned}$$

This error is so small (corresponding to less than $2\frac{1}{2}$ yards at 1,000 yards) that the adjustment may be considered correct.

Note.—When observing on the moon the range-finder must be held so that the dividing line cuts the edge of the moon at right angles, and observations must of course be made on the bright, clearly defined edge. If observations are made on a star, it is best to select a star near the horizon (so that observations can be made with comfort), and to use the astigmatiser.

CAUTION.—It is absolutely forbidden to look through the range-finder at the sun, even with the aid of smoked or coloured glasses. If this is done the range-finder may be permanently damaged, and the observer's eyesight also.

The coloured glasses in the eyepiece of the Barr & Stroud range-finder are for use when taking ranges in very bright weather. Either the blue or the neutral-tinted glass may be used, as found most convenient. They are a great assistance to accurate observation when the light is very bright. The blue glass is sometimes of assistance when the atmosphere is hazy.

(3) ADJUSTMENT ON AN ARTIFICIAL INFINITY.

Referring to Fig. 26, in which A B represents the range-finder, and O_1, O_2, O_3 the target, it is clear that the further away the object is from the range-finder the larger does the angle A B O become. When the object is at an infinite distance, the angle A B O becomes a right angle, and the lines A O, B I are parallel, the distance between them being equal to the base A B of the range-finder. Hence, the rays of light from an infinitely distant object, which enter the two ends of the range-finder, are parallel; and if the two images are seen in coincidence in the range-finder, and the adjustment is correct, the scale should read infinity.

The converse of this is also true, namely, that if, when the scale is set to infinity, the lines of sight from the two ends of the instrument are parallel, then the adjustment is correct.

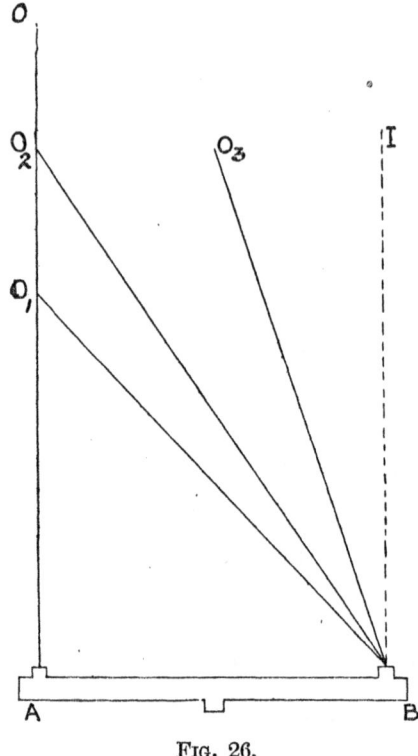

Fig. 26.

Consequently the adjustment of the instrument can be tested by seeing whether the lines of sight from the two ends are parallel when the scale is at infinity. This is done as follows:—

On the adjusting lath are painted two vertical lines, the distance between which, centre to centre, is exactly equal to the base of the range-finder. This base length is marked on the lath and is also engraved on the range-finder. The range-finder is set up on its stand, and the adjusting lath is placed on the "Stand, F.A. Telescope" which is set up about 150 to 250 yards away from the range-finder. By means of the open sights on the adjusting lath, the lath is laid on the centre of the range-finder, and the degree scale of the stand is clamped. The lath is then turned through 90° exactly. This places the lath parallel to the range-finder, and consequently the lines joining the lines on the lath to the windows of the range-finder are parallel to one another.

The observer then looks through the range-finder and sees the lath as in Fig. 27.

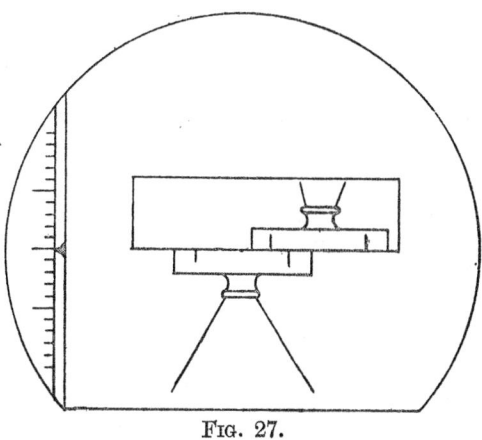

Fig. 27.

When the scale is set to infinity, the left-hand line on the adjusting lath in the upper field should be seen in exact coincidence with the right-hand line in the lower field. (See Fig. 28.)

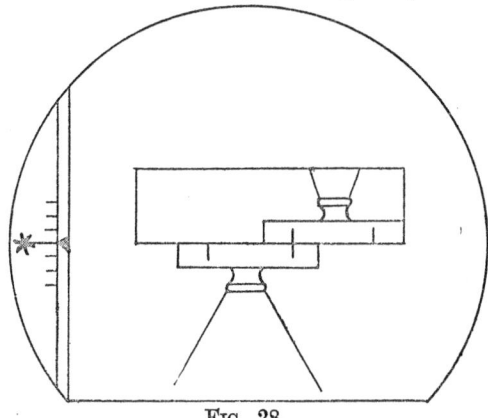

Fig. 28.

If it is not, the coincidence should be adjusted, and the procedure is as follows :—

    (1) Set up the range-finder on its stand, and adjust the halving (if necessary).
    (2) Take the lath some 200 yards away and set it up as described above.
    (3) Take a series of observations on the lath, writing down the result each time, and work out the mean of the readings.
    (4) If the mean is not between $+ \cdot 3$ and $- \cdot 3$ divisions, set the scale to infinity and correct the coincidence by turning the coincidence adjusting head.
    (5) Take another set of observations, and work out the mean. When the mean is between $+ \cdot 3$ and $- \cdot 3$ divisions, the adjustment is correct.
    (6) Cover the adjusting head.

Instructions for setting up and using the Zeiss pattern adjusting lath will be found on page 155.

The method of using the laths is the same, whether the range-finder is of the erect or inverted image type.

Results of Incorrect Halving.

Unless the halving adjustment is correct, it is difficult to make a really accurate coincidence, since any error of halving results in different parts of the object being cut by the dividing line.

Figs. 21 and 22 show the appearance of the images of a bell tent in a range-finder of the erect image type when the halving is not correct, and it is obvious that very different ranges would be given if coincidence were made on the right or left side of the tent; one would be too long, and the other too short. (Similar errors would of course be made if the range-finder were of the inverted image type.)

The correct range would be shown if one image overlaps the other by the same amount on each side; or, if the range-finder is tilted until the dividing line is at right angles to one edge of the tent, and coincidence is made, the correct range will be obtained, and the same range will be obtained if the range-finder is tilted in the opposite direction and coincidence made on the other side of the tent.

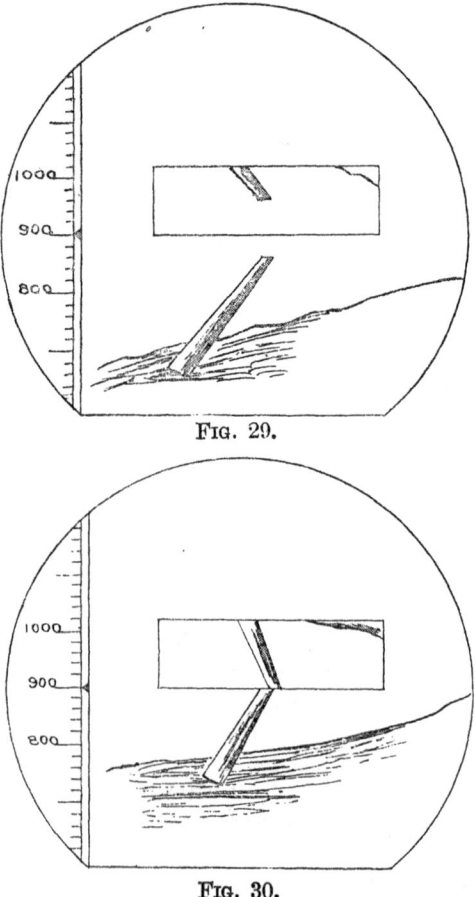

FIG. 29.

FIG. 30.

Again, Fig. 29 shows the images of a sloping post as they would be seen in a range-finder of the inverted image type if the range-finder were held horizontal and the halving were not correct; here, correct alignment has been obtained, and the range scale is showing the

[*To face page* 149.

PLATE XLI.

ZEISS ARTILLERY RANGE-FINDER (FRONT VIEW).

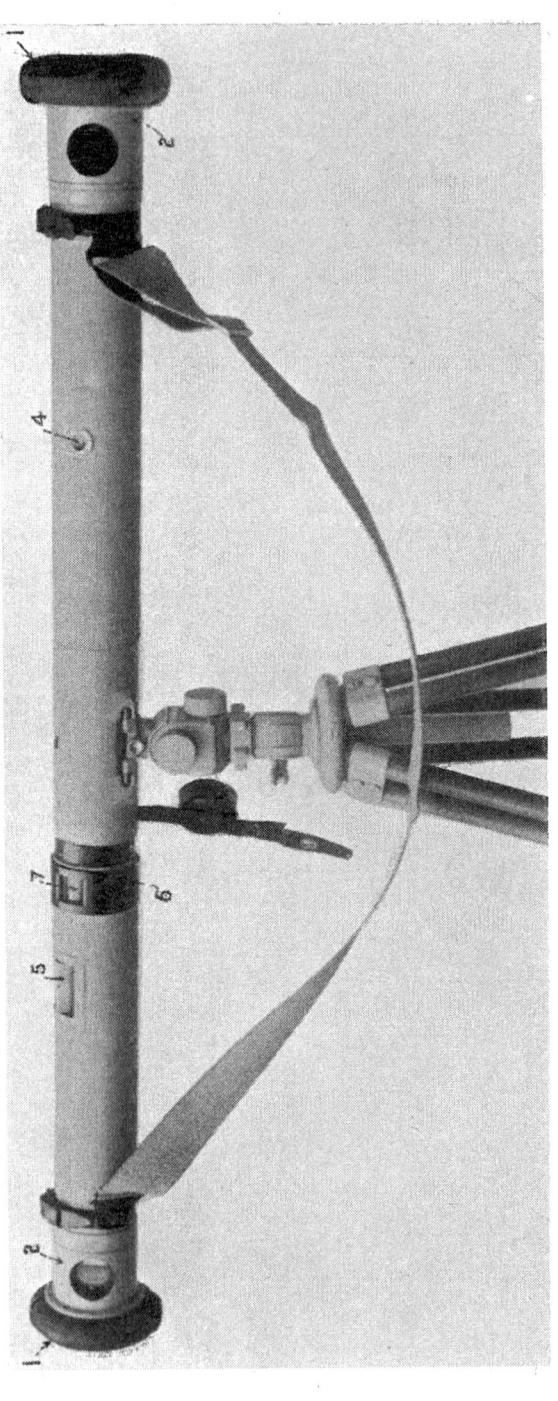

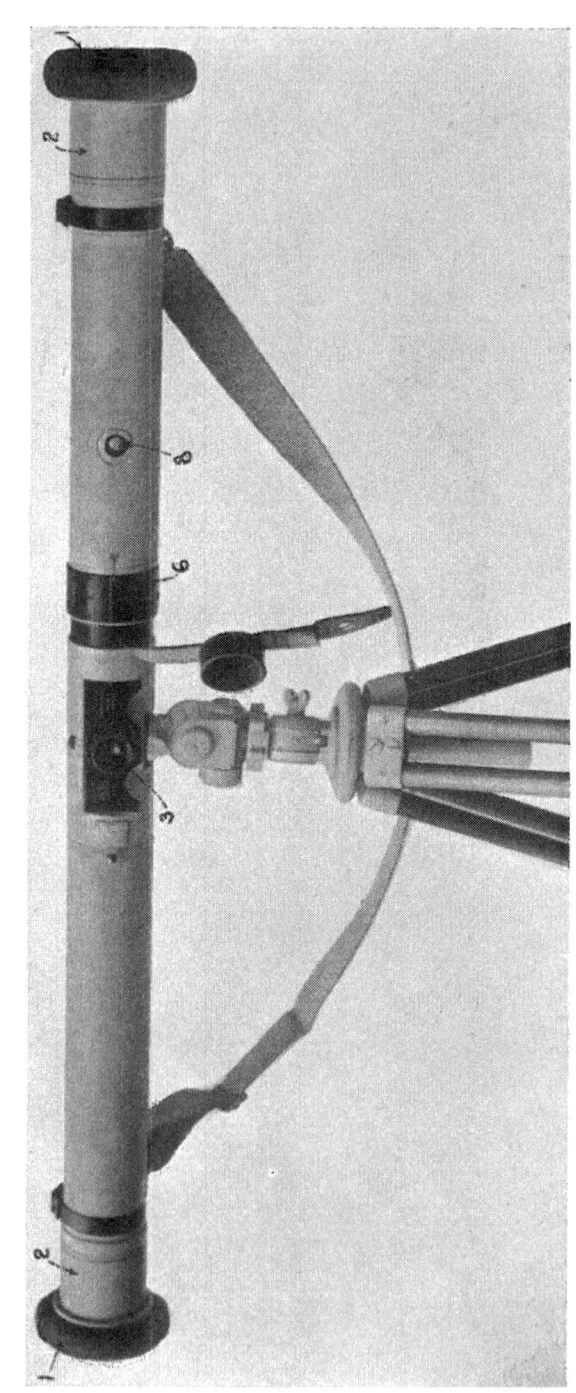

PLATE XL.

ZEISS ARTILLERY RANGE-FINDER (REAR VIEW).

correct range; but if the range-finder is depressed so as to bring the images together, they would appear as in Fig. 30, and would *seem* to be out of coincidence. If, however, the range-finder is tilted so that the dividing line is at right angles to either side of the post, the images would appear as in Fig. 31, and the coincidence would be seen to be correct.

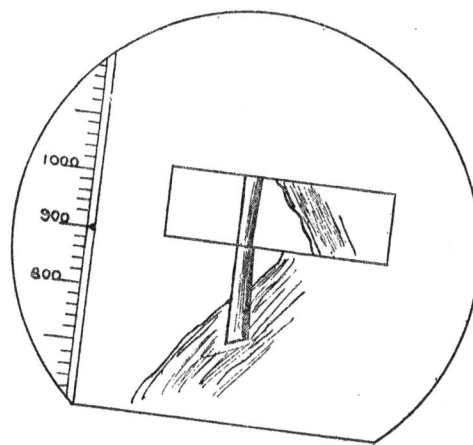

Fig. 31.

The *apparent* error of coincidence in Fig. 30 is due to the fact that, owing to the halving being incorrect, the dividing line is cutting different parts of the post in the two images.

The above cases show the importance of having the halving adjustment correct, and as the adjustment can be so easily and quickly carried out, the range-finder should never be used with the halving incorrect.

The Zeiss Pattern Range-Finder.

Plates XL and XLI show the Zeiss pattern range-finder on the Zeiss stand.

The instrument consists of a tube about 43 inches long. At either end is a leather covered pad (1) attached to a revolving end cap (2). The end cap has a circular aperture cut in it; by turning the cap this aperture can be brought opposite the window in front of the end prism.

The eyepiece (3) is placed at the centre of the tube. It is focussed by screwing it in or out. The eyepiece is provided with a diopter scale similar to those used on the eyepieces of prismatic binoculars.*
To the left of the eyepiece is a small window (4). This admits light for illuminating the range scale. When the window is covered up

---

* Every range-taker should know the setting of the eyepiece required to focus the telescope for his own sight, so that when he wants to use the instrument it is only necessary for him to turn the eyepiece till the correct division is opposite the index. To ascertain your diopter number, proceed as follows:—Set up the range-finder on a stand, lay the instrument on some clearly defined object, some 500 yards or more away, and screw the eyepiece in or out until the object is seen most distinctly. Note the reading of the diopter scale. Suppose it is $-1\frac{1}{2}$, that is your diopter number. Any telescope or binocular which is provided with a diopter scale can at any time be set to your focus by simply turning the scale till the division $-1\frac{1}{2}$ is opposite the index. The diopter number should be ascertained separately for each eye, in case of any inequality of vision. Thus you might find that your right eye is normal (diopter No. 0), and your left eye requires $+1$.

the range scale cannot be seen. When using the range-finder at night a light must be placed opposite the window to light up the scale. During preliminary instruction it is advisable for the instructor to cover up the window while the range-taker is making coincidence, and so make the scale invisible. This prevents the range-taker from being influenced by the readings on the scale when making several consecutive coincidences on the same object, and enables the instructor to see whether the range-taker is consistent.

To the right of the eyepiece on the upper part of the tube is a milled roller (5). This is the " working head," which actuates the deflecting prisms.

The " adjusting heads " are situated between the eyepiece and the working head, and are protected by a revolving ring (6) with a rectangular opening cut in it. Normally this ring is in the " closed " position, and both adjusting heads are covered. By turning the ring until the words " Rectification of altitude," or " Halving adjustment," are opposite the arrow on the body of the range-finder the rectangular opening is brought opposite the halving adjusting head (7).

A catch is provided which prevents the ring from being turned any further. This catch takes the form of a screw, the head of which is flush with the milled ring and has a wide slot cut in it. In order to uncover the coincidence adjusting head the screw catch must be turned through half a circle, as indicated by the arrow. The milled ring can then be turned round until the words " Rectification of stadia," or " Coincidence adjustment," are opposite the arrow on the body of the range-finder, when the rectangular opening will be opposite the coincidence adjusting head.

Except when adjustments are actually being carried out the milled ring should be in the " closed " position, and the catch locked. On the right of the ring covering the adjusting heads is a window (8) through which a scale and reader can be seen. This scale shows the setting of the coincidence adjustment, and is of assistance when adjusting the range-finder, as described on pages 144-145.

Two ray-shades (india-rubber tubes about $1\frac{1}{2}$ inches long) are provided with the instrument. They fit into the openings in front of the end windows, and are used to protect the end windows either from the sun or rain. When not in use they are carried in a pocket on the range-finder case.

The key (carried in the same pocket) is for the purpose of removing the end caps when they require cleaning or lubricating.

The following are the principal dimensions, &c., of the Zeiss range-finder :—

Length, $45\frac{1}{2}$ inches. Base length, 1 metre (39·3 ins.).
Diameter of body, 3 inches.
Maximum diameter (over end caps), $4\frac{1}{2}$ inches.
Weight, 12 lbs. 3 ozs.
Range scale graduated from 400 to 10,000 yards.
Magnification of telescope × 10.
Field of view, circle, 3° 50' ⎫
    „   inset rectangle, 2° by 30'* ⎬ approximately.

---

* For Mk. I Insts.
In the Mk. II Insts. the inset rectangle is 1° 30' by 30'.

[*To face page* 151.

PLATE XLII.

THE BARR & STROUD RANGE-FINDER (REAR VIEW).

[*To face page* 151.

PLATE XLIII.

The Barr & Stroud Range-Finder (Front View).

The Zeiss Range-finder is so constructed that it cannot be taken to pieces except by expert workmen provided with special tools and appliances. It is claimed for this instrument that it can be used for years without requiring to be taken to pieces, and that the internal optical parts are so protected that they cannot get dirty. The eye lens and the end windows should be cleaned with a clean chamois leather, and the metal parts wiped with a clean rag. The ray-shades and revolving end caps may occasionally be wiped over with a little vaseline on a rag to make them work easily. For this purpose the end caps can be removed by means of the forked key provided. Any external screws which work loose should be tightened up by the range-taker.

If the instrument sustains any serious damage, it should be returned to Woolwich for examination; no attempt should be made to dismantle or repair the instrument locally.

The Barr & Stroud Pattern Range-finder.*

Plates XLII and XLIII show the Barr & Stroud range-finder.

The instrument consists of a tube (1) about 36 inches long and 3 inches in diameter. The ends of the tube are formed of hollow castings, slightly larger in diameter than the tube, within which are the seatings for the pentagonal end prisms (3). A screwed cap (4) closes the ends of the tubes, a leather pad being attached to each cap to protect the instrument from blows.

Circular openings (5) are cut in the end castings and are fitted with glass windows. The windows can be closed by means of the revolving rings (6). Studs are provided on the revolving rings for the attachment of the ray-shades. Brass stops (2) are fitted to the end castings and act as guides for the revolving rings and also as stops to prevent the screwed caps (4) from becoming unscrewed. In the centre of the tube are two eyepieces (7 and 8). That on the right (7) is the eyepiece of the telescopes through which distant objects are seen: it is provided with a focussing lever (9). The left eyepiece (8) is for viewing the range scale. In front of the right eyepiece is a direct vision view finder (10). A detachable rubber face piece (11) surrounds the two eyepieces.

In front of the left eyepiece is the scale window (12). This window admits light to the range scale and allows a second observer to read the range scale if required. At night a light must be held in front of this window to make the range scale visible.

Two handles are provided: they are hinged so that they can be folded parallel to the body of the instrument when not in use. Close to the right handle is the working head (13), and attached to the left handle is the astigmatiser lever (14).

The two adjusting heads (for the "halving" and "coincidence" adjustments) are situated in the left end casting, and are protected by a revolving ring (32).

Normally this ring should be turned so as to cover up both the milled heads. When making adjustments turn the revolving ring so as to uncover the required adjusting head.

* The following remarks refer to the earlier pattern instruments. For details of the Mark II see page 158.

Surrounding the body of the instrument, close to the eyepieces, are two bands (15) which attach the instrument to the carrier (16). The carrier is fitted with a socket and catch by means of which it can be attached to the Stand Artillery Range-finder.

The inner frame of the range-finder which carries the objectives, deflecting prism and range scale, centre prisms and astigmatisers, is a steel tube of square section, and is shown in Plate XLIV. It is supported in the outer tube by two bearing rings (24). The objectives are not seen in the plate, but are situated within the inner frame, near its ends. The deflecting prism mount is seen at (25) and the range scale (which is attached to it) at (26).

The clutch which connects the working head to the deflecting prism rack is seen at (27), and the lever for actuating the astigmatisers at (28), and the centre prisms at (29). The screw (30) screws into a screwhole under the right handle, and serves to hold the inner frame in position, its point fitting into a recess (31) on the right bearing ring of the inner frame.

The following are the principal dimensions, &c., of the Barr & Stroud range-finder :—

Length, over all, $44\frac{1}{4}$ inches. Base length, 1 metre (39·3 ins.).
Diameter of body, 3 inches.
Maximum diameter (over end caps), $5\frac{1}{2}$ inches.
Weight, $13\frac{1}{2}$ lbs.
Range scale graduated from 500 to 20,000 yards.
Magnification of telescope × 13.
Field of view, horizontal, 3° 10'.
     ,,   vertical, 2° 40'.
Eyepieces inclined to the horizontal at 60°.

The Barr & Stroud instrument can be readily taken to pieces by a qualified artificer, and Plate XLIV shows the instrument in pieces.

To Dismantle the Instrument.

(1) Loosen and swing aside the stop (2) preventing the rotation of the right end cap.

(2) Unscrew and remove the right-hand end cap.

(3) Loosen the two set screws and slide outwards the plate retaining the end of the pentagonal flat spring.

(4) Loosen the plug locking screw and then unscrew the plug holding the spherical pivot of the pentagonal holder.

(5) Withdraw the pentagonal holder. When replacing the pentagonal holder care must be taken that the projecting arm (33) engages the inner recess in the tube.

(6) Disconnect and remove the working head (13) by loosening the two screws, and turn the cover plate through 90°, when it can be lifted out.

(7) Swing up the right handle, so as to expose the head of the screwed plug in the socket, and then remove the plug (30).

(8) Turn the instrument over, *i.e.*, handles downwards, and slightly incline the instrument downwards at the right-hand side, and allow the inner frame to slide out.

PLATE XLIV.

THE BARR AND STROUD RANGE-FINDER.

[*To face page* 152.

To re-assemble the parts, the above operations should be performed in the reverse order.

Great care must be exercised in taking the instrument to pieces and putting it together again. No force must be used. All the parts go together easily when correctly manipulated, and no force is necessary. If the parts do not slide into position easily that is due to their not being correctly brought together, and a little manipulation, turning or tilting the parts, will make them go together.

When withdrawing the inner frame it is advisable to remove the scale window (12) so that the finger can be inserted to start the inner frame. As the inner frame slides out hold your right hand over the right end of the tube to catch it. The frame holding the centre prisms (29) will catch in the frame of the right end window and the inner frame must be given a quarter of a turn (clock-wise) in order to clear it before the inner frame can be completely withdrawn.

When putting the inner frame back again, place the body of the range-finder on a table, handles down : insert the inner frame carefully turning it round as necessary to clear the end window frame ; when the centre prism frame is clear of the window frame turn the inner frame into its correct position (*i.e.*, with the slot (31) downwards) and push it in. As the inner frame is much shorter than the body tube it will be found convenient to make a small handle with which to manipulate the inner frame into position. The handle can be made of a piece of wood, one end being cut square to fit into the end of the inner frame. A stop must be provided to prevent the end of the handle from touching the object glass in the inner frame.

Push the inner frame in until the reader on the scale is opposite the scale window. Then turn the range-finder over, with the handles uppermost. The clutch (27) should be opposite the centre of the opening for the working head, and the recess (31) should be **exactly** opposite the centre of the hole in the handle for the screw plug (30). If not, the inner frame must be manipulated until it is in the correct position. If this is not done the inner frame may be bent, or the screw cross-threaded. The screw plug (30) should then be inserted and screwed home.

When replacing the pentagonal prism the plug holding the spherical pivot must be screwed up until there is no shake at all between the spherical pivot and its seating, but it must not be so tight as to bind the pivot.

Care must be taken that the arm (33) is correctly entered in the slot prepared for it in the end casting.

The instrument should only be taken to pieces indoors, and care must be taken to keep all the parts perfectly clean and dry.

Cleaning the Barr & Stroud Instrument.

The presence of dirt on the optical parts of the range-finder will be more or less evident in the field of view according as the parts affected are more or less nearly in the focus of the eyepiece.

Particles of dirt on the windows, or the pentagonal faces, or the objective will not be visible in the field of view, but will cause a general darkening of the whole field ; greasy smears or finger marks on these parts may, however, cause a very noticeable deterioration of the definition of the images.

The focal plane of the eyepiece is contained within the centre prism combination, and is therefore entirely protected from dirt.

Any dirt on the optical parts should be removed by using first a fine brush to remove any grit, and then a soft cloth of fine linen, or silk. Unless the parts are so dirty that the clearness of the images is affected, the instrument should not be dismantled.

The outer tube should be kept clean by rubbing frequently with the chamois leathers provided.

THE CASE, ARTILLERY RANGE-FINDER (ZEISS PATTERN).

This case is of cane and canvas, and is for carrying the range-finder on horseback.

The case is carried on the off side of the horse. The surcingle is passed through the steadying arm. The steadying strap (*i.e.*, the upper of the two straps) is passed round the rear arch and support of the saddle. The supporting strap is passed over the steadying strap and round the rear arch and support of the saddle.

The steadying girth is passed under the horse and connects the case to the case of the stand which is carried on the near side of the horse.

A leather case is issued for the Barr & Stroud range-finders. It is generally similar to the Zeiss case and is carried in the same way.

*THE STAND ARTILLERY RANGE-FINDER, MK. I.

Plates XLV to XLVII show the Stand Artillery Range-finder, Mark I.

The stand consists of three mahogany legs pivoted to a baseplate which carries the head of the stand.

The legs are in two parts, the lower part sliding in the upper part so that the height of the stand can be adjusted as required. Two clamps (1 and 2) with butterfly nuts are provided so as to ensure rigidity at the junction of the two parts of the legs. When the stand is set up both clamps should be tightened up.

The upper part of each leg is pivoted to a lug on the base plate and a clamp (3) is provided. This should be tightened when the stand is set up, so as to minimise play between the base plate and legs.

The head of the stand consists of a pivot (4) with toothed arc (5), a steel arm and ball (6) with clamp (7) acting on the toothed arc, and a gunmetal socket (8) in which are formed the trunnions (9) and catch (10) by which the range-finder is attached to the stand. A screw clamp (11) is provided for tightening the socket on the ball.

The steel arm can be folded down into the horizontal position (Plate XLVII) when it is required to use the range-finder vertically; it can also be clamped in intermediate positions. The ball and socket

---

* The stands shown in Plates XL to XLIII are now obsolete. They have been superseded by the Stand Artillery Range-finder shown in Plates XLV to XLVIII. This stand is suitable for use with either the Zeiss or Barr & Stroud pattern range-finders.

[To face page 154.]

PLATE XLV.

Stand, Artillery Range-Finder, Mk. I.

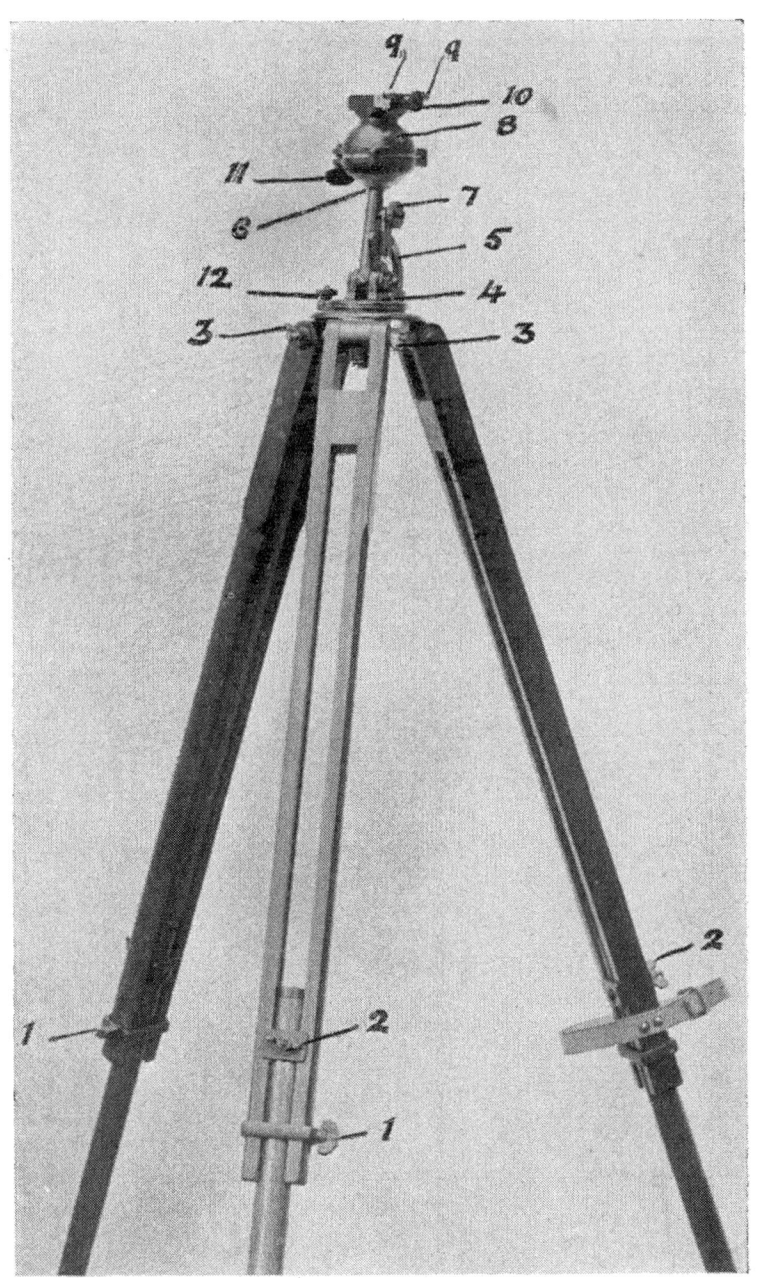

PLATE XLVI.
STAND, ARTILLERY RANGE-FINDER, MK. I.

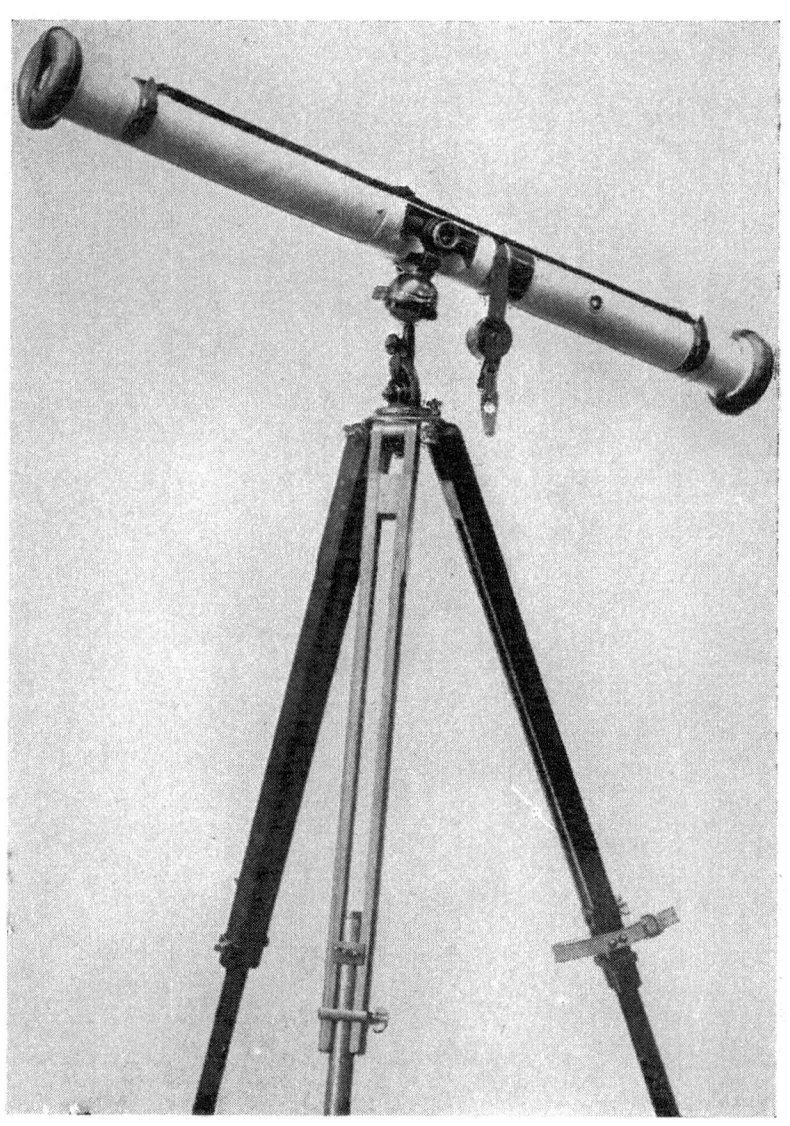

PLATE XLVII.

STAND,
ARTILLERY RANGE-FINDER,
MK. I.

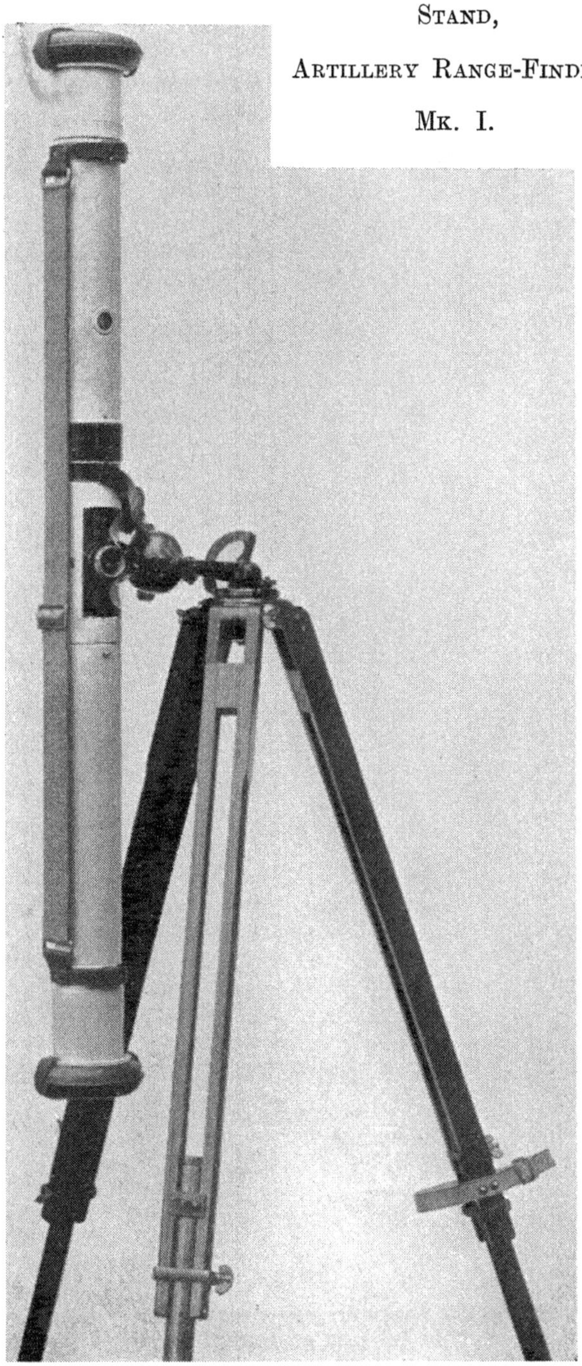

[*To face page* 155.

PLATE XLIX.

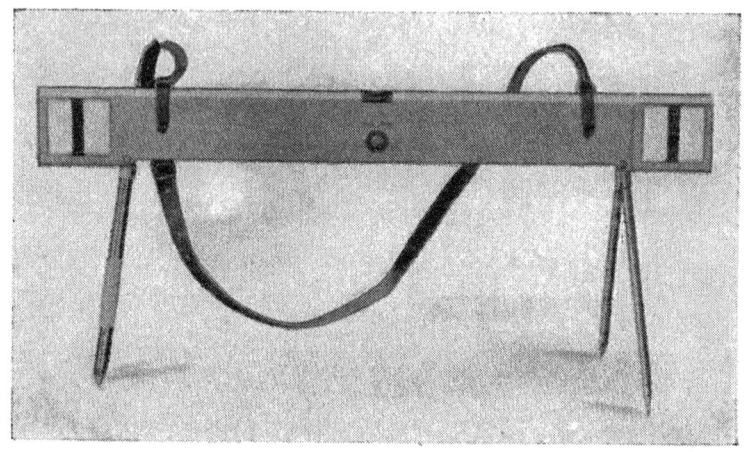

LATH, ADJUSTING ARTILLERY RANGE-FINDER, MARK I.
(ZEISS PATTERN.)

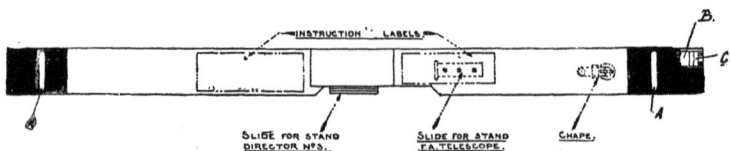

LATH, ADJUSTING ARTILLERY RANGE-FINDER, MARK II.
SCALE $= \frac{1}{6}$.

[*To face page* 155.

PLATE XLVIII.

STAND, ARTILLERY RANGE-FINDER, MARK II, IN CASE, STAND, ARTILLERY RANGE-FINDER, MARK II.

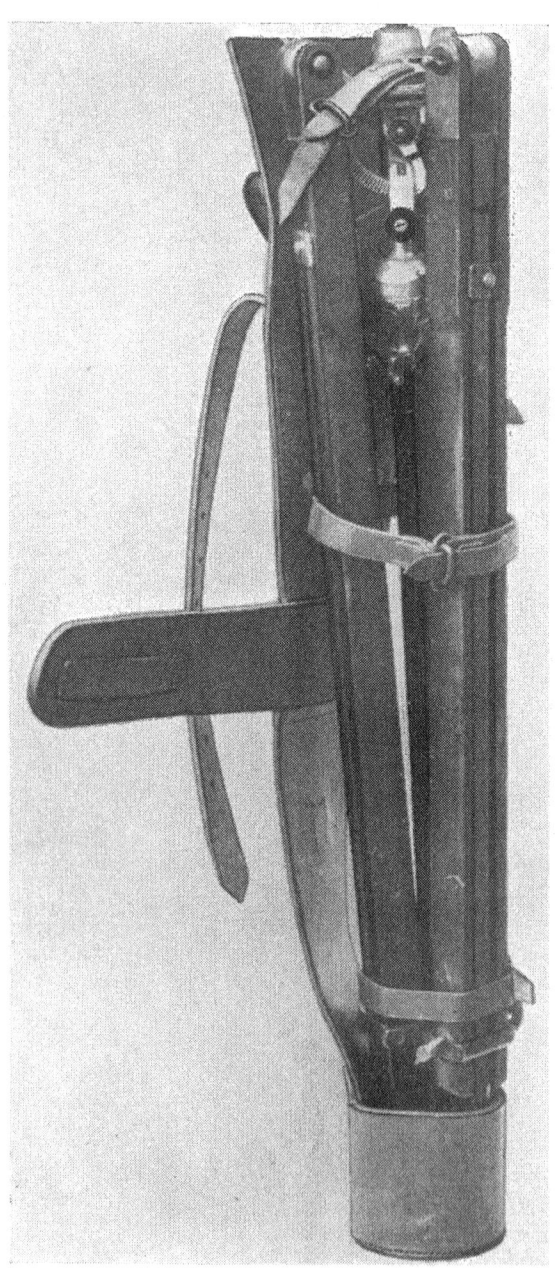

joint provides for all the movements which are required when using the range-finder.

The clamp (11) should be tightened up as required. It will be found best when using the instrument in the horizontal position to have this clamp fairly loose so that the movement of the ball and socket joint is quite free. When the range-finder is used in the vertical position the clamp should be rather tighter. The ball should be occasionally lubricated and must on no account be allowed to rust.

The pivot which carries the ball and socket can revolve in the base plate, and is provided with a clamp (12). When the arm is vertical this clamp should be tightened up, as any traversing movement required can be obtained on the ball and socket joint. When the arm is horizontal this clamp may be loosened or tightened, as preferred.

Except when the maximum height is required the legs should not be fully extended, but should be clamped as shown in Plates XLV to XLVII, *i.e.*, with a space of 3 or 4 inches between the clamps (1 and 2). This adds considerably to the rigidity of the legs.

THE CASE, STAND ARTILLERY RANGE-FINDER, MARK I.

This case is a leather bucket for carrying the stand on horseback.

It is carried on the near side of the horse. The surcingle is passed through the steadying arm. The steadying strap (*i.e.*, the upper of the two straps) is passed round the rear arch and support of the saddle. The supporting strap is passed over the steadying strap and round the rear arch and support of the saddle.

The steadying girth is passed under the horse, and secured to the "D's" on the "Case, Artillery Range-finder," and "Case, stand."

THE STAND ARTILLERY RANGE-FINDER, MARK II.

The Mark II Stand is generally similar to the Mark I, but is lighter, and is so constructed that the legs fold up over the head.

Plate XLVIII shows the stand folded up in the case.

THE CASE, STAND ARTILLERY RANGE-FINDER, MARK II.

This is a leather bucket for carrying the Mark II Range-finder Stand on horseback. It is attached to the saddle in the same way as the Mark I Case. The upper strap on the case should be passed over the boss on the base plate of the stand, as shown in Plate XLVIII, to prevent the stand from being jolted out of the bucket.

THE ADJUSTING LATHS.

There are three patterns of adjusting laths in use, one of Messrs. Zeiss' manufacture, one made in the Ordnance Factories and the Mark II.

(1) The Zeiss Lath (Plate XLIX).

This is a hollow brass lath about 44 inches long by 4 inches wide, provided with three folding legs and a view-finder. On one side of the lath are two vertical black lines whose centres are exactly 1 metre apart.

The method of using the lath is as follows:—

Set up the range-finder on its stand. Take the lath some 150 or 200 yards away and set it up on its legs with the black lines towards the range-finder. The exact distance does not matter and need not be known; it must not be less than 100 yards, and provided the lath can be clearly seen the further away it is the better, up to about 200 yards. Kneel down behind the lath and look through the view-finder; turn the lath as required until the pointer in the view-finder is laid on the centre of the range-finder. This places the lath parallel. to the range-finder. The adjustment of the range-finder is then carried out as described on page 146.

(2) The Ordnance Factory Lath.

This is a wooden lath about 44 inches long and 4 inches deep, on one side of which two vertical lines are painted, their centres being exactly 1 metre apart. The lath is provided with a pair of open sights and a fitting for mounting it on the Stand F.A. Telescope. The method of using this lath is described on page 146.

The Lath Adjusting Artillery Range-Finder Mark II.
(Plate XLIX.)

This lath consists of a board about 45 inches long and 4 inches deep, the ends being painted black. It has two strips of celluloid (A A), whose centres are 1 metre apart, let into it.

A sighting groove is cut along the top of the lath, and an acorn foresight is fixed in the centre of the groove at one end of the lath. At the other end of the lath a prism* (B) is fixed in a metal mount (C). The top of the prism is level with the bottom of the groove.

Two metal slides are provided, one for mounting the lath on the "Stand Director No. 3," and the other for mounting it on the "Stand, Field Artillery Telescope."

A brass cap is provided for covering the prism end of the lath when not in use. The lath is carried in a waterproof canvas cover.

Instructions for using the lath are printed on two labels which are glued to the front face of the lath.

The lath is intended for use with any coincidence range-finder of 1 metre base, and can be used—

 (*a*) With the Stand, Field Artillery Telescope.
 (*b*) With the Stand Director No. 3.
 (*c*) Without a stand.

Instructions for Using the Lath.

(*a*) Set up the range-finder on its stand. Take the adjusting lath and Stand, Field Artillery Telescope some 150 or 200 yards away from the range-finder. Screw the slide for Stand, Field Artillery Telescope to the bottom of the lath, and place the lath on the stand. Lay the lath, by means of the groove and foresight, on the centre of the range-finder.

Clamp the degree scale on the stand at 0°.

Turn the lath through 90°.

The lath is then in position for use.

Care must be taken that the lath is not moved while the range-finder is being adjusted.

---

* For details of this prism, see Appendix A.

(b) Set up the range-finder as before, and set up the Stand No. 3 Director some 150 to 200 yards away from it. Screw the slide for the Stand No. 3 Director to the bottom of the lath, and place the lath on the stand. Place the lath roughly parallel to the range-finder. Stand in prolongation of the lath and look into the prism, which reflects a right angle, and traverse the lath, inclining and tilting it as necessary, until the acorn at the far end of the groove on top of the lath is seen in the centre of the groove and vertically above the reflection of the right end pad of the range-finder, as seen in the prism.

The lath is then in position for use.

In order to see the image of the end pad of the range-finder in the prism at the same time as the foresight it is necessary not only to tilt the lath in the direction of its length (*i.e.*, to raise or lower the prism end), but also to incline the front face of the lath by working the cross-levelling screw on the Director Stand, until the image of the end pad of the range-finder is seen near the top of the prism. The foresight and the end pad of the range-finder can then be seen simultaneously, one above the other. If the lath is, so to speak, " leaning backwards " or " leaning forwards " it is difficult to see the two objects together and to make sure that the lath is correctly laid.

Care must be taken that the lath is not moved while the range-finder is being adjusted.

(c) Place the lath on a limber, wagon or other suitable support with the side on which the white lines are marked towards the range-finder. Set up the range-finder on its stand some 150 to 200 yards away from the lath.

Place the lath roughly parallel to the range-finder, and then looking along the lath and into the prism as described under (b) above, get the lath accurately parallel to the range-finder.

The Hanger.

This is an adjunct to facilitate the use of the range-finder without a stand, and is used with all Artillery range-finders. When used with the No. 2 Mark I, it is necessary to bend the supports slightly outwards until they are clear of the handles of the range-finder.

It consists of a leather breast plate and shoulder strap with a pair of iron wire supports.

For use the shoulder strap is passed over the head so that the breastplate lies on the range-taker's chest. The range-finder rests on the iron supports, and its height is adjusted by shortening or lengthening the shoulder strap as required.

Accuracy.

The accuracy of one-man range-finders of the type described in the foregoing pages varies directly as the base length and as the magnifying power of the telescope. Considerations of size, weight and handiness in use, limit the length of an instrument for use in the field, and it has been decided that a base length of about 1 metre (39·3 inches) is the most suitable for a Field Artillery range-finder.

The power for the telescope to be employed is governed by a number of considerations which need not be entered into here. At present a magnifying power of from 10 to 13 is used. The accuracy obtainable from any given instrument varies inversely as the square of the range. The greatest accuracy which can be expected under favourable conditions from a 1 metre base range-finder is that the ranges recorded by consecutive observations on a well defined object shall be within about $\pm$ ·5 per cent. per thousand yards of range; *i.e.*, if the object is a thousand yards distant the ranges recorded should be within ·5 per cent., or 5 yards ; if the object is at 2,000 yards, within 2 × ·5 per cent. of range, or 20 yards ; at 3,000 yards, within 3 × ·5 per cent. of range, or 45 yards, &c.

RANGE-FINDER, ARTILLERY, NO. 2, MARK II (BARR & STROUD).

This range-finder is similar in principle to the one described on page 151; but it is lighter and of smaller diameter. The principal details of it are as follows :—

Length over all, 43·75 inches. Base, 1 metre.
Diameter of body, 2·25 inches.
Maximum diameter, 4 inches.
Weight, 9¾ lbs.
Magnification, 14 diameters.
Field of view, horizontal, 3° 10′ ; vertical, 2° 11′.
Upper image inverted.

ANGLE OF SIGHT INSTRUMENT.

PLATE L—*continued.* [*To face page* 159.

ANGLE OF SIGHT INSTRUMENT—*continued.*

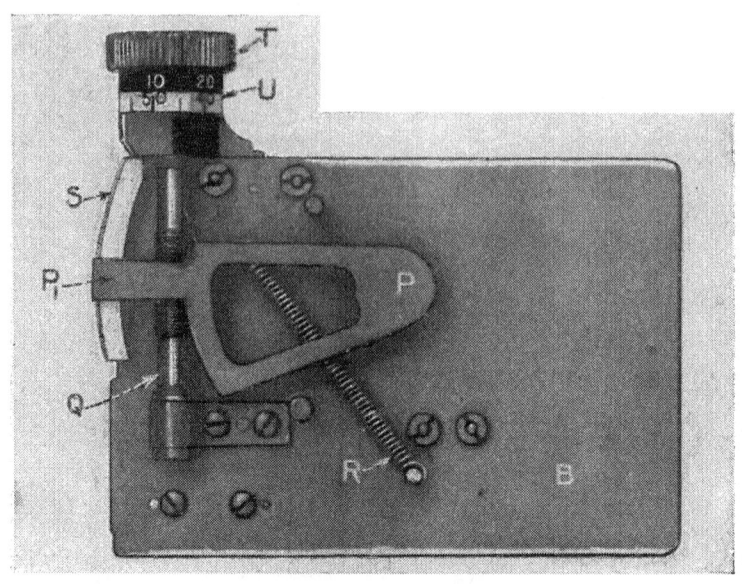

SUPPORTING PLATE. RIGHT SIDE.

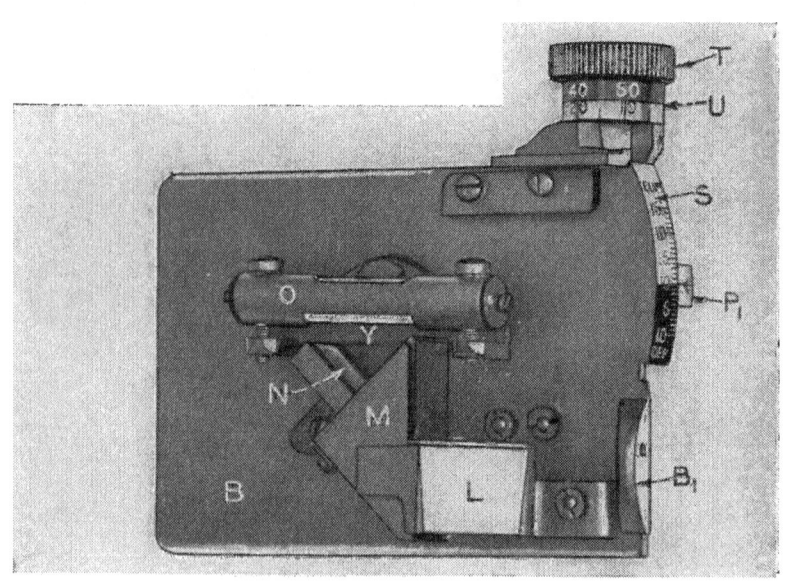

SUPPORTING PLATE. LEFT SIDE.

CHAPTER VIII.

VARIOUS INSTRUMENTS.

ANGLE OF SIGHT INSTRUMENT.
(Plate L.)
Mark I.

This instrument is used for finding angles of sight with reasonable accuracy from positions, to which it is not convenient to carry a larger instrument on a stand (*e.g.*, a No. 2 or 3 director).

It consists of a brass box forming a prismatic telescope, the eyepiece of which is so arranged that besides the view and a horizontal line in the instrument, a spirit bubble can be seen. The bubble can be inclined to the line of sight, and the inclination read off degree and minute scales :—

Magnification	4 diameters.
Field of view	4° horizontal × 5° 30' vertical.
Weight of instrument in case	1 lb. 8 ozs.
Overall dimensions of case	$5\frac{1}{4}''$ × $4''$ × $2\frac{1}{4}''$.

It consists of the following parts :—

The brass body (A) is fitted internally with guides for the supporting plate (B). A flap (C) is hinged to the rear end and holds the eyepiece adapter (K) and eyepiece (D). It is kept in position by the screw (E). A glass window (F) admits light to the bubble. The two serrated discs (G) are for the fingers of the left hand to rest on, when taking angles. A flat aluminium plate (H) is riveted beneath the body and forms a suitable surface for supporting the instrument, as well as protecting the hinge.

The object glass is mounted in front of the body and a ray shade (J) fits over it. It consists of two lenses balsamed together and is adjusted so that the horizontal line on the prism (M) is in its focal plane.

The eyepiece (D) fits in the eyepiece adapter (K) and is focussed by sliding it backwards or forwards. It has two lenses, the front one is cut away for a third of its breadth, so that the view, which is seen through both lenses, and the bubble, which is seen through the rear one only, are in focus simultaneously.

The supporting plate (B) fits accurately in the guides in the body. A small projection (B_1) is formed on it to facilitate withdrawal.

On the left side are mounted two double reflecting prisms (L, M), the latter having a horizontal line engraved on its rear surface, and a mirror (N) in which the reflection of the bubble is seen.

A pivot passes through the plate and on it are mounted a cased spirit bubble (O) and an arc (P). The bubble, which is sensitive to a movement of between 4' and 5', is supported on the bubble bracket (Y) by two screws which allow of it being adjusted if the degree and minute scales do not correspond. The arc has teeth cut on it, which gear with the worm spindle (Q), and a projection (P_1) on which an arrow for reading the degree scale is engraved.

Play is taken up by a spiral spring (R).

Attached to the plate is the degree scale (S) with graduations in single degrees from 0° to 15° elevation and 10° depression, the latter being filled in white on black.

The worm spindle (Q) is fitted in bearings and is squared at its upper end to take the milled head (T), beneath which is an adjustable skin (U). The latter is graduated every 5 minutes, numbered every 10', in both directions, and coloured to agree with the degree scale. It can be loosened for adjustment by slackening the two screws (V).

CASE.

The leather case is padded and has a shoulder strap fitted to it.

EARLY PATTERNS.

Nos. 1 to 39 differ slightly from the above. The base is formed to fit on the "Stand, F.A. telescope," the degree scale reads from 15° elevation to 5° depression, and the case is not padded.

Mark II.

The Mark II differs from the Mark I in the following particulars:—

(a) A vertical cross-line, in addition to the horizontal line, is etched on the large prism. The two lines intersect each other at the centre of the field of view.

(b) A light gunmetal slide, to fit on the "Stand, Telescope, Field Artillery," is fitted to the base of the instrument instead of an aluminium plate.

(c) The fittings in the case are made to suit the altered dimensions of the instrument.

When mounted on a "Stand, Telescope, Field Artillery," the instrument can be used instead of the "Director, No. 1" or "Telescope, Field Artillery," for measuring angles in horizontal and vertical planes.

Mark I*.

A certain number of Mark I instruments have been altered as in (a) and (b) above, and are known as Mark I*.

TO TAKE AN ANGLE OF SIGHT.

Focus the instrument by sliding the eyepiece backwards or forwards.

Set the degree scale at the estimated angle by turning the milled head (T).

Grasp the instrument firmly with the left hand, two fingers resting on the serrated discs (G).

Lay the *right end* of the horizontal line on the target, and keep it there.

Turn the micrometer head with the right hand until the centre of the bubble is opposite the horizontal line.

To *raise* the bubble turn to the *right* and to *lower* it turn to the *left*. Always turn to the left last.

Read the degrees off the degree scale and the minutes off the corresponding minute scale.

If time admits make three observations and take the mean.

To Test and Adjust the Instrument.

Lay out a horizontal line as described on page 174. Set the degree and minute scales at zero. Place the object glass at one end of the horizontal line, and lay the right end of the horizontal line in the instrument on a point at the other end of the line laid out. The centre of the bubble should then be in line with the horizontal line in the instrument.

If it is not, turn the milled head until it is so. Loosen the two screws (V) in the milled head and revolve the skin (U) until it reads zero. Tighten the screws (V).

If the degree scale is found to be more than a few minutes off zero it will be necessary to start afresh and manipulate the screws supporting the cased bubble (O) until, the scales being at zero, the horizontal line in the instrument is laid on a distant point in the same horizontal plane, and at the same time is opposite the centre of the bubble.

BUBBLES, SPIRIT, GLASS.

Bubbles are made in certain definite sizes, so that if one becomes broken it can easily be replaced by a similar one. The different natures also vary in their sensitiveness.

Each bubble consists of a hermetically sealed glass tube, partially filled with absolute alcohol. The inside of the tube, where the air bubble will be, is carefully ground away to a certain curve, upon which the sensitiveness of the bubble will depend.

The upper surface of the tube has lines engraved on it at equal distances from the centre.

Owing to the expansion of the alcohol when heated, the air bubble will become smaller as the temperature increases.

The L and M bubbles, which are also known as Cat's-eye bubbles, are of the same dimensions as the A and B bubbles respectively, but differ from them in sensitiveness and colour. The underside of the glass is white with a blue line on it, and the liquid is amber-coloured.

All instruments of recent manufacture take the standard bubbles, but some of the older natures have to have special bubbles made for them. When these are damaged, and new ones demanded, their diameter and length, and the nature of instrument for which they are required should be stated. It is not necessary that the glass bubble should fit the casing exactly, as the plaster of Paris, by means of which it is fixed in position, can be used to fill up any gaps.

When a bubble is demanded, it should always be made clear if the glass bubble only, or the bubble fixed in its case, is required.

The following table shows the details of the standard glass bubbles in the service :—

Name.	Length in Inches.	Diameter in Inches.	Sensitive to a Movement of—	Each Division represents—
A	1·6	0·3	30″	30–35″
B	1	0·35	30″	30–35″
C	1·8	0·48	30″	30–35″
D	2·7	0·44	15″	25–30″
E	2·4	0·61	15″	25–30″
F	5·3	0·61	15″	15–18″
G	7·3	0·88	15″	15–18″
H	1·1	0·3	30″	30–35″
J	2·82	0·56	15″	15–18″
K	1·3	0·5	30″	30–35″
L	1·6	0·3	2′	1–2′
M	1	0.35	2′	1–2′

The different natures are used with the following instruments. (For other instruments for which they may be suitable see L. of C., para. 14213) :—

Bubble A.—*Clinometer, sight, Q.F. 13- and 18-pr., and B.L. 2·75 inch.
   *Sights, dial, Nos. 2, 3, 4, 5 and 6.
   Sight, Oscillating, B.L. 60-pr. (transverse).
   *Sight, Rocking Bar, B.L.C. 15-pr.
   *Carrier, No. 7 dial sight, No. 1, Mark I.
   *Telescope, Sighting, No. 6, Marks II and III.
   Director, No. 3.
Bubble B.—Director, No. 2.
   Clinometer, Field, Mark I.
   Observation of fire, instrument.
Bubble C.—Clinometer, Field, Mark III.
   Clinometer, B.L. 10-pr., Mark I.
Bubble D.—Clinometer, large, Mark I.
   Clinometer, Inspectors, Mark II.
Bubble E.—D.R.F. Marks II, II* and III, short body.
   D.R.F. Mark I, long body.
Bubble F.—D.R.F. Marks II and III, long body.
   D.R.F. Marks II and III telescope.
   D.R.F. Mark II*, long body (probably).
Bubble G.—P.F. long body (except C.O., P.F.'s.).
Bubble H.—15-pr. Q.F. hind sight.
Bubble J.—D.R.F. Mark II* telescope.
Bubble K.—D.R.F. Mark II*, short body.
Bubble L.—*For future manufacture, and to replace unserviceable bubbles in those instruments which use the "Bubble A" and are marked with a * above.
Bubble M.—Telescope, Sighting, No. 6, Mark I (except a few of early manufacture).

BUBBLE, SPIRIT, CIRCULAR, CASED.

This bubble is used with Nos. 2 and 3 directors and observation of fire instruments, where very accurate levelling is not required.

It consists of a brass body (Fig. 1) in the top of which is fixed a

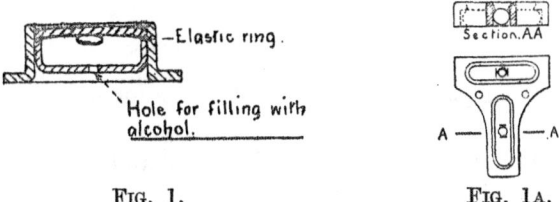

FIG. 1.   FIG. 1A.

glass disc (the underside of which is curved), having a small ring engraved on it. The alcohol is retained in the body by means of a metal cap pressed in from below, against an elastic ring which is in contact with the glass, so as to make an airtight joint. The base of the body is surfaced, so that when it rests on a horizontal plate the air bubble will be concentric with the ring engraved on the glass.

The bubble is sensitive to a movement of two minutes, and its exterior dimensions are as follows :—

Diameter of base	1·2 inches.
Height overall	0·45 ,,
Diameter of top portion	0·8 ,,
Thickness of base	0·075 ,,

If exposed to very high temperatures some of the alcohol may escape, which is shown by the air bubble becoming larger. If this occurs the bubble must be replaced.

BUBBLE, SPIRIT, CASED, No. 1.

This bubble (Fig. 1A) has been introduced to supersede the "Bubble, Spirit, Circular, Cased," which was found to leak in tropical climates.

It consists of a T-shaped brass mount in which are fitted two small glass bubbles. The latter are sensitive to a movement of 8'.

The overall dimensions of the cased bubble are 1" × 1·25" × ·25".

COLLIMATOR, TELESCOPE SIGHTING.

This instrument consists of a long flat iron stand mounted upon a base board. At one end of the stand is mounted a tube and at the other end two V-brackets in which the telescope to be collimated is supported. The rear bracket can be adjusted both horizontally and vertically.

Cross wires and a ground glass background are mounted in the tube, and at the end nearest the V-brackets is mounted a lens, so constructed that the cross wires appear to be at an infinite distance, the rays of light from the cross wires emerging from the lens parallel to one another.

When the instrument is in adjustment, a No. 1, 3 or 7 Sighting Telescope placed in the V-brackets, can be rapidly collimated by making its crosswires coincide with those in the collimator.

A chest is provided to carry the collimator, and is fitted with two boxes which contain screw-drivers, tommies, spare pointers and other parts, and cleaning material.

Full instructions for its adjustment and use are provided with each instrument.

IRIS DIAPHRAGMS.

There are four patterns of iris diaphragms for use with telescopes, viz. :—

    No. 1.—For sighting telescopes, Nos. 1, 3 and 7.
    No. 2.—For P.F.s.
    No. 3.—For Mark I D.R.F.s.
    No. 4.—For Marks II, II* and III D.R.F.s. and horizontal transmitters.

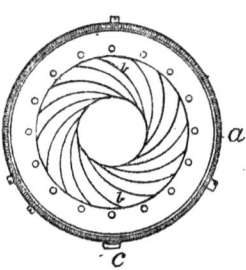

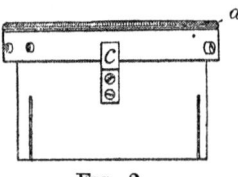

Fig. 2.

They are for use in a very bright light, and prevent too much light coming through the telescope, and so tiring the eye. They fit on to the telescope in front of the object glass. By turning the milled ring (a) (Fig. 2), the leaves (bb) are caused to move inwards and cover part of the object glass. A stop (c) is fitted to prevent undue strain being put on the leaves. The figure shows the diaphragm half closed.

    SWITCH AND RESISTANCE COIL.
    FOUR-VOLT LAMP.
    FLEXIBLE LEAD.
    JUNCTION BOX.

In order to see the graticules or cross wires in a telescope at night it is necessary to illuminate them, and the following apparatus has been designed for this purpose :—

The switch and resistance coil (Figs. 3 and 4) consists of a base board H, having mounted on it the following parts :—

Ebonite block, F, with brass socket, G, for reception of one end of flexible lead.

Lever, C, one end of which can make electrical contact with six studs, D_2 to D_7.

A stop stud, D_8, which prevents the base board being incorrectly inserted into the junction box.

Two contact pieces, E E, which make electrical contact with the two springs in the junction box.

SWITCH AND RESISTANCE COIL (MARK IV).

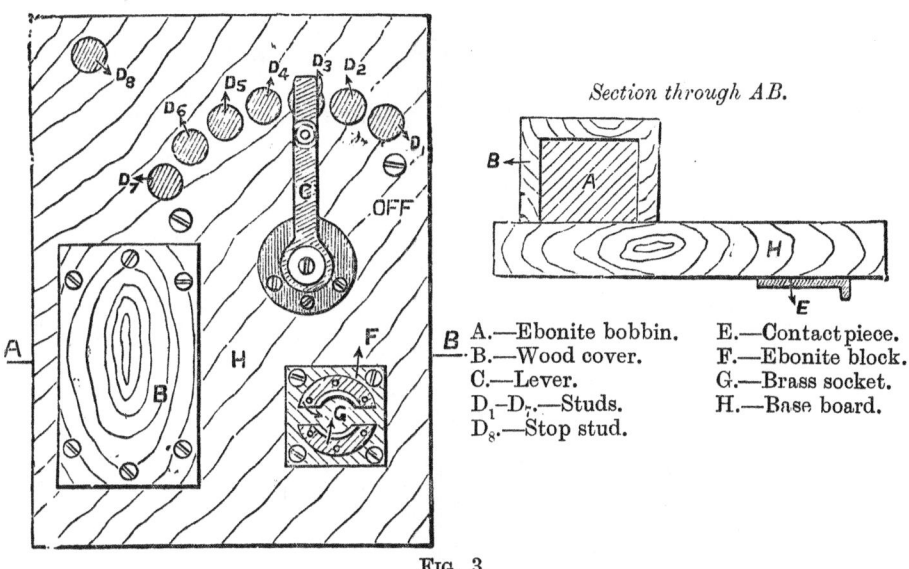

A.—Ebonite bobbin.　　E.—Contact piece.
B.—Wood cover.　　　　F.—Ebonite block.
C.—Lever.　　　　　　　G.—Brass socket.
D_1–D_7.—Studs.　　　　　H.—Base board.
D_8.—Stop stud.

FIG. 3.

CONNECTIONS OF SWITCH AND RESISTANCE COIL (MARK IV).

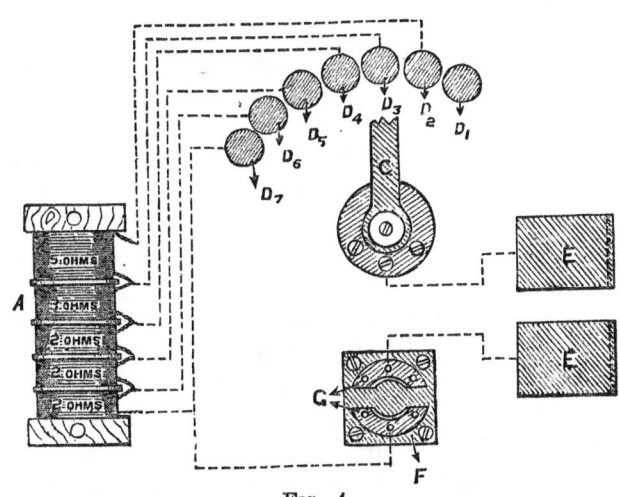

FIG. 4.

A.—Ebonite bobbin.　　EE.—Contact pieces.
C.—Lever.　　　　　　　F.—Ebonite block.
D_1–D_7.—Studs.　　　　　G.—Brass socket.

An ebonite bobbin, A, wound in sections with silk covered copper wire, the resistance of the sections of the copper wire being 5, 3, 2, 2 and 2 ohms. The ends of the wire are connected to the lower half of the socket G. The lever can thus be used to insert, between its pivot and the lower half of the socket G, resistances of 14, 9, 6, 4, 2 and 0 ohms, when it is in contact with the studs D_2 to D_7.

A wood cover B is fitted over the bobbin. The pivot of the lever and the upper half of the socket G are connected by insulated wires to the two contact pieces E, E at the back of the baseboard.

The 4-volt lamp (Fig. 5) consists of a small 4-volt incandescent electric lamp 0 mounted on an ebonite plug D, the ends of the filament being electrically connected with the two halves of the socket PP.

4-VOLT LAMP, MARK II.

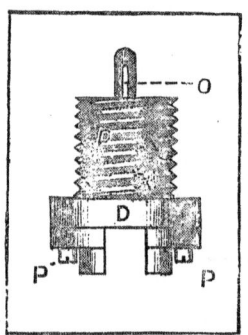

FIG. 5.

The ebonite plug is screw threaded and fits into the lamp socket in the telescope behind the wires.

The flexible lead consists of a convenient length of twin insulated copper wire. At each end is an ebonite plug having two brass contact pieces, one of which is connected to each strand of copper wire. It is used for connecting the S and R coil to the lamp.

The junction box (Fig. 6) consists of a wooden slide to take the switch and resistance coil. In it are mounted two springs (a a), which press against the contact pieces (e e) at the back of the switch and resistance coil. Two lugs (b b), which are in electrical contact with the springs, have the two leads from the battery soldered to them. The leads pass through the hole (e) and along the groove (f). A block

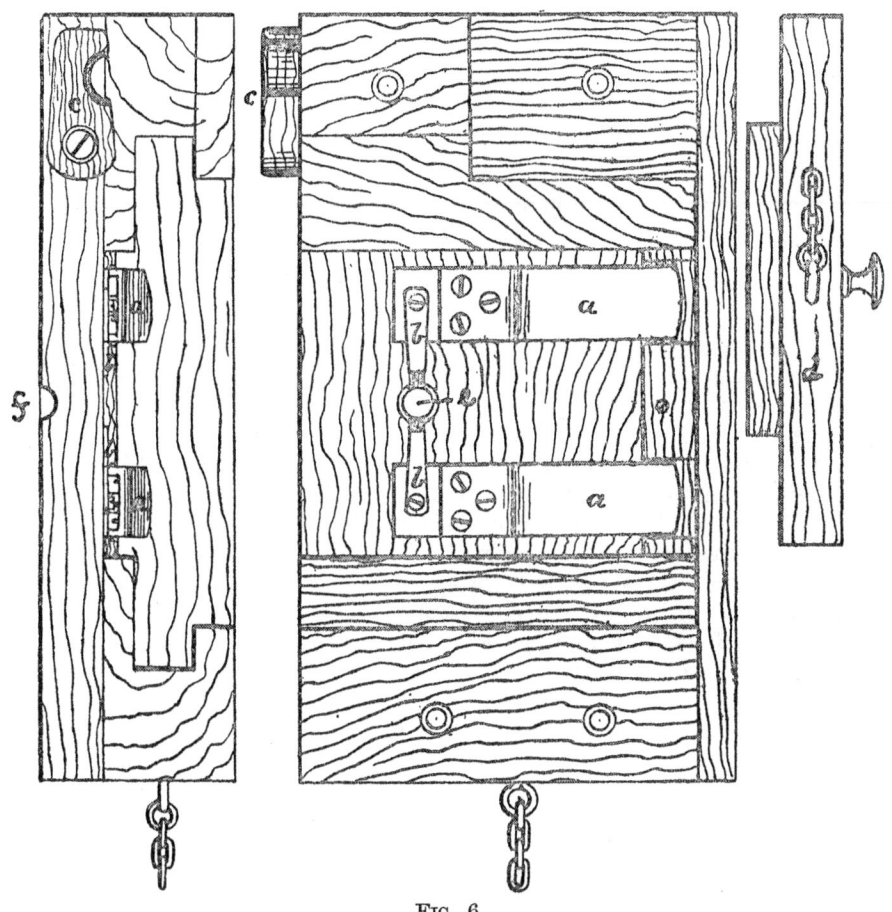

Fig. 6.

(d) is inserted in the slide when the switch and resistance coil is removed. A small wooden stop (c) keeps the S and R coil, or block, in position.

Instructions for Use.

Screw the lamp into the telescope socket, slide the switch and resistance coil into the junction box and prevent it from moving by bringing the small wooden stop (c) in contact with it. Connect the two leads from the junction box to a battery of four Le Clanché or other cells. See that the lever of the S and R coil is at "off." Insert the two plugs at the end of the flexible lead into the sockets of the S and R coil and of the lamp. Move the lever slowly to the left until the crosswires are sufficiently illuminated.

Great care must be taken not to pass too much current through the lamp or the filament will be fused. The lamp should not be tested in daylight, but at night or in a dark place. The current should always be turned off when the telescope is not being used.

SIGHTING RULES.

(Plate LI).

There are three patterns of sighting rules, which differ from one another only as regards the scales to which they are constructed.

Scale.	Graduated from.	To.	Length.
1½″ to 1 mile	2,000 yds.	20,000 yds.	25·15″.
2″ ,, ,,	2,000 ,,	15,000 ,,	25·15″.
3″ ,, ,,	1,000 ,,	14,000 ,,	31·9″.

They are used in conjunction with B.C. charts, which must be made to the same scale. If the battery commander is directed to engage a target in a certain square, the rule is swung round until its right edge cuts the centre of the square. The approximate range of the target can be read off the scale, and its training off the B.C. chart. This information can be passed on to the range-finders and guns. The target can be identified by noting which target (at approximately the range indicated) is approximately in line with the vanes.

The rule consists of a boxwood rule (A), to which are attached two folding vanes (B). A range scale is engraved on it, being divided every hundred yards and figured every thousand. A brass fitting (C), having a pivot projecting downwards, is screwed to it, the centre of the pivot being in line with the right edge. A socket (D) to take the pivot is secured to the B.C. chart, at the point representing the B.C. post, by two screws.

WATCHES, STOP, ONE-FIFTH SECOND.

(Plate LI).

There are two marks of this watch, which is a centre seconds stop watch reading from one-fifth of a second to 30 minutes. One revolution of the seconds hand (A) registers one minute, the hand moving in steps of one-fifth of a second above a dial (B), which is divided every one-fifth of a second. The minute hand indicates single minutes from 1 to 30 on the minute dial (C).

A leather thong (D) for attaching the watch to a button, and a chamois leather bag (E) are provided.

The Mark I is the more suitable watch for ordinary timing, when each record is complete in itself, as its " start, stop and flyback " action is more convenient for this purpose than the slide action of the Mark II. But if the period of time which is to be recorded is liable to interruptions (such as, when timing a series at practice, the firing has to be stopped for any reason), the Mark II is the more suitable.

The watches are not compensated for temperature, and they should consequently be occasionally checked with an accurate clock.

[PLATE LI.

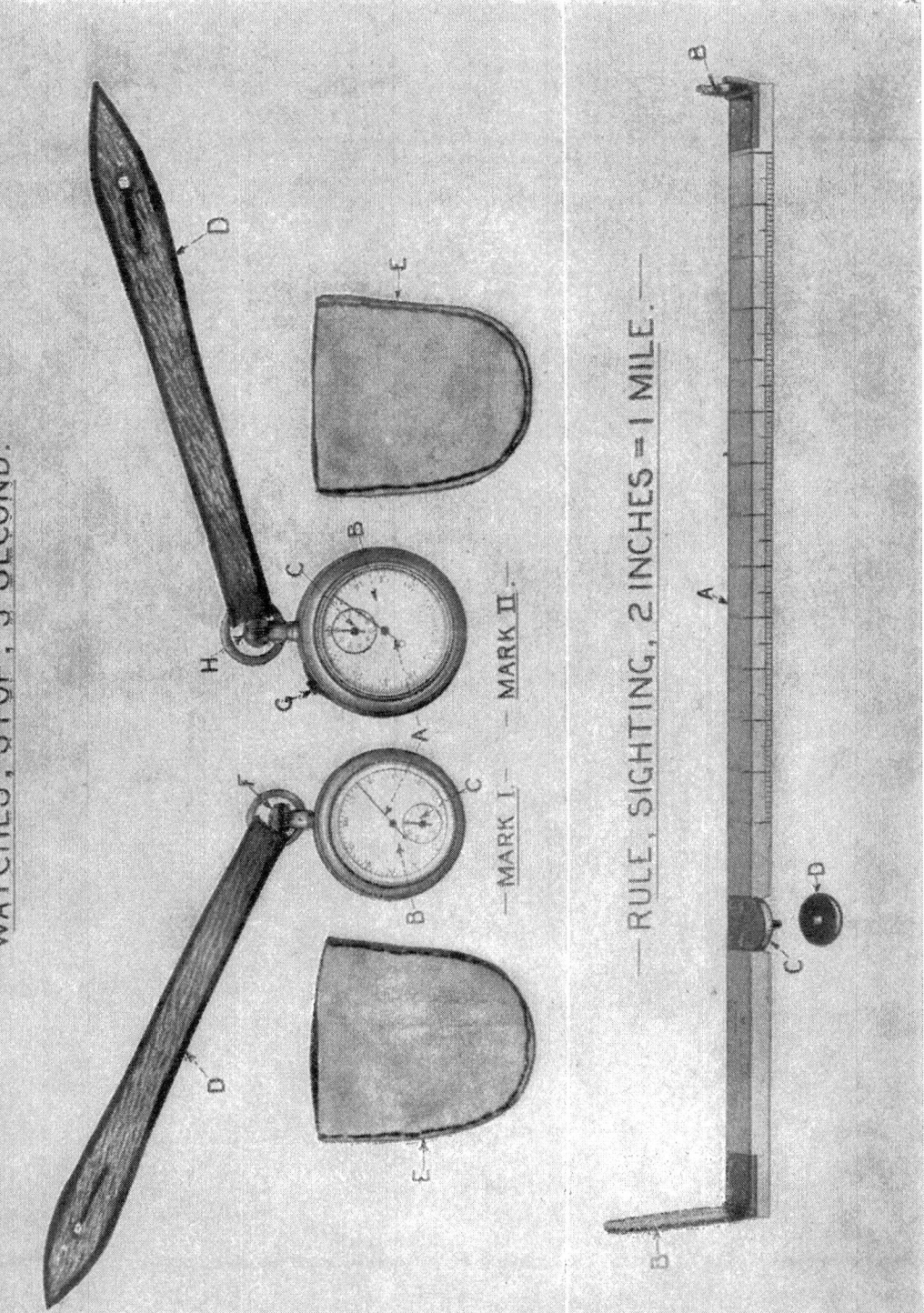

Mark I.

The case is made of silver, and watches which have been converted to the Mark II pattern are still accounted for as Mark I on account of their different value.

The " start," " stop " and " flyback " actions are all actuated by successive pressure of the keyless button (F).

When starting and stopping this watch, care should be taken to put no pressure on the keyless button before the actual movement of " start " and " stop," when the button should be pressed sharply.

Mark II.

The case is made of nickel.

The " stop " and " go-on " movement is actuated by a slide (G) which is slid upwards (towards the pendant), to start the watch, and downwards to stop it.

The " flyback " movement is actuated by pressing down the keyless button (H) which, however, does not stop or start the watch.

CHAPTER IX.

CARE AND PRESERVATION.

All instruments must be treated with the greatest care in order to keep them serviceable and ready for immediate use. It is the duty of everyone, who has charge of them or who uses them, to see that they receive careful attention and treatment.

They must not on any account be taken apart in any way except by persons who have passed through courses of instruction, and who are in possession of certificates showing that they are competent to do so. The specialist, or person who is responsible for their care, will only clean the outer surfaces, and occasionally clean the lenses of telescopes.

TELESCOPES AND BINOCULARS.

On no account must oil or grease be allowed on any of the lenses. Lenses should only be cleaned with a chamois leather, silk cloth or soft camel's hair brush which is used for no other purpose. Very dirty lenses may be cleaned with alcohol.

The exterior metal surfaces must be wiped clean with a dry cloth; if very dirty, a little turpentine or paraffin may be used.

Metal caps, if stiff, should be lightly lubricated with a thin oil, only traces of which should be allowed to remain. The part of the telescope, over which the cap fits, should be treated in a similar way.

Lenses, or their cells, must never be removed unless their inner surfaces require cleaning. It should be remembered that the collimation of a telescope will probably be upset if—

(1) The object glass is removed from its cell.

(2) The object glass cell is not screwed home to its original position.

The incorrect assembling of lenses in their cells, and the incorrect replacing of the cells in their tubes may cause a telescope or binocular to become unserviceable, and is likely to result in the fracture of the lenses or the destruction of the screw threads on the cells. As a rule, only one lens should be removed at a time. For the correct method of assembling object glasses see p. 3.

The screw threads of most tubes or cells are very fine, and are easily crossed and rendered useless. When screwing in any tube or cell first turn to the left as if unscrewing until the threads " snap " then turn to the right in the usual way. If the thread seems to work stiffly, unscrew and repeat the process.

When telescopes or binoculars are not in use, their caps and eyepiece covers should be carefully replaced, focussing gears racked home, and the instrument placed in its case (when such is provided).

Telescopes and binoculars should be kept in a dry place, especially in tropical climates, where a fungus is apt to form on the lenses. If it appears it should be immediately cleaned off with very dilute sulphuric acid, no traces of which should be allowed to remain.

When carried, telescopes and binoculars should be kept in their cases, and any unnecessary shaking or jolting avoided.

The bearing surfaces, or bands, of sighting and other telescopes must be very carefully protected.

Any burrs or dents in these surfaces throw the telescope out of adjustment, and probably necessitate its return to the makers. When not in use they should be covered with a thin coat of vaseline, which should be thoroughly cleaned off before using the telescope, as otherwise grit, which may have become embedded in the vaseline, might tear the bearing surfaces.

Telescopes and binoculars should be frequently tested to see that they are in order and fit for use. Damaged lenses, dented tubes, binoculars out of parallelism (which is denoted by the object viewed being duplicated), and other similar defects are easily noticed. Steps should be at once taken to have these defects reported and the instrument repaired or exchanged.

The *testing* of collimation can be carried out by any one; but the *adjustment* must only be undertaken by persons holding certificates of proficiency.

DERMATINE AND RUBBER EYEGUARDS.

1. They should not be unnecessarily exposed to extremes of temperature, to the sun's rays or bright light.

2. Oil and grease will inevitably destroy dermatine and rubber and prolonged contact with benzole, petrol and chemicals is undesirable. If, however, oil or grease gets on the eyeguards it should be immediately removed, either :—

   (a) By wiping with a clean rag soaked in petrol or benzole.
   (b) By washing in water to which a little soap and soda have been added, and finally well rinsing in clean water.
   (c) By wiping off with a clean dry rag.
   N.B.—French chalk, or even fine road dust, are useful to absorb oil from rubber, &c., if none of the methods of cleaning above enumerated are possible.

3. They should be washed occasionally with soap and water. If any soda is used in the water, all traces of it should be removed by further washing in clean water. Any iron rust formed on the surface should be immediately removed by washing.

4. Spare eyeguards should be stored in a wooden box completely filled with French chalk (so as to exclude air). The box should be as nearly air-tight as possible. The eyeguards should be packed in such a way that they are not distorted. If French chalk is not available, eyeguards should be kept under water. A temperature of about 60° F. is the most desirable for storage purposes.

If after being in store for some time the eyeguards lose their pliability, they can be generally rendered supple, when required for use, by steeping them in warm water.

Instruments.

All steel parts and working surfaces should occasionally be oiled and then wiped dry with a soft cloth, as otherwise the oil tends to collect grit. Pivots of instruments should be cleaned occasionally with a chamois leather and a very little pure watch oil.

If dust gets on the cross-wires it may be removed by taking out both the eyepiece and the object glass and blowing *very lightly* through the tube. If moisture gets inside the telescope the eyepiece should be removed and the moisture allowed to evaporate. If moisture gets between the object glass lenses, they should be removed from the telescope and dried with a gentle heat before a fire or lamp, but they should not be taken apart unless absolutely necessary.

Great care must be taken when removing instruments from their cases that they are not held by weak parts ; and when replacing them, that they rest correctly in their fittings, and that the lids of the case can be closed down without damaging them. Keys for locks, if kept in the cases, should be wrapped up to prevent them injuring instruments during transport.

Cases.

Leather cases or coverings may be cleaned with any good leather preservative or a little castor oil, which must, however, be wiped off again with a dry rag.

Polished or varnished wood cases should be cleaned with a rag and a little sweet oil.

General.

When an instrument has been removed from its case or box the latter should be closed so as to prevent wet or grit getting into it.

CHAPTER X.

REPAIR AND ADJUSTMENT OF INSTRUMENTS.

As these can only be undertaken by specially trained persons detailed descriptions are not as a rule included in this handbook, but the following points should always be carefully attended to :—

(1) When any part of the instrument is taken to pieces, the pieces should be replaced in the same position. Screws should not be interchanged.

The cells of most telescopes are marked on the sides to show how far they should be screwed home.

When milled heads, &c., are mounted on squared spindles, one side of the square and the part of the head, which it should fit against, are marked. The milled head of a micrometer screw must have the central screw, which attaches it to the worm spindle, screwed well home. If this is not done the worm spindle may be able to move axially, and the micrometer will give inaccurate readings.

Object glasses are always carefully marked to guard against incorrect assembling (see page 4).

(2) Screwdrivers, which *fit* the heads of the screws, should always be used, and the greatest care taken not to damage the heads. It should be remembered that the grooves in screw heads are usually cut with a saw, and are rectangular in section, and that the point of the screwdriver should consequently be of approximately the same shape. Tommy holes are cylindrical, and the points of the tommies should be nearly so, and of approximately the same diameter.

(3) Great care should be taken that the parts of an instrument gear together without unnecessary play, and at the same time that they do not work too stiffly. This is especially the case with stands, the accuracy of the instrument being often neutralized by having the legs fitting loosely to the stand.

Tightening up a few nuts and screws will often make an enormous difference in the serviceability of an instrument.

(4) With telescopes having the pointer or graticules fixed in the focal plane of the object glass, the greatest care must be taken, when collimating, that parallax is not introduced.

(5) When a new bubble is being mounted in an instrument, which will not always be cross levelled, the greatest care must be taken to mount it parallel to the base or pivot on which it rests. Thus with a "clinometer, sight," used with field guns, if the bubble is mounted parallel to its bearings

and consequently to the axis of the gun, practically correct elevations will be given even if one wheel is higher than the other. If, however, it is not parallel to the axis of the gun, incorrect elevations will be given when the wheels are not level, although the bubble is in the centre of its run.

Refilling Graduations.

Graduations and figures should be wiped over occasionally with a soft rag or chamois leather to prevent them becoming tarnished. If the black filling comes out it can be replaced by rubbing in heel ball, and afterwards cleaning off any superfluous deposit with a dry cloth. Defective white filling can be replaced with enamel, any superfluous deposit being wiped off with a dry cloth just before the enamel sets.

If the black background is defective it may be touched up with black enamel or a good spirit black.

The "right" scales of some instruments have the graduations filled with a white metal on a black background. This metal is an alloy, known as Wood's metal, which melts at about the temperature of boiling water. It can easily be removed if it is heated with the flame of a spirit lamp, and brushed out with a stiff brush. It should never wear out. If, however, the black background comes off, and cannot be touched up around the graduations it may be found necessary to remove the Wood's metal, reblack the background, and fill in the white graduations with white enamel. The Wood's metal will only take on a perfectly clean surface, and cannot be applied to graduations which are not freshly cut.

To Obtain a Horizontal Line for Adjusting Instruments, which Find Angles of Sight.

This may be done in the following ways :

(1) If there is available a telescope having a pointer or cross wires, which can be collimated, bearing rings and an adjustable spirit level, proceed as follows :—

(a) Collimate the telescope.

(b) Support the bearing rings of the telescope in bearings, such as those on a rocking sight bar.

(c) Elevate or depress the telescope until the bubble is in the centre of its run.

(d) Lift the telescope out of its bearings and replace it end for end. If the bubble remains in the centre of its run, any distant object seen on the tip of the pointer (or the intersection of the cross wires), when the bubble is in the centre of its run, is in the same horizontal plane as the axis of the telescope.

(e) If the bubble does not remain in the centre of its run, get it half way there by the elevating gear, and half way by the adjusting nuts or screws. When the telescope is turned end for end again the bubble should remain in the centre of its run. If it does not do so, repeat the operation until it remains in the centre of its run whichever way round the telescope is placed.

(2) If a straight gun, and a clinometer are available :—

(a) Place cross wires diametrically across the muzzle, and remove the lock from the breech, using the vent as a peep hole.

(b) Place the clinometer, set at zero, on the clinometer plane and bring its bubble to the centre of its run by the elevating gear.

(c) Distant objects in line with the vent and intersection of the cross wires will be in the same horizontal plane as the *axis of the gun*.

If the gun is not straight and the angle of droop is known, an allowance must be made.

(3) If only the instrument to be tested is available :—

(a) Select a position where there are two walls or upright posts, &c., about 200 yards apart (Fig. 1).

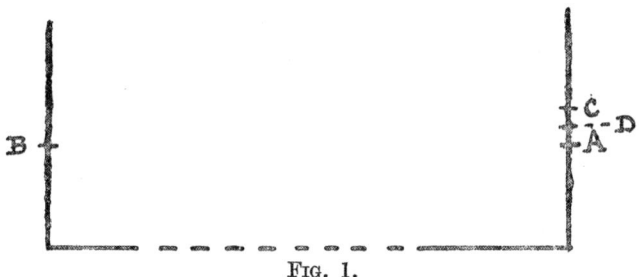

Fig. 1.

(b) Take the instrument to one wall (A), if possible at the corner of a house. Set the angle of sight scale to zero, direct the telescope at the other wall, and bring the bubble to the centre of its run. Look through the telescope and direct someone to mark the point where the pointer or cross wires cut through the distant wall (B). Mark the wall where you are standing, at (A), the same height as the *object glass* of the instrument.

(c) Take the instrument to the distant wall (B) and place the object glass against the mark made on it (B). Set the angle of sight scale to zero and bring the bubble to the centre of its run. If the instrument is in adjustment the pointer or cross wires should be in line with the mark

(A) on the first wall, and the line between the two marks is in a horizontal plane.

(*d*) If such is not the case, direct someone to mark on the first wall (A) the point (C) on which the pointer or cross wires are laid when the bubble is central.

(*e*) Make a third mark (D) on the first wall exactly halfway between (A) and (C).

(*f*) With the instrument still at (B) on the second wall, elevate or depress the telescope until the pointer or cross wires are laid on the third mark (D). Whilst keeping it laid on this point, move the micrometer head of the angle of sight gear until the bubble is in the centre of its run, and adjust the adjustable minute skin until it reads zero. If the degree scale does not read approximately zero it will be necessary to mark a fresh reader for it, or adjust the nuts or screws supporting the bubble, which can only be done by an expert.

(*g*) Check the adjustment using the marks (B) and (D). If correct, a line between these marks is in a horizontal plane.

When once a horizontal line has been obtained, any number of instruments can be checked and adjusted on it.

To Fix Spider's Web, Cross Wires or Graticules.

Remove the eyepiece and the four diaphragm adjusting screws from the telescope, and allow the diaphragm to slide out.

Take a frame with spider's web wound round it (see below) and lay the web carefully in the lines cut on the diaphragm, keeping it fairly taut. Fix the ends with a small drop of varnish or shellac applied on the pointed end of a match.

Cut a piece of stick, long enough to reach down the telescope body as far as the positions of the diaphragm, point one end of it, and insert it in one of the screw holes of the diaphragm. Using the stick as a handle, insert the diaphragm in the telescope and secure it there with two adjusting screws which are opposite one another, being careful that the diaphragm is the right way up. Remove the stick and revolve the diaphragm by the screws already in it until the web is nearest the eyepiece, and the two other adjusting screws can be inserted. Collimate in the usual manner.

Method of Taking and Storing Spider's Web.

In the British Isles the best time for collecting web is in August and September. Thick web should be obtained from large garden spiders, and thin web from small ones. The spider should be kept without food for a day previous to winding. The web should be examined through an eyepiece to see that it is of suitable thickness.

Brass wire frames should be prepared and coated with hard brown varnish, a suitable size being 6″ × 2″ × 0·1″.

The spider should be placed on the end of a stick and breathed upon, this will probably make him drop and hang suspended by his web. The top of the web should be attached to the frame, which is then revolved, so that the web is wrapped around it in a spiral, and the end secured.

It is as well to have a box with grooves in it to take a number of frames, and so arranged that the web does not come in contact with the wood.

If kept in a hermetically sealed box, the web will last for years, but when practicable it should be renewed annually.

To Replace a Broken Bubble.

Remove the bubble case from the instrument; pull off the bubble caps and take out the broken glass and old plaster. Insert the new one, which will be found to fit loosely in the tube and will have to be packed up with paper. Cut from a sheet of good notepaper a slip the width of which is equal to the cylindrical length of the bubble glass, fold it into a zig-zag, the first fold of the paper being about one-third of the circumference of bubble glass, the next fold about 0·1-inch less, and so on.

Place it under the bubble glass with the narrowest fold against the case, and push them together into the bubble case, seeing that the graduations are on top and equidistant from the edges of the opening of bubble case. The glass bubble should fit just tightly enough to support its own weight in the case when held vertically. Care must be taken to see that the packing bears equally on either side of the glass bubble, otherwise it will not be set accurately enough for roll. Mix some plaster of paris with water until it is of the consistency of cream. Stand the bubble vertically on one end, and pour the plaster of paris into the upper end of the bubble case until it just covers the pip of the glass tube. Allow it to stand until nearly dry, then reverse the case and repeat the operation. Before replacing the bubble caps, scrape away the plaster from the glass pips with a piece of hard wood having a chisel shaped edge. If this is not done, when the plaster gets thoroughly set it will, most probably, break them off.

If the casing has an opening beneath it for admitting light to the bubble, a corresponding opening must be made in the paper packing after the plaster of paris has set.

Adjustment of Roll.

In an instrument which may be used when it or its support are not cross levelled (*e.g.*, the mountain clinometer or No. 3 director), it is very important that the bubble should be made parallel to the base of the instrument or support of the bubble mounting (see p. 74). In the case of the mountain clinometer, one edge of its base is placed parallel to the side of the clinometer plane, and when the clinometer is in adjustment, set at zero and levelled, and is tilted on this edge, the bubble should remain in the centre of its run. If it does not do so, the two side screws (see p. 74) must be adjusted.

In the case of the bubble of the clinometer level of the No. 3 director, when the instrument is in adjustment, set at zero, and levelled, and the clinometer level is swung sideways the bubble should remain in the centre of its run. If it does not do so the bubble is not parallel to the trunnions of the clinometer level. There is no adjustment for this, but the position of the bubble in its casing must be corrected by trial and error.

To Fit a Circular Bubble.

All circular bubbles are issued in adjustment with reference to their own bases, but it will, probably, be found necessary, when fitting a new one to an instrument, in consequence of the seating on the top plate not being truly at right angles to the vertical axis, to effect some further slight adjustment.

A new circular bubble should be fitted as described below :—

Remove the defective circular bubble from the top plate of the instrument; if the new one has not been drilled to take fixing screws, place them base to base, with their rims concentric, and mark off the position of the holes with a pointer, and drill the three holes. If the holes are already drilled, they should be made to coincide, if necessary, with the screw holes on the top plate by drawing them over with a small "Swiss mousetail file." Fix the bubble with the three existing fixing screws, and level the instrument with the telescope, or clinometer level bubble, everything being at zero.

The air bubble should coincide with the ring marked on the glass.

If it does not, the part of the base of the circular bubble immediately beneath the air bubble requires to be slightly reduced in thickness. This should be done with a four or six-inch super-smooth file, or, if a super-smooth file is not available, with a coarse emery stick. This done, fix and test it with the telescope pointing in different directions. This operation may have to be repeated several times before complete adjustment is obtained.

When it is correct the air bubble should remain steady at all readings of the horizontal scale.

APPENDIX A.

Notes on Reflecting Prisms.

Right Angle Prisms.

Prisms used in telescopes and binoculars are usually right angled ones, a section through them being a right angle isosceles triangle. Either one or two surfaces may be used for reflecting. The reflection at the reflecting surfaces is total, *i.e.*, all the light reaching them is reflected, and none passes through the surface (*see* Notes on Optics, 1908, para. 31). This, however, is the case only when the reflecting surfaces are perfectly polished and clean. If moisture, dirt, &c., are present on the surfaces a certain amount of light will pass through the surface into the moisture, &c. The above can be noticed by looking into a prism from a point normal to one side and observing an object such as a light (O, Fig. 1). If the reflecting surface A B is perfectly polished and clean, the

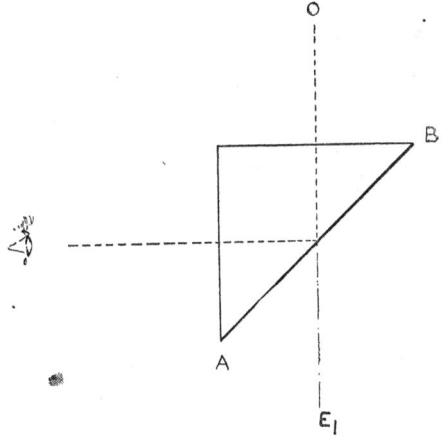

Fig. 1.

reflected image will appear to be nearly as brilliant as if the object were seen direct. If, however, the surface A B is breathed on, the reflected image will appear very dull. If a spot of ink is placed on the surface, it will be seen to blot out a part of the object.

If the eye is placed at E1 in prolongation of the line from the light to the prism, no sign of the light will be seen in the prism. This shows that none of the light passes through the surface A B, but that it is all totally reflected. If the surface A B were silvered, it would reflect better than if it were dirty, but not nearly so well as if it were perfectly clean. It is not customary to silver prisms unless satisfactory reflection cannot be otherwise obtained.

A prism used as in Fig. 1 acts in the same way as if the surface A B were a mirror. If this surface is moved in any direction, objects seen reflected by it will also appear to move. Prisms, one reflecting surface of which is made use of, are employed in the Stereoscopic Telescope (page 30) and at the top of the No. 7 Dial Sight (page 92). In the latter case, however, the reflecting surface has to be silvered or some of the light would pass through the surface when the prism was much elevated or depressed.

When two reflecting surfaces are made use of the action is similar. The prism A B C (Fig. 2) may be considered as being made up of two smaller right

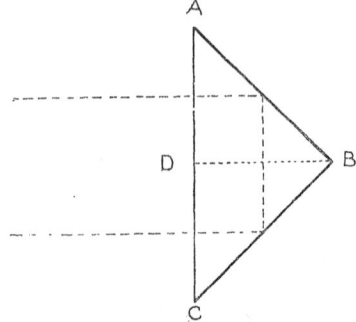

Fig. 2.

angled prisms A D B, C D B. The path of a ray of light is shown in dotted lines. As, however, A B and B C are reflecting surfaces at right angles to one another, a ray of light will always emerge from the prism parallel to the direction in which it entered. Prisms, two reflecting surfaces of which are made use of, are employed in prismatic binoculars (page 36) and other instruments.

Prisms which Reflect a Constant Angle.

It is very necessary that the end prisms in one man range-finders should always reflect rays of light through some definite angle as, otherwise, if the tube in which they are mounted became bent or warped, the coincidence adjustment would be upset. They are usually made to reflect a right angle and are known as Prandl or pentagonal prisms. A section of one is shown in Fig. 3. The surfaces A B and A E are at right angles to one another, and

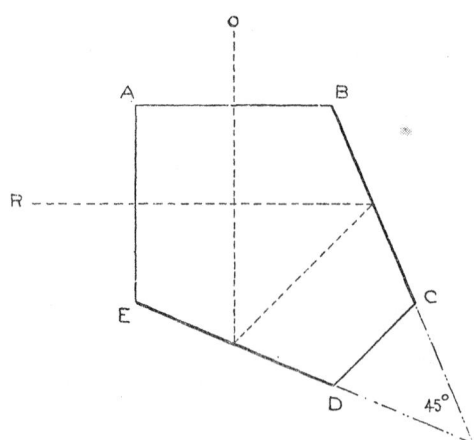

Fig. 3.

B C and E D are at 45° to one another. The path of a ray of light from an object O to the interior of a range-finder R is shown in dotted lines. The surfaces B C and D E are silvered. If they were not, the ray of light would pass through them instead of being reflected by them. Rotation of the prism in the plane of reflection will not alter the angle through which the ray of light is reflected. The prism acts in the same way as the two mirrors, inclined at 45° to one another, in a sextant, left mekometer, &c.

The same effect is obtained by the prism which is used in the Weldon Rangefinder and the " Lath, Adjusting, Artillery Range Finder, Mark II." It is shown in section in Fig. 4. The angles to which it is cut depend upon the

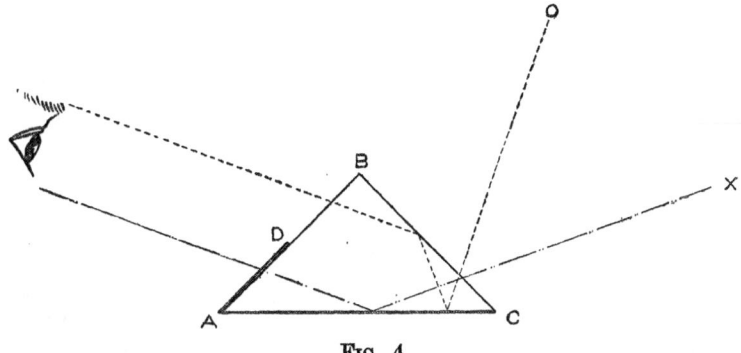

Fig. 4.

angle which it is required to reflect. The surface A C is silvered. A ray of light coming from an object O will be reflected by the silvering on the surface A C on to the unsilvered surface B C, from which it will again be reflected. As B C and A C are reflecting surfaces inclined to one another at some definite angle, they will in combination always reflect a ray of light at some constant angle. The magnitude of this angle is also dependent upon the form of the triangle C A B. When using such a prism the eye must be placed near the apex B. If it is placed near A an object in the direction of X will be seen, its image being reflected by the surface A C only. Half the surface of A B (from A to D) is, therefore, left unpolished, or is covered over.

APPENDIX B.

TEST FOR RANGE TAKERS USING RANGE FINDER, ARTILLERY, No. 1.

85 per cent. of full marks must be obtained in each of the three following tests in order to qualify:—

TEST 1.

1. A suitable position for an observing station should be selected, with cover about 50 to 100 yards away, from which the range-taker can work.

Three natural objects will be selected (not previously pointed out to the range-taker) not less than 5 degrees apart, and at ranges from 2,500 yards to 4,500 yards, at least one object being at a range exceeding 3,500 yards.

A reference point will also be selected from which to point out the targets.

2. The battery commander, with the battery sergeant-major, will be in position at the observing station. The range-taker, mounted, with instrument and stand properly secured in their places, together with his horse-holder, will be halted 100 yards in rear of the observing station under cover.

3. On the order "Dismount"—The range-taker dismounts, takes the instrument and stand from their cases, and reports to the battery commander. The battery commander points out the three objects selected by means of the reference point. The range-taker then moves at least 50 yards away and selects suitable cover from which to work. He sets up the stand if possible, using the legs in the short position, and fixes the instrument. He then takes the ranges to the objects in the same order as pointed out by the battery commander, and as soon as taken, semaphores each range to the battery sergeant-major (or signaller) at the observing station, at the same time noting it on his range card for reference.

4. Time allowed, 4 minutes, to be taken from "Dismount" to the receipt of the last range.

Full marks, 50.

Deduct 1 mark for every 10 seconds or fraction of 10 seconds over time.

Deduct 5 marks if the best use is not made of the available cover.

If the ranges taken are within the limit of error shown below, full marks will be allowed for accuracy, but for every 10 per cent., or fraction of 10 per cent. over and above such limit of error, 1 mark will be deducted.

Limits of error allowed.

Range.	Error allowed.
2,500	50 yards
3,000	80 ,,
3,500	110 ,,
4,000	140 ,,
4,500	180 ,,
5,000	220 ,,
5,500	270 ,,
6,000	320 ,,

TEST 2.

1. The battery commander, battery sergeant-major and range-taker will be in position as in Test 1.

2. At the order "Dismount," the range-taker dismounts, removes stand and instrument, and reports to the battery commander.

The battery commander points out a reference point in a zone covering about 25 degrees, and orders the range-taker to make out a range card showing the ranges to six prominent points in that zone at ranges from 2,500 to 6,000 yards. Three ranges must be at a range of 4,000 yards or over. The range-taker chooses a position for his instrument as in Test 1, takes the ranges and lateral angles to the points selected by him, fills in the range card, as shown in Field Artillery Training, omitting the angles of sight and the minutes of lateral angles. He then hands in the range card to the battery sergeant-major at the observing station.

3. Time allowed, 15 minutes, to be taken from "dismount" to the receipt of the range card.
Full marks, 125.
Deduct 1 mark for every 10 seconds, or fraction of 10 seconds, over time.
Deduct 5 marks if the best use is not made of the available cover.
If the ranges taken are within the limit of error laid down above, no marks will be deducted, but for every 10 per cent., or fraction of 10 per cent., over and above such error 1 mark will be deducted.
If the lateral angles are measured correctly within 1 degree, no marks will be deducted. If the error is over 1 degree and under 2 degrees, 3 marks will be deducted; if over 2 degrees, 5 marks will be deducted. If an object cannot be located by the description on the card, 15 marks will be deducted. The six prominent points shown on the card must be such as would assist a battery commander in rapid ranging.
In order to measure the lateral angles the range-taker may use graticuled glasses or a scale.

TEST 3.

ADJUSTMENTS.

(a) Adjusting the instrument for coincidence by means of the adjusting lath and by a known range.

(b) Halving adjustment.
Each adjustment is to be explained to the examining officer, and then carried out practically.
Full marks, 20.
No time limit.
Deduct 1 mark for each mistake made in explanation. All marks will be deducted if either of the adjustments in (a) and (b) are not carried out correctly in practice.

INDEX.

A.

	PAGE.
Adjustable focus object glasses, Telescopes with	11
Adjustment of instruments	173
Angle of sight instruments (*see* Instruments, angle of sight).	
Apparatus, observation of fire—	
Base plate, 62. Instrument, 54. Slide rule	63
Method of using	58
Apparatus, testing clinometer	82
Apparent field, Definition of	2
Artillery telemeter (*see* Telemeter, Artillery).	

B.

Base Plate, Apparatus, observation of fire	62
Binocular—	
Mark III, 35. Mark IV, 35. Mark V	35
Night	36
Binocular, prismatic—	
No. 1, 38. No. 2, 39. No. 3	40
Binoculars—	
Care and preservation of, 170. Construction of Galilean, 33. Construction of prismatic, 36. Table of service	33
Boxes (*see* instruments with which used).	
Box, junction	166
Bubble, Replacing a broken	177
Bubbles—	
Cased No. 1, 163. Circular, 163. Spirit, glass	161

C.

Calculations with a slide rule	64
Carriers, No. 7 dial sight how attached to	84
Care and preservation of instruments, 170. Eyeguards	171
Cases, care and preservation of	172
Cases (*see* instruments with which used).	
Circular spirit bubble	163
Clinometer—	
Field, Mark II, 76. Field, Mark III.	79
Inspectors, Mark I, 75. Inspectors, Mark II.	76
Large, 75. Sight, 80. 10-pr. B.L.	76
Clinometers—	
Apparatus for testing	82
General	72
Instructions for setting, testing and adjusting Watkin type, 77. Field, Mark III, 80. Sight	82
Collimation—	
Definition of, 7. Means of adjusting	7
Collimator, telescope sighting	163

D.

	PAGE.
Dermatine, care and preservation of	171
Dial sight No. 7—	
Consideration of optical arrangements	84
Description	92
General arrangements	83
Instructions for use	96
Diaphragms, adjustable, in telescopes	9
Diaphragms, iris	164
Diopter, definition of	31
Director, No. 1. Description, 41. Instructions for use	52
Director, No. 2. Description, 42. Instructions for use	52
Director, No. 3. Description, 45. Instructions for use	53
Director, No. 3. General remarks on, 50. Tests for	51

E.

Eccentric rings for adjusting collimation	7
Effective aperture, Definition of	2
Eyeguard, Care and preservation of	171
Eyepieces, Focussing arrangements of	12
Eyepiece lenses	4

F.

Field Artillery telescope, 28. Stand for	41
Field plotter	69
Focussing	6
Formula for Siege Artillery	68
Four-volt lamp	166

G.

Galilean binoculars	33
Garrison telescope	29
Graduations, refilling	174

H.

Horizontal line. To obtain a	174
Hanger for Artillery Range finders	157

I.

Instrument, angle of sight, Description, 159. Method of use, 160. To test and adjust	161
Instruments—	
Care and preservation of	170
Repair and adjustment of	173
Iris diaphragms	164

J.

Junction box	166

L.

	PAGE
Lamp, 4-volt, 166. Flexible lead for	166
Lenses, Eyepiece, 4. Object glass, 3. Cleaning	170

N.

Night binoculars	36
No. 7 dial sights (*see* Dial sight No. 7).	

O.

Object glass lenses	3
Object glass, Telescopes with adjustable focus for	11
Observation of Fire, Apparatus (*see* Apparatus, observation of fire).	
One man range finders (*see* Range finders, one man).	

P.

Parallax, Definition of	6
Plotter, field	69
Prismatic binoculars (*see* Binoculars).	
Prisms, Notes on reflecting	179

R.

Range finders, one man—

Accuracy of	157
Adjusting lath for	156
Adjustments...	140
Arrangements of the field of view	127
Barr and Stroud pattern—	
Cleaning, 153. Description, 151. Dismantling, 152. General arrangement of, 131. Use of astigmatisers in	140
Hints to range takers	140
Range taking with	135
Results of incorrect halving	148
Stand, Artillery Range finder. Mark I, 154. Mark II.	155
Zeiss pattern. Case for, 154. Description, 149. General arrangements	133
Rubber, care and preservation of	171

S.

Sine, To find the, of an angle	69
Sight, dial, No. 7 (*see* Dial sight No. 7).	
Sighting rules	168
Sighting telescopes (*see* Telescopes, sighting).	
Slide rule, Apparatus, Observation of fire, 63. 10-inch, 68. Calculating by means of a	64
Spider's web, fixing on diaphragms, 176. Method of taking and storing ...	176
Stands (*see* instruments with which they are used).	
Stereoscopic ; Telescope...	30
Stop watches	168
Switch and resistance coil	164

T.

PAGE.

Tables—
    Artillery telemeters, 99. Binoculars, 33. Clinometers, 72. Iris
        diaphragms, 164. Sighting rules, 168. Telescopes... 1
Tangent, To find the, of an angle 69
Telemeter, Artillery—
    Description, 99. Drill with, 113. Preliminary drill with, 113.
    Testing and adjusting, 122. Theory, 118. Use of 107
Telescope, Field Artillery 28
Telescope, garrison 29
Telescope, sighting—
    No. 1, 14. No. 2, 16. No. 3, 17. No. 4, 17. No. 5, 18. No. 6, 19.
    No. 7, 22. No. 8... 24
Telescope, stereoscopic 30
Telescope, variable power—
    No. 1, 24. No. 2 27
Telescopes—
    Care and preservation of, 170. Focussing, 6. General remarks on, 1.
        Table of 1
Tests for Range Takers (Appendix B.) 182

V.

Variable power telescope—
    No. 1, 24. No. 2 27

W.

Watches, stop 168
Wrench for No. 7 dial sight and carriers 98

(B 10585) Wt. 10070–811   15m   8/14   H & S   P 13/16